ORDER IN COURT

David Osborne

The author wishes to acknowledge with gratitude the assistance given by John
Plimmer, who proof-read the book and made a number of editorial suggestions.

ISBN: 1499735847
ISBN 13: 9781499735840

ABOUT THE AUTHOR

David Osborne is a successful English barrister, author, public performer and public speaker. Some years ago, he hit the headlines nationwide and made legal history when he delivered his final speech to the jury entirely in verse. For this *tour de force* he was dubbed 'The Barrister Bard' by the popular press.

He followed this with the publication of a short humorous book on the law entitled **No Holds Barred** and written under the pseudonym of Ivor Bigg-Wigg QC. This is available as an e-book on Kindle.

He has appeared regularly on radio and television as a legal commentator, and has written a number of articles for the national and regional press, as well as various journals. His blog can be found at: http://www.david-osborne.com/blog

In the recent past, David has also written and presented two legal revues, both times to full houses. See his website for an excerpt of one of his live performances. http://www.david-osborne.com/theatre.

He is regularly in demand as a keynote and after-dinner speaker, and has written a short book on the Art of Public Speaking, available on Amazon.

He is married with four children and lives in Somerset.

Last year, David's first book in what is planned to be a series of humorous legal books was published. It is based on the fictional character of Toby Potts, a young and aspiring criminal barrister climbing the greasy pole to fame and fortune, or so he hopes. It is entitled **May it Please Your Lordship**.

Book 3, provisionally entitled **My Learned Friend,** is due for publication very soon.

To Sir Leicester Dedlock

CONTENTS

CHAPTER 1
PARTING IS SUCH SWEET SORROW

Thankfully, January had all but blown itself out, with February just around the corner. For me at least, February heralded Valentine's Day, with chocolates, flowers, a sexy card and a romantic *diner à deux* with Susie, the love of my life and with a spring wedding in the advanced stages of planning, soon to be Mrs. Toby Potts.

If I had my way, I'd abolish January altogether, a totally depressing month. After the euphoria of Christmas and the false dawn of New Year's Day, January was a month of gritting the teeth through the sleet and snow and a biting North wind, incessantly grey skies and a pervading air of gloom and doom made worse, if that were possible, by the taxman knocking loudly at the door.

As I was also to discover, January was the month when divorce petitions were hitting the courts in record numbers for all sorts of reasons. The rictus grins around the Christmas dinner table as the in-laws made merry mischief with carping comments about the Brussels sprouts and the congealed gravy, and the fourth bottle of *vin ordinaire* releasing the usual inhibitions that had been maintained, with difficulty, since Christmas Eve. Then there were the presents round the tree which never failed to disappoint, with the breadwinner giving "her indoors" a shiny new set of saucepans and oven gloves with a cheeky motif. The kids were screaming the house down because they hadn't received a new Playstation or DVD player or BMX bike which Santa, smelling of mothballs and strong peppermint sweets, had promised them when they visited Hardy's department store, and besides, they'd told him they'd been good children, and to have their word impugned by some beery Bozo from Neverland simply added insult to injury.

With the in-laws barely out of sight and wending their way home, the recriminations began. "Her indoors", who had kept up the pretence of *bonhomie* with the help of copious slugs of cooking sherry, finally snapped and flung the new set of shiny saucepans at the breadwinner, telling him to shove them where the sun never shines. For his part, the breadwinner brought up the subject of the Brussels sprouts, bad move, and not even the congealed gravy could pour oil on the troubled waters.

The final straw was usually the New Year's Eve dinner dance, overpriced and overhyped, with enforced jollity the order of the night. It was when the breadwinner asked that gorgeous dolly bird on the next table for yet another dance that "Her Indoors" lost the plot, told him to drop dead, and stormed out.

Belinda Beveridge, known as Bee, was one such casualty of a marriage that had broken down irretrievably after four short years of wedded bliss with only Hugo, now two years old, to show for it.

The brief to represent Bee came by the usual circuitous route. I was not Counsel of first or even second choice, but I was available, and Michael, Chambers' first clerk, had put me forward.

Bee had petitioned for divorce on the grounds of unreasonable behaviour and infidelity, and reading her account, she was spot on. The lead up to the petition had all the usual ingredients: Tom, her husband, had suddenly taken to working late at the office; there was the pungent aroma of a different perfume when he returned in the early hours and no amount of showering could loosen its tacky grip; and the disconnected calls on his mobile phone on the rare occasions Bee answered it, usually when Tom was taking yet another shower.

Her suspicions were finally confirmed when she was driving 'by chance' past his office in the City and saw him emerge with a younger and very attractive girl firmly attached to his arm. He could hardly take his eyes off her, the cheating bastard! And after all she had done to make the marriage work, the culinary delights she had created in the kitchen, sex freely available on demand, the son and heir they had both craved, all this came crashing down in a few short weeks.

Bee, with nothing else to do but sit at home and rue the day she ever met the slimy toad, decided to play the part of the gumshoe to plan her revenge, so one evening she waited outside his office, and when she saw Tom and Miss Right emerge, she followed them to a small mews house in Belsize Park. As she was later to discover, and to rub salt into the wounds, Tom was paying the rent on this sordid little love nest!

She drove home in a blind fury, went through the house, gathered up everything that belonged to him and threw the whole lot out of the window. Into the car again, she drove back to Belsize Park, where she posted a pack of his favourite condoms through the letterbox, small, Featherlite and seductively flavoured with *eau de rat*. Tom was small in that department, but what he lacked in size, he more than made up for in effort. As Tom and Miss Right looked out of the window, Bee could be heard screaming obscenities by all the neighbours for miles around.

The police were called, and Bee was arrested. She was later charged with threatening behaviour and criminal damage to Tom's property, which included several sharply tailored Savile Row suits.

Tom was an investment banker, which meant giving investment advice to the super rich and being paid obscene amounts of money for the privilege. Coupled with his annual bonuses, he was already well on his way to his second million, and the sky was the limit. With his cheque book at the ready, he instructed a very smart and expensive firm of divorce solicitors to represent his best interests, and the divorce battle lines were drawn.

For his part, Tom had no wish to press the charges brought against Bee by the police, but Miss Right was having none of it. She could just about stomach the ranting and raving outside their love nest, but the packet of small condoms was the last straw. The slight on her lover's manhood was too much to bear!

Bee's parents stepped up to the plate. Her father knew somebody who knew a solicitor in a small firm who specialised in divorce, so he was duly instructed together with a down payment. Her solicitor didn't do crime, who in their right mind would, but he knew somebody who knew a small firm of solicitors who specialised in crime, so he farmed the criminal matters out in return for a small referral fee. As Bee's only source of income was Tom's monthly allowance, as small as his marriage tackle, she was eligible for legal aid. Small was very much the order of the day! As for me, it was an irresistible combination: a scorned woman on legal aid! Hardly likely to excite my bank manager!

A conference was duly booked in Chambers at 4.30, the traditional time of the day when busy practitioners return from a busy day in court. Busy was very much the order of the day!

Bee was accompanied by a trainee solicitor, in keeping with the legal aid certificate. I didn't catch his name, and it didn't matter, as he knew absolutely nothing about the case. Clutching the file, he seated himself at the back of the room and began doodling in his notebook, leaving me and Bee to strut and fret our hour upon the stage.

As was my wont, I began with a review of the evidence. A good tactic, as it showed the client I had mastered the complexities of the case as well as bringing the Trainee up to speed. After my recital, time to put flesh on the bones. This meant gently exploring her defence, which, if the truth be told, I hadn't yet spotted.

"Now, Mrs. Beveridge," I smiled reassuringly for no obvious reason, "I need to know what you say about all this." Legal aid hadn't extended to taking any evidence whatsoever from the client. The brief contained the cryptic comment: "Counsel is instructed to take the client's instructions and to represent her at trial". This was a euphemism for me to do all the spadework and for the solicitor to take the lion's share of the legal aid payment. Were it ever thus!

"Bailey," she replied, "Ms. Bailey. I prefer to be known by my maiden name. I don't wish to be associated with that scumbag of a husband in any shape or form!"

Start as you mean to go on was her Mantra!

"Of course," I replied soothingly.

"Have you read the background to this?" she asked, glaring at me.

"I've received a copy of your statement in support of your divorce petition, helpfully forwarded by your divorce solicitors. It's all very sad."

"Sad!?! Is that all you can say!?!" she exploded. This was not going to be easy, and the trainee solicitor was no help at all. He had wisely chosen to stay well out of it, and was now doodling frantically in his notebook, head down. "I gave that bastard the best years of my life, and what do I get in return?!? Tossed aside for a slapper!"

"Well," I was beginning to feel uncomfortable, "We're not here to discuss whose fault it is that the marriage broke down...." Wrong tack.

This was like a red rag to a bull. "Why not?" she shot back, "If you'd bothered to read my statement, you wouldn't be asking such stupid questions!"

"I *have* read your statement," I was not going to be brow beaten, "and I'm sure the court will take into account the background to these charges, but that's mitigation, not a defence."

There was long and awkward silence.

"Are you married?" Bee suddenly demanded.

"Not yet," I replied cheerfully. "Engaged, with the wedding fixed for the spring."

"Well I hope your fiancée has better luck than me," she retorted, with hot tears welling up. "You men are all the same, sex mad, can't keep it zipped up! And it's not as if the little prick has anything worth showing!" An unfortunate choice of words.

This was going from bad to worse, and very little to show for it. Time to bring the conference back on track.

"Looking at the charges," I began firmly, "you're charged with threatening behaviour. The prosecution case against you is that you used threatening, abusive or insulting words or behaviour towards the occupants of the mews house. Now, as we know," I continued before Bee could interrupt me with another outburst, "there is a witness statement from the female occupant Ms. Harmony Young setting out exactly what you said and did, and if she's believed by the court, that amounts to threatening behaviour."

Bee glowered back, but mercifully said nothing. I had lift off.

"As for the criminal damage of your husband's property, as I understand it, you didn't damage it but simply threw it all into the garden?"

"Yes, that's right." Bee had had her rant, and was now a spent force.

"Good. The fact there was a steady rain all night may not help, but nothing that a good dry clean wouldn't put right."

Bee nodded. Did I detect the faintest smile of appreciation? Almost too much to hope, but I pressed on. "We need a short statement from Mr. Beveridge's tailor," I looked pointedly at the trainee solicitor, "confirming that a Savile Row suit is for life, not just for Christmas, if you follow my meaning."

He took a moment or three to come on board, reluctant as he was to enter the evidential arena, but slowly he turned to a doodle free page, grunted, and made a note. Hallelujah!

Bee had calmed down a little. "So what do you suggest?"

"The Crown Prosecution Service are always open to offers. If they can tick the right boxes and come in on budget, they'll play along, and as I understand it, your husband isn't pressing charges, which is more than we can say for his suits."

Bee didn't see the humour. "OK, whatever you say. I'm past caring."

I smiled encouragingly. "If we can get the CPS to drop the criminal damage charge, they'll want something in return, so I suggest you plead guilty to threatening behaviour, and with a lot of good mitigation, I'll try for a conditional discharge. No promises," I added quickly to cover my back, "but I'm hopeful."

To my relief, her solicitors came up with the goods. A short and pithy statement from Messrs. Mellish & Sanders, Savile Row tailors to the Great and the Good since 1839, confirmed that many of their clients married, divorced and died in one of the best suits money could buy, and true to form, the CPS played their part. They dropped the criminal damage charge, Bee pleaded guilty to threatening behaviour, and after mitigation that was a model of its kind, though I say it myself, she was given a conditional discharge. At one stage it was touch and go. The Chairman of the Bench was a bloke, who looked singularly unimpressed, but he was outflanked and outnumbered by two women, one of whom nodded vigorously throughout my submissions. I felt I'd touched a raw nerve.

Bee was gracious enough to thank me through clenched teeth before leaving court to pick up the pieces of her broken marriage. Mercifully, the trainee solicitor was nowhere to be seen, no doubt back at the office protecting the public purse.

⟫⟪

My encounter with Bee left me shell-shocked. Here was a pleasant if somewhat hot-headed woman whose dreams had turned into a nightmare in four short years. Although I knew nothing about divorce law, I expected her to be well looked after financially by the errant Tom, and little Hugo's future was assured, but that was cold comfort to her as she faced an uncertain future.

I couldn't understand why Tom had decided to throw it all away for a life of unbridled passion with Harmony, or until he tired of her allure and moved on to his next conquest. If Bee was right, and the little prick couldn't keep it zipped up, Harmony's tenure of the love nest was far from secure.

The statistics of marriages breaking down in the first four years were frightening, in the region of 40% at the last count. Even though the Lord had blessed their union till death do them part, it seemed to make little difference, and divorce lawyers were kept fat plying their trade in human misery. Still, I comforted myself in the knowledge that 60% of marriages made it past the four year benchmark, and anyway, as they say, there are lies, damned lies and statistics.

I loved Susie and she loved me, and as far as I was concerned, that counted for everything. And besides, a life of unbridled passion with the likes of Harmony sounded positively exhausting. After a long day in court, defending the innocent and holding high the sword of justice, it would be back to the love nest, off with the kit and a torrid tumble in the sack satisfying her every demand, and all before a drink and a chance to unwind. I felt faint at the very thought!

It wasn't going to happen to us, but I suppose Bee had said exactly the same when she and Tom were being showered with biodegradable confetti, shortly after they had plighted their troth.

I hadn't seen Susie properly since the New Year's Eve celebrations at the Cricket Club. Not that I was much of a cricketer, although I knew Ted Dexter, so that was something, and according to village gossip, it was the best bash for miles around, with fireworks and dancing till dawn to the accompaniment of the Chiltern Valley Stompers. It was supposed to be 'black tie', but that pretence was quickly abandoned by the young and active, leaving only the Wrinklies to bring a thin veneer of respectability to the proceedings. They pushed off soon after the chimes of Big Ben heralded the New Year, leaving the field to the Hooray Henrys and Henriettas, with copious quantities of alcohol to keep the party going and fuel what my parents' generation would describe as 'inappropriate behaviour'. Cricket with lager cans was a particular favourite.

One thing and another kept me in Town for the following weekends, although we phoned each other regularly, so I was greatly looking forward to Valentine's Day and a night of romantic bliss with Susie all to myself.

As luck would have it, I was out of court the following day, so I had no professional commitments to dull the appetite. The true romantic in me had booked a double room at the Feathers Inn, within easy walking distance of La Bella Italia, fine Italian dining, or so they claimed, and all was set for the big night.

Was it just me, or was there a certain unspoken tension between us? I sensed it from the moment I picked Susie up. The meal was good enough, although fine Italian dining was a relative term, and the wandering troubadours were a bit naff in their Neapolitan outfits belting out endless renditions of 'O Solo Mio', but they meant well. We made love that night, but I had an uneasy feeling that something was wrong. I put it down to Big Match nerves, with the nuptials rapidly approaching.

It was over breakfast that she dropped the bombshell.

"Toby Darling," she took my hand in hers and looked intently into my eyes, "I've got something to tell you."

Oh my God, she's pregnant! The shame of it all, and what would the parents say? We'd be social pariahs, unable to hold our heads up in polite society.

"It's been a lovely evening, and one I shall treasure for years to come." This sounded ominous. "The truth is, Clarence House have been in touch." She paused, looking for the right words. "I told you about my work in Lesotho, it's Prince Harry's project in memory of his mother." I nodded. "Well, he's asked me personally to go back, he phoned me last week."

I was stunned. I was being second bested by Prince Harry, and what did he have that I didn't? OK, he was a Prince of the Realm, and called the Queen 'Grannie', and he had an apartment in Clarence House, and a country estate, or several for that matter, and he was dashingly handsome, and an accomplished sportsman, and the ultimate party animal, but was he a qualified barrister?!? No he was not! One in the eye for him!

"When? And for how long?" I stammered.

"It's just for a year," she replied, "and if I go, I leave at the end of the month." She paused, still squeezing my hand. "I told him I'd discuss it with you first, and let him have my answer in the next few days."

I was groping for the right words. "It's come as a bit of a shock," I said, trying to control my emotions. "I'm not sure what you want me to say."

"If you don't want me to go, I won't, and that's that, but," she continued, "we're still very young," I'd heard that one before, "with the rest of our lives before us, and I can't think of anybody I'd rather spend it with than you." She smiled reassuringly. "I love you, and always will, and it's only for a year."

There was a long silence.

"Then you must go," I smiled, putting on a brave face, "and if I read in the press you've got engaged to Prince Harry, I shall never forgive you."

Susie laughed. "There's only one man for me, and that's you!"

"What about the wedding plans? You know the parents have been flapping around like wet hens for months."

"I've told Mummy and Daddy they might have to postpone it for a year, they're disappointed of course, but they understand." She paused. "Thank you for being so kind and considerate, my darling. I do love you, you know that, it's only for a year, and it will soon fly by."

"Not for me it won't. Every day I'm parted from you will seem like an eternity. I wonder if there's a job for an aspiring lawyer in Lesotho," I added as an after-thought. "Perhaps Prince Harry could pull some strings."

Susie laughed. "We'll keep in touch of course, emails and phone calls, although the postal service from Lesotho is not the most reliable in the world."

Predictably, the parents took the news well enough, although the two Georges were less than pleased. Costs had been incurred, and with the postponement, deposits lost, so the carefully controlled balance sheet was shot to pieces. Still, as the mothers were fond of saying, you can't put a price on happiness. Not what the Georges wanted to hear.

Two weeks to the day, I drove Susie to Heathrow airport in my father's car. Terminal Three was like a refugee camp, with the flotsam and jetsam of life sprawled around in a mound of empty crisp packets and cans of drinks, either waiting to go back home or hoping to persuade the Border Agency to let them in without a visa. Some had been there for months. It was a depressing sight.

And then it was time to say goodbye. A last lingering kiss, with both of us putting on a brave face. Susie promised to email me the moment she landed, and I promised to email her every day to keep her abreast with my burgeoning practice, so that wouldn't take long.

It was like that scene in Casablanca, with Humphrey Bogart doing the noble thing as Ingrid Bergman walked slowly towards the plane, one last look back, a fleeting smile from both of us, the music reaching a crescendo, and then she was gone.

I stood by the window in the terminal hall, watching as the plane taxied out and took off into the leaden grey sky. Suddenly I felt terribly alone.

CHAPTER 2
MAN'S BEST FRIEND

As the days passed since Susie's departure, my mood of depression slowly lifted and life returned to some sort of normality. Susie was as good as her word, with regular emails about her work at the orphanage, the fabulous sunsets, herds of wildebeest sweeping majestically across the Serengeti plains, and mercifully, no mention of Prince Harry dancing attendance on her every whim and fancy round the campfire.

A year was a long time as I began my self-imposed celibacy, so no more torrid tumbles with the likes of Camilla Foster-Ward and her endless supply of fruit-flavoured condoms, or the fragrant Harmony Young on the rebound. I was sure I could cope, the months would fly by, or so I kept telling myself, and then it was down the aisle and happy ever after.

My emails in reply couldn't match Susie's for excitement and magic moments under a star-spangled sky. Mine were confined to telling her how much I loved and missed her, and counting the days to her return. Nothing earth-shattering, all things considered, but trying to excite her, or me for that matter, about another day at Snaresbrook Crown Court locking antlers with Judge

'Bonkers' Clarke and coming off second best, was not exactly the stuff of tabloid headlines.

Life went on, and as a fully qualified barrister with aspirations, I was instructed to represent a client charged with having a dangerous dog in a public place. Not exactly red meat, but something to get my teeth into, so in that regard, the dog and I had something in common. The client's name was Bill Sykes, and his dog was called Bullseye. Somewhere in the deep recesses of my mind, these names rang a faint bell, but I couldn't quite put my finger on it.

My instructing solicitors were Messrs. Bumble & Beadle, a small firm specialising in small cases with an office abutting the mud-flats of Slade Green near the Thames estuary. I could almost smell the cockles and mussels alive, alive ho!

The good news was that Bill was paying for my services privately, and had deposited the princely sum of £200 in sweaty banknotes with Mr. Bumble, to be released to Counsel at the conclusion of the case. Were it ever thus, last in the pecking order again.

The short summary, which mirrored my instructions, told me that Bill Sykes was the chieftain of a group of travellers who had pitched their caravans on a piece of derelict land close to the river, and were intent on staying for a while. The menfolk tinkered, the womenfolk sold clothes pegs and lucky heather, and the kids did a bit of pocket picking just to keep their hands in. It was all very Dickensian, with shades of yesteryear.

All was going swimmingly well until one of the three respectable people who lived within smelling distance of the site complained to the local council. The complaints had an all too familiar middle class ring to them. The animals were fouling the land, which was saying something in Slade Green, the adults were hostile and the children downright rude. Where did they learn that sort of language at such a tender age? And besides, they should be in school where that sort of language is daily fare to the long-suffering teachers, and not out and about upsetting law-abiding taxpayers, or at least one of them.

The matter eventually reached the ear of Jack Dawkins, the compliance officer with the Health & Safety Department at the council, who received the call to arms with as much enthusiasm as a man on the eve of his public execution. His first reaction was to put the complaint into the pending tray and hope it would go away. It was like a hornet's nest. If you left it alone, you could just about live with it, but if you poked it with a stick, all hell broke loose. But his best laid plans went up the Suwannee when the Slade Green Gazette had got wind of it and ran it as their lead story. Bloody journalists!

With some trepidation, Jack organised a posse of junior officials to visit the site and serve an eviction notice. If he could persuade the travellers to up sticks and move on, at least as far as the adjoining borough of Crayford, he could wash his hands of the lot of them – job done!

Sadly, it was not to be. The posse, with Jack leading from the rear and waving his eviction notice like Chamberlain's return from Munich, were not universally welcomed, and as he predicted, all hell broke loose. Bill Sykes, with his trusty Bullseye at his side, and a dozen or more of his fellow travellers, built to a man like brick barns, met the posse at the entrance to the site. After a full and frank exchange, they were scattered to the four winds, the eviction notice trampled underfoot, and Jack ended up in a slurry pit which served as the camp's evacuation point. It was not a pretty sight.

Battered and bruised, it was time to fall back and regroup with as much dignity as his high office could command, but Bullseye had other ideas, and gave the retreating Jack a nasty nip in his thinking parts.

Jack returned to work after a week's sick leave, which included a trip to his local hospital for treatment and a tetanus shot. With his usual attention to detail, his injury was photographed as evidence to be used if a prosecution were to be brought against the offending animal and his master. For reasons never satisfactorily explained, and in his absence, the photograph, in glorious technicolour, found its way onto the office bulletin board. Jack was decidedly unamused.

Jack called a Council of War, but not before he had completed an application, in triplicate, for one week's paid leave of absence, not to be deducted from his paid holiday entitlement pursuant to Rule 46 (a) (iii) of the Paid Leave of Absence Regulations, as amended by Rule 46 (c) (iv). This was forwarded to the Paid Leave of Absence officer, applications thereto, to be delegated in the fullness of time to the appropriate sub-committee for consideration thereof.

In addition, Jack also lodged a formal complaint, again in triplicate, reference the unauthorised display of confidential material on the office bulletin board, contrary to Rule 17 (j) (vii) of the Council (Confidential Material) Regulations. This, in turn, was forwarded to the Acting Complaints officer, as the Complaints officer was on paid leave of absence, to be delegated in the fullness of time to the appropriate sub-committee for consideration thereof.

Jack's posse were summoned to attend, a totally useless bunch in his opinion, and found wanting under fire. There was also a flippancy in their manner which ill-behoved the conduct expected of responsible council employees, and the quip at the beginning of the meeting about getting to the bottom of it was unhelpful, and duly noted. The area beat police officer, Constable "Proper" Charlie Bates, had also been invited to attend, and wished he hadn't. He didn't fancy going head to head with the travellers, he was not alone in that regard, and in his considered opinion, it was best to let sleeping dogs lie. It wasn't so much a hornet's nest, more like the lion's den, and he was no Daniel.

Dawkins was having none of it. After all, his pride and more besides had been wounded, and council officials going about their properly delegated business were entitled to the full protection of the law. Against his better judgment, but mindful of his public duty, Constable Bates agreed to investigate, collect evidence and prepare a report for the consideration of the Crown Prosecution Service, where, in the fullness of time, it would be delegated to the reviewing lawyer for a decision. Delegation was very much the order of the day.

The identification of the dog and its owner came from the posse who, from the safety of their council van, had observed Bill Skyes calling Bullseye back, and Bullseye immediately responding. The two had walked back to Bill's gaily decorated caravan and out of sight. A reconnaissance visit a few days later, with the help of binoculars from a safe distance, confirmed that the two were inseparable companions, and a statement to this effect was completed. Dawkins had completed his own statement, describing Bill as the ring leader of the reception committee and their spokesman. The dog, an ugly-looking brute with no trace of pedigree, had been at his side during the opening exchanges, growling ominously. With the photograph of Jack's thinking parts taking pride of place on the CPS bulletin board, the reviewing lawyer authorised a prosecution. It was an open and shut case as far as he was concerned, a bit like Bullseye's mouth.

A conference in Chambers had been arranged that Thursday afternoon, promptly at 4.30, the traditional hour of the day when conferences took place for the convenience of busy practitioners. As I knew absolutely nothing about the Dangerous Dogs Act, other than what the title implied, it was time for some serious research.

Opening my well-thumbed copy of Archbold, the criminal practitioner's bible, I was directed to the section headed "Offences Against Public Morals and Policy". At first blush, I couldn't see the connection. Quite how Bullseye could offend against public morals and policy by allegedly biting Dawkins was not immediately obvious. Going straight to the meat and potatoes of the offence, Bill had been charged with having a dog dangerously out of control in a public place, and if the dog while so out of control injures any person, he is guilty of the aggravated offence. This was an "either way" offence, which meant that the prosecution or Bill could elect to have the charge tried by a judge and jury in the Crown Court, or agree to summary trial by the Magistrates. Something to consider in conference.

Promptly at 4.30, or sixteen thirty hours as Ronald Berger, my former pupil master, would have put it, there was a knock and Paul, the Chambers gopher, put his head round the door.

"The client and his solicitor are here, Mr. Potts, if you're ready."

"By all means Paul, show them in."

He hesitated. "What about the others?"

"What others?"

"There's at least another twelve in the waiting room. They came mob-handed. It smells like a farmyard," he added helpfully.

"Well, let's leave them where they are for the time being, and see how we get on."

"What about the horse and caravan? They've parked it in the Chambers bay, and Mr. Gazzard might put in an appearance. You know what I mean."

I did indeed. Nigel Gazzard, the eccentric Head of Chambers, was wont to turn up unannounced, and would brook no nonsense. "I'm sure Mr. Gazzard and the car park attendants will be able to sort it out," I replied, although I didn't fancy their chances.

Paul grunted, disappeared and returned a minute later with Bill Sykes and Bootsy Farmer, the darling of the Metropolitan Police until he was "invited" to take early retirement. To top up his pension plan, he now offered his services as an "outdoor" clerk to small firms of defence solicitors, where he was expected to sit in on conferences, take notes, and generally make himself useful.

A classic case of gamekeeper turned poacher, but old habits die hard, and he was always trying to get the clients to cop a plea. The last time we were together was at Larry King's porn trial, a triumph of my forensic skills if I say so myself.

"Good Lord, Mr. Farmer," I said with as much enthusiasm as I could muster, which was precious little, "we meet again."

"We do indeed, Mr. Potts, just like old times."

I wondered if Bootsy had tried to work his charms on Bill Sykes to cop a plea, but one look at the man dispelled any such notions. He was man-mountain, at least six foot six in his hobnailed boots, and almost as broad. He was eccentrically dressed to put it mildly, with a battered top hat, a large knotted spotted red handkerchief around his neck, a scruffy waistcoat under what looked like a frock-coat, and knee breeches.

There was an overpowering smell of horse droppings as he advanced towards me. "Is it yourself, Mr. Potts," he boomed in a broad Irish brogue, as he gave me a bone-crushing handshake.

"It is indeed, Mr. Sykes, and thank you for coming." I glanced out of the window. "I see you've come by horsepower, but as we're in a smokeless zone, perhaps you could turn down the stove before we get a complaint."

"Be Jasus you're right!" He opened the door and bellowed across the hall. "Seamus, tell Mickey to kill the stove for Chrissake! If you want a brew, ask the tea boy, but nicely!" He sat down and glowered at me. "Complaints, complaints, that's all we get, day in, day out, it's more than a man can bear. And why, I hear you ask?" I didn't. Bill leaned across with his enormous hands on the desk, his mood darkening, "because we're travellers, and your so-called piss-pot middle classes don't like us, that's why!" He rounded on Bootsy, giving him a mighty slap on the back. "Am I right, Bootsy, or am I right?" Bootsy grinned through clenched teeth. "There, Mr. Potts, Bootsy agrees with me, to be sure."

19

I had already decided this conference would need careful handling if we were to make any progress at all, at all. Best to let Bill make the running, with Bootsy and me following at a respectful distance.

"Let me assure you Mr. Sykes, there's no prejudice against travellers in this room," I lied, avoiding eye contact with Bootsy, whose list of prejudices ran to biblical proportions. As far as he was concerned, the sooner the lot of them were back in the Emerald Isle, the better all round. Bloody Pikeys!

"I suggest we turn to the matter in hand and the charge against you."

"Good t'inking, Mr. Potts," boomed Sykes.

"Now as you know," I tried to sound purposeful, "Jack Dawkins and the council officials have made statements identifying you as the owner of the dog."

"Have they, Begorrah?"

"Yes they have." I paused. "I assume you've read through their statements?"

"Now why would I be wasting my time with statements when I've got you and Bootsy to look after me?" he shot back. "And besides, I don't read or write, never seen the need for it in my line of work."

"And what exactly is your line of work?" I asked.

"A bit of dis and a bit of dat, if you catch my meaning, enough to keep body and soul together," he chuckled.

Now was not the time to explore dis and dat, the more so as Bootsy had now opened his notebook, pen poised.

I moved swiftly on. "Well, they say they saw you with the dog, and an unidentified female, entering your caravan."

"That'll be Nancy," Bill volunteered.

"And I take it Nancy is your good lady wife?" I asked in all innocence.

Bill threw back his head and roared with laughter. "Bless your cotton socks, Mr. Potts, you've obviously never met Nancy. She's only good when she wants to be, which isn't often, she's certainly no lady, and she's not my wife!" He dabbed his eyes with his filthy knotted spotted red handkerchief.

Time to move on. "Tell me about the dog, Mr. Sykes. According to Mr. Dawkins, it answers to the name Bullseye. Is that right?"

"It is indeed. A loveable little scamp, wouldn't hurt a fly."

"Well," I continued, passing a photograph of the dog across the desk, "I doubt if the court would agree with your description. It looks pretty terrifying to me. And as for not hurting a fly, it bit Mr. Dawkins, and he's got the injury to prove it." I passed the second photograph across the desk, which Bill studied with interest.

"No," he said at last, "dat doesn't look like Bullseye's teeth marks at all at all. We have a dozen or more dogs in the camp, all trained to see off bailiffs and interfering council busybodies, any one of them could have bit the dozy bugger. Has Bullseye been identified as the guilty party?"

Good point, and one to squirrel away for my incisive cross-examination. "Not as such," I replied, "Mr. Dawkins was in full flight at the time, but shortly after the attack, he claims he heard you calling Bullseye to heel, so to speak. Do you remember doing that?"

"Not really," Bill replied, "I was laughing meself silly at the time!" Another dab of the eyes with the filthy knotted spotted red handkerchief as he relived that action-packed afternoon. "Anyway, if he didn't see what dog bit him, why am I here?"

"It's what we barristers call 'drawing inferences' from the evidence," I replied pompously.

"And it's what we travellers call a load of codswallop! If that's the law, then the law is a ass!"

I'd heard that expression before, but where? No matter, as I decided to change tack. "Can you tell me about Bullseye? Does he belong to you?"

"Lord love us, Mr. Potts, Bullseye doesn't belong to anyone. He's a free spirit! He wandered into our camp about four or five years ago, let me t'ink," he paused, obviously t'inking, "that's right, we were in the Ring of Kerry, God's green acre if ever there was. Have you been to the Emerald Isle, Mr. Potts?"

"As a matter of fact, I have," I replied, "two memorable weeks, and it rained every day."

"Fed and watered by God's almighty hand, Mr. Potts," said Bill waxing lyrical.

"If that's the case, I don't know how you can bear to leave it," Bootsy muttered. Bloody Micks! He looked pointedly at his watch, and then at me. Time to draw proceedings to a close.

"So if you're not the owner, who is?" I asked.

"Nobody, Mr. Potts. I've already told you, Bullseye's a free spirit. He's free to come and go."

"Every dog has to have an owner," snapped Bootsy irritably, "otherwise it's against the law."

"Lord love us, Bootsy," replied Bill, giving him another slap on the back, "and here was I t'inking you was just a pretty face! Two lawyers for the price of one!"

Bootsy had that coming, and it served him right. The cheek of it, being upstaged by an ex-plod.

"Well," I said, standing up, "I think that's as far as we can take it today. Thank you for coming, Mr. Sykes, and I'll see you again at court."

"God bless you, Mr. Potts, until then. Now," he turned to Bootsy, "can I be giving you a lift?"

"No thanks," replied Bootsy, "I'll make my own way home." The thought of a bone-shaking ride in the back of a Pikey caravan through the streets of London was more than he could bear, and if word got out, he'd be the laughing stock of the Met, the finest bunch of lads you'd never wish to meet.

"Just one last thing," I said as Bill was leaving, "if you lose the case, they might come for Bullseye."

"Now why would I be losing the case, Mr. Potts, with you representing me? And besides, if they come for Bullseye, I wouldn't fancy their chances."

Nor would I.

⚔

The more I lived and worked in London's concrete jungle, the more I was amazed at the number of absolutely ghastly places calling themselves 'Green'. There was Wood Green, the scene of one of my greatest forensic triumphs in the murder trial of Andrew Stubbs, although in fairness, I was ably assisted by Sir James 'Jumbo' Bingham QC, one of the foremost advocates of his time.

Then there was Slade Green, on the outer margins of civilisation, where 'Green' was conspicuous by its absence.

And finally, to add insult to injury, the case against Bill and his dog was listed for hearing at Camberwell Green Magistrates' Court, and light years away from the Emerald Isle and God's green acre.

No matter, work was work, and after a tortuous journey by Underground from my spacious one-bedroomed flat just off the Earls Court Road, I arrived ready for the cut and thrust of the courtroom drama.

The sight that greeted me was like a Hogarth cartoon. There were six or more gaily painted caravans randomly parked along the road, each with their respective dobbins munching lethargically from nosebags of oats. To them it was just another day at the office. Not knowing much about the internal workings of your average dobbin, it seemed to me that the oats went in one end, spent precious little time providing essential nourishment before coming out the other end in record time, with loud farts and mounting deposits creating a potential health hazard. Another assignment for Jack Dawkins and his posse, I thought, although they had other things on their mind. It was just as well it was early March, as we were spared the swarms of flies normally associated with dobbin's nether regions.

Paul had warned me in advance that Bootsy would not be coming, so I had to live with the disappointment. Apparently Bill's £200 had been all but exhausted, so I was on my own. As it turned out, I had all the moral support I could handle. Bill, still wearing the same clothes he had sported at the conference, detached himself from the group of forty of his fellow travellers and came over to greet me with another of those bone-crushing handshakes. Almost immediately there was a spontaneous burst of applause, and mob-handed, we advanced like a Roman phalanx towards the front doors and into court. Let battle commence!

The Crown Prosecution Service in their wisdom had decided to hand on the sword of justice to Counsel, as none of their 'internal advocates' stood up to be counted, a bit like Dawkins's posse, found wanting under fire. The sword, also known as the poisoned chalice, had been passed to Noah Claypole, in his dotage and well past his sell-by date, but ready and willing to feed off the occasional scraps thrown his way. He was profoundly deaf, but it didn't seem to matter, to him at least, and to the CPS, he had one redeeming feature. He was cheap.

In the main hall, Dawkins, his posse and Constable 'Proper' Charlie Bates huddled together at one end, deep in conversation with Claypole, which as it transpired, was a fruitless exercise. Claypole's hearing aid was on the blink, and it was too late to dash out for new batteries. Even over the hubbub Claypole could be heard shouting "speak up!" and "what's that you say?" to Dawkins, who was shouting back as discreetly as he could in these difficult circumstances.

Promptly at ten, the court door was unlocked, and the usher, with the froth of her first coffee of the morning playing seductively around her pursed lips, announced: "The case of Sykes will now be heard in Court Three." In reply, Claypole could be heard shouting back: "What's that she's saying?"

I made my way into court, pressed from behind by the phalanx. Fortunately Court Three was the biggest court Camberwell Green had to offer, so to the accompaniment of much grunting and pushing and shoving and cursing, the phalanx managed to seat themselves under the disapproving eye and increasingly pursed lips of the usher. However, with discretion the better part of valour, she said nothing. After all, it was a public court of law, and it wasn't in her job description to bring forth order out of chaos. Bill, still sporting his top hat, was escorted to the dock to await his date with destiny.

Five minutes later, and in keeping with his own sense of importance, Jeremiah Brownlow, the court clerk, marched purposefully into court, took one look at the phalanx, almost keeled over from the overpowering smell of the farmyard, and marched purposefully straight back out again.

As we waited, the court's extractor fans cranked noisily into life, maximum power, creating an audible whirring sound that had Claypole shaking his hearing aid. Moments later, back came Brownlow, with a less than purposeful stride, and swaying visibly behind his desk, nodded to the usher.

"All rise," she intoned. There was a loud knock on the door at the back, and to the accompaniment of much grunting and pushing and shoving and cursing from the phalanx as they staggered to their feet, the three magistrates, two male and one female, trooped in.

The proceedings began with Brownlow addressing the court through me.

"Mr. Potts," I rose to my feet, "we have received a complaint from the council traffic warden that there are six caravans and horses parked illegally in the road outside court, with the pavement being fouled by waste matter. They will have to be moved immediately."

Pompous jackass I thought. Might as well start as I mean to go on. "I'm not sure what concern it is of the court, as they are not parked on court land, but if you will give me a moment." I turned to Bill and asked in a stage whisper, "do any of the caravans outside belong to you?"

"No they do not," replied Bill, entering into the spirit of things. No fool he!

"You may have heard the defendant's reply," I continued mischievously, "they are equally no concern of his, and *my* only concern is the defendant's right to a fair trial."

There were mutterings of approbation from the phalanx as Brownlow considered his options. He chose to pass the buck.

"Mr. Dawkins, you're a council official from Health & Safety," Dawkins stood up to even louder mutterings as the colour drained from his face, "can you help?"

"No I can't," Dawkins shot back, as life and limb were on the line, "it's not my department."

There was a long pause as Brownlow considered his further options. He chose to pass the buck again.

"Mr. Claypole, can you help?"

Claypole was right out of it, staring blankly into the middle distance. As Dawkins was on his way down, he tapped Claypole firmly on the shoulder.

"The court clerk is addressing you."

"What?" he shouted. "Speak up man!"

"The court clerk is addressing you," Dawkins shouted back.

"Is he by Jove?" Claypole stood up.

"Can you help?" asked Brownlow, like a dog with a bone.

"What's that you say?" shouted Claypole, cupping his hand to his ear, "can you speak up, I'm a little hard of hearing."

This was going nowhere, as everybody in court except Brownlow had realised several minutes ago. But still he blundered on. "Can you help?" he shouted back.

"Oh, I see, yes of course." He turned to the Bench. "May it please your worships," he was off and running, "the defendant is charged with having a dog dangerously out of control..."

"No, no, no," Brownlow interrupted, shouting back, "we haven't got to that part yet. Can you help about the illegal parking outside court?"

"I have certainly not parked illegally," replied Claypole with righteous indignation, "and I resent this unfounded accusation. I came by bus. Now if I may continue without further unwelcome interruptions?"

Brownlow waved Catchpole back down, and mindful of stirrings on the Bench behind him and stirrings in front of him from the phalanx, finally threw in the towel and addressed Bill.

"Are you William Skyes?"

"No I am not," came back the firm reply.

There was a long pause. "If you are not William Sykes, who are you?"

"I'm an innocent man falsely accused," Bill replied without the trace of a smile.

"That's not what I meant. What is your name?"

"Bill Sykes. I've never been known as William Sykes in my entire life."

Progress of sorts. "Before we proceed to trial, Mr. Sykes, the court has noticed you're wearing a top hat." Dear Lord, here we go again. "It is usual for defendants to remove headgear in court unless they have a particular religious conviction, such as a Sikh turban or one of those funny little skull caps worn by members of the Jewish faith, I forget the name."

"It's called a kippah," interrupted the Chairman of the Bench, tapping his own, and looking singularly unamused.

"Thank you sir," Brownlow replied, totally unfazed. After all, this was his court, he made the rules, which required the magistrates to listen, to be advised by him, and to do as they were told.

He turned back to Bill. "So do you have a particular religious conviction?" he repeated.

"I do indeed," came back the firm reply.

"And what is it?"

"I believe in God the Father, God the Son, God the Holy Ghost, the Blessed Virgin Mary and all the Saints, and especially the Blessed St. Patrick." There were loud cheers from the phalanx and the stamping of heavy boots. The usher, who had played very little part in the proceedings so far, sprang into action.

"Order!" she shouted. "Order in court!"

"In that case, make mine a pint of the black stuff," shouted some wag from the back of the phalanx to even louder cheers.

Brownlow waited for the cheers to subside before turning to the Bench. "The defendant is professing a belief in the Christian faith," he advised, "and as the Christian faith does not fall within the defined category of particular religious convictions, he should remove his hat."

The Chairman conferred briefly with his colleagues. As he had just had his kippah described as a funny little skull cap by this pompous jackass, it was a slight he was not prepared to overlook if given the chance. "The Bench has no objection to the defendant wearing his top hat," he ruled to more loud cheers. That'll teach him.

Brownlow had spent the best part of half an hour trying to stamp his authority on the proceedings but getting nowhere fast. The extractor fan was running red hot, and the female magistrate, fighting off a rising sense of nausea, was fanning herself like a Spanish Dueña. She'd obviously had enough, and she was not alone. The Chairman addressed Brownlow with a firmness that took even him by surprise. "Mr. Clerk," he said, "I suggest we now move on to why we are all here, which is to try the case against the defendant, otherwise further valuable court time will be frittered away."

"Very well sir," replied Brownlow through clenched teeth. He turned back to Bill. "Do you own a dog of indeterminate pedigree that answers to the name Bullseye?"

"No I do not."

Brownlow's mouth snapped open. "If you don't own the dog, who does?"

I was up on my feet like a jackrabbit. "With respect, sir," I said, addressing the Chairman, "that is not a proper question, and I advise the defendant not to answer it. The law is clear," I continued, opening my copy of Archbold, "and I refer you to section 3 (1) of the Act. The prosecution must prove on admissible evidence that the defendant was the owner of the dog at the material time. Unless and until this is proved to your satisfaction, the defendant is under no obligation to provide the prosecution or the court clerk with this or any other information."

There followed a crashing silence as Brownlow plucked his copy of Archbold from the rack. "In order for me to assist the Bench, can you direct me to the relevant passage?"

"I can indeed," I replied, "page 2666." Archbold was a very t'ick book.

Brownlow found the passage which he read carefully and deliberately, his concentration broken only by the noise of the two fans flailing away in the background. Finally, the Oracle spake:

"It would appear that learned counsel for the defence is right. Ownership is for the prosecution to prove." He looked over to Catchpole. "Can you help, Mr. Catchpole?"

Catchpole rose to his feet. "I've already explained, I came by bus."

Brownlow's mouth snapped open again. "The Bench wants to know if you have any admissible evidence that the dog in question belonged to the defendant," he shouted.

The penny finally dropped as Catchpole rounded on "Proper" Charlie Bates.

"Can you help?" he whispered for all to hear.

As it turned out, Constable Bates had not arrested and interviewed Bill, it was more than his life was worth, so he'd relied on the evidence of Dawkins and his posse.

"The dog was with the defendant at the time it attacked Jack," he whispered, "so that's the evidence of ownership."

"What's that you say? Speak up man! And who's Jack?"

Bates repeated what he'd said, only louder. "Jack's Mr. Dawkins, and he's sitting right behind you. And anyway, aren't you supposed to advise the CPS?" The buck was being passed again, and if the ship was going down, he wasn't going down alone.

"Not at these prices," boomed Catchpole, waving his backsheet with the agreed fee of £100 written on it. "You prepare the case, and I present it, that's the way it works."

Bates glared back. "Why don't you call the evidence and see where that gets us?"

"Is that the best you can offer?" Catchpole was unimpressed. "What about the dog's collar? Didn't that give you a clue? And presumably the dog had a licence?"

Mr. Catchpole," Bates was losing his composure, "these are Pikeys we're dealing with, they don't obey our rules, in fact they don't obey any rules, so their dogs aren't licensed, and they don't have collars!"

"Pikeys?" boomed Catchpole, unfamiliar with the term, "what are Pikeys?"

The phalanx was beginning to stir, and it was not a pretty sight. Bates had had enough, and it was time to abandon ship. "You're in charge, Mr. Catchpole, so I leave it to you." The buck came bouncing back.

Catchpole turned to face the Bench. "Thank you for your patience, your worships. I have now taken instructions, and we have compelling evidence that the dog was owned by the defendant. I suggest we proceed to conviction." Catchpole was completely oblivious to the fact that the whole court had heard every word of his lively exchange with Bates.

To the Chairman, the use of the word 'Pikey' was almost as bad as describing his kippah as a funny little skull cap, and he and his colleagues had been enjoined by the Lord Chancellor to be ever vigilant when it came to the pejorative use of racial stereotypes. He motioned Brownlow towards him, and the four of them huddled round in animated conversation for several minutes.

Finally, Brownlow resumed his seat and addressed Bill. "Please stand up, Mr. Sykes." Bill did as he was asked. "The court has concluded that there is no evidence that you owned the dog at the time of the incident, so the charge against you is dismissed. You are free to go."

As fast as decency would allow, Brownlow and the magistrates headed for the door just as the phalanx rose as one and erupted in loud cheering and stamping of hobnailed boots. Bill left the dock and gave me another bone-crushing handshake and a Bootsy-style slap on the back.

"You're a star, Mr. Potts, for sure for sure, me and the boys never doubted you for a minute."

The boys all crowded round, and before I knew it, I was being carried shoulder-high from court. Once outside, it was time to saddle up and keep those wagons rolling, Rawhide. The only people missing were John Wayne, Robert Ryan and Jimmy Stewart, but they were probably in the saloon enjoying a pint of the black stuff.

As Bill was about to mount up, he turned to me. "Are you a betting man, Mr. Potts?" he asked.

"Not really," I replied, "the occasional flutter on the Grand National and the Derby, but nothing serious."

"Well, here's a tip for you. There's a horse called Ginger Watt running in the 3.30 at Limerick this coming Saturday, with odds of 200-1 to win. A rank outsider, but who knows? You could have the luck of the Irish," and so saying, he climbed into the caravan and trotted off.

As chance would have it, I passed a bookmaker's on my way to the Underground, so I popped in and placed ten pounds on Ginger Watt to win. The bookmaker looked at me as if I were some kind of an idiot, but my money was as good as anybody's. It was like taking candy from a kid.

More in hope than expectation, I checked the results in Sporting Life, and to my astonishment, Ginger Watt had romped home by five clear lengths. The bad news was that the stewards had ordered an inquiry, as Ginger Watt had never even been placed before, let alone won a race, and it all looked highly suspicious. Understandably my bookmaker refused to honour the bet, but a week later, to my delight, the win was confirmed.

Now where had I put that betting slip?

CHAPTER 3

IN THE LYON'S DEN

I was feeling quite pleased with my handling of the Bill Sykes case, although I had Catchpole to thank for unwittingly helping me on the way. Preparation was the key, as I had been told repeatedly in my first months of practice, so "mastering" the complexities of the Dangerous Dogs Act was well worth the effort. After several reminders from my clerks, Messrs. Bumble & Beadle were finally persuaded to hand over my £200 which, after deductions, left me with the princely sum of £50.

Susie's emails were a welcome relief, although her life, like mine, was settling into a routine. After all, one jolly night around the campfire was very much like another, and with mosquitos the size of London buses buzzing around, it had limited appeal.

Her exciting news was that the new school block was taking shape, and the King had sent one of his wives to lay the foundation stone. As nobody knew until the last minute which wife would be favoured with this signal honour, the inscription was left blank, to be added at a later date.

As for me, it was business as usual. Swings and roundabouts, peaks and troughs. One day I was the toast of the town, the next

I was the forgotten man. But then, as the clerks were fond of reminding me, variety was the spice of life.

⟞⟝

It was one of those days. I was unemployed and surplus to requirements, which placed me on the horns of a dilemma. I could either stay at home, get up late, wander down to Domino's Pizzeria in Earl's Court Road for an American Hot and a pint of lager, then back to the flat for a dose of afternoon television, or I could wander into chambers and look interested until it was time to go home, in the hope that this devotion to duty might be rewarded by some crumb of professional comfort for the following day. I decided to compromise, so I got up late, dressed soberly, breakfasted lightly, and was heading for the door when the phone rang. It was Mike the first junior clerk. "Mr. Potts? I hope I didn't wake you." Ouch! "I've had Mr. Finnan on the line wanting to speak to you urgently. I've told him you're on your way into chambers…" Derek Finnan, or Del to friend and foe alike, was a 'one man band' solicitor practising in the twilight zone south of the river. His office was a back room in his house just off Camberwell Green, ably manned by his wife Topsy, who did the accounts, kept a record of clients past and present, and answered the phone. Everything about Del was unremarkable. In his mid fifties, he was of average height and build, war weary leaden features with thinning over combed hair plastered to his pate. He favoured spectacles that went out of fashion in the sixties and a suit, just the one, which he slept in at night. Del specialised in quantity rather than quality, always crime, get the punters in, cop a plea and get them out again as fast as decency would allow. The 'not guilties' were a drain on his limited resources to be avoided at all costs. Still, from my perspective at least he was loyal to a fault, and loyal solicitors were a rare breed indeed.

"Just leaving, Mike," I replied, still smarting from the rebuke, "unavoidably detained."

"Quite so, sir." He paused. "Always best to get in early, then we know where to find you."

"Yes, thank you for the advice Mike, see you shortly." Too far up himself for his own good, but Golden Rule Number One, never upset the clerks. As Lyndon B. Johnson once famously remarked about J. Edgar Hoover, better to have him inside the tent pissing out than outside pissing in. He had a way with words, did Lyndon B. Johnson, if nothing else. I wondered what the 'B' and 'J' stood for, but that could wait, and turning my mind to more pressing matters, I phoned Del Finnan.

"Del? Sorry I wasn't in chambers to take your call. I was working at home," I lied, "and just leaving when Mike rang."

"No sweat, Tobes," replied Del.

"So what can I do for you?"

"I've had an urgent call from a former client, well actually from the father of a former client, I represented his son a few years ago charged with murder, copped a plea to manslaughter on the grounds of diminished, with parole he'll be out next year, but that's by the by," Del had a remarkable gift for compressing everything into a few sentences, he'd make a very poor barrister, "anyway, his dad's been charged with various benefit frauds, nothing exciting, but by all accounts he needs careful handling, so I immediately thought of you, what with your silver tongue and smooth manner." I chuckled. I hoped that was a compliment. "Thing is, Tobes, he's a bit of a recluse, like Dracula, only comes out after dark, that sort of bloke, clinging to the masonry like a vampire bat and baying at the moon." Del had a way with mixed metaphors.

"Sounds interesting, Del," I replied hesitantly. In my experience, arguing the toss with a lay bench of magistrates in the face of local officialdom was a sterile exercise and downhill all the way, but work was work. "So what do you suggest?"

"I'm going to see him this afternoon, and as you're not in court, I'd hoped you might join me, killing two birds with one stone, so to speak. He lives just up the road from you on Adelaide Road between Swiss Cottage and Chalk Farm, in one of those tower blocks. Two thirty outside, OK?"

"Of course, see you there."

"Oh, I nearly forgot," Del added as I was about to put down the receiver, "do you have a fax machine?"

"I do indeed," I replied proudly, ever at the cutting edge of technology.

"I'll fax something through to you now, sent to me this morning by our client. It doesn't make any sense, but you might as well see it. Forewarned is forearmed. Cheers."

I sat patiently by my fax machine, purchased at no little expense from '**Computers R U.S**', a small shop specialising in second hand equipment off Warwick Road. It was steam driven with thermal paper that curled up like an over exercised lapdog, but it was better than nothing. Very much a collector's item, or so I was told when I bought it.

At last the machine connected, and painfully slowly the crumpled message revealed itself. It contained one word in bold type:

illiterati

Del's geography north of the river left a lot to be desired, and after a long bone shaking ride on the Underground, with one change, I emerged from the bowels of Swiss Cottage station and a ten minute brisk walk found me outside a clutch of grey dismal concrete tower blocks, a monument to local council planning gone mad. I spotted Del, peering at the array of buzzers on the communal door.

"Hello, Tobes," he called, peering on, "I'm trying to locate our client's buzzer." Del consulted a scrap of paper. "Ah, here we are,

Flat 1204." He pressed and waited. After a minute or two, a disembodied voice crackled over the intercom.

"Who's there?"

"It's Del Finnan," Del bellowed into the speaker, "you're expecting us."

"Us? Who's us?"

"I've brought Mr. Potts with me, he's your barrister."

There was a long pause. "Can you vouch for him?"

"Of course."

Another long pause. "Were you followed?"

Del and I exchanged glances. "No."

Yet another long pause. "Very well. Now listen carefully. Upon entry to the lobby, go to the lifts and take the one on the right. Then push the button **12.** Is that clear?"

"Absolutely," Del bellowed back, "seems obvious to me."

"Do not underestimate the task ahead of you," snapped the disembodied voice, "you do so at your peril. You have precisely three minutes from the time of entry to reach my door. Any longer and you will not be admitted. Is that clear?"

"Crystal," replied Del, looking back at me and shrugging his shoulders. Before we had time to reflect on these strange instructions, the entry buzzer sounded and we were off and running, straight to the lift, which thankfully was waiting for us. Del pushed the button, the doors clanged shut, and the lift juddered into life. Time to take stock of the situation.

"Did you get the fax?" asked Del.

"Yes," I replied. "All I got was one sheet with the word

Illiterati

printed on it. Sorry to sound unhelpful, Del, but what's it supposed to mean?"

"Join the club, I haven't the foggiest, but I suspect we're about to find out."

The lift juddered to a halt, and we decanted onto a dimly lit landing. As I peered around trying to get my bearings, a door at the end opened a crack, and a bony finger emerged, beckoning us furiously. There was a sense of urgency as we approached.

"State your business," said the owner of the bony finger from behind the door.

"Del Finnan, solicitor, and…" he turned to me.

"Toby Potts, counsel."

"And why are you here?"

"You're charged with various benefit frauds, and we're here to help you," replied Del.

"Very well, come in! Quickly! Quickly!" The door half opened to admit us, and slammed shut behind us.

The living room was as dimly lit as the hallway, and as I peered into the gloom, I took stock of my surroundings and the owner of the bony finger.

Seated before me, and confined to a wheelchair, was a wizened old man, taller than he looked, probably in his seventies, emaciated, with sunken almost opaque eyes, wispy grey hair and a moist beak like nose, on which were perched a pair of half-moon spectacles. His clothes were obviously handpicked from a top of the range charity shop, and a large travel rug covered his legs.

He motioned us impatiently towards two commode style chairs facing him, the sort you find in the Twilight Home for the Bewildered where incontinence is a real problem and where the professor clearly belonged.

"Now," he began in an American drawl, the firmness in his voice jarring with his apparent frailty, "introductions are in order. I am Professor Dan D. Lyon," I stifled a giggle, "and I am, amongst many things, Emeritus Professor of Astrophysics at the University of Albuquerque."

"A bit off your patch, Squire," Del commented flippantly, not knowing his Albuquerque from his elbow, and immediately wished he hadn't. The professor's eyes narrowed into an icy stare.

"I hope, Mr. Finnan," he snapped back, "you'll do me the courtesy of according me some respect. I don't welcome smartass remarks." There was a long pause. "Now, to the business in hand." His wintry features softened. "May I offer you both a cup of coffee after your long journey?"

"Please don't go to any trouble on our account," I replied for both of us, mindful of the professor's infirmity.

"No trouble at all," and with one bound, the professor was out of his chair and walking purposefully to the kitchen. Oh dear, I thought, as I exchanged glances with Del, bang goes the disability allowance defence. "I've sent my trusty retainer away for the afternoon," he continued as the kettle began to boil, "a very good man, been with me for years, I call him Jocky," he added with a faint chuckle.

Back with three steaming mugs of coffee, the professor settled back into his wheelchair and took a sip. "Now to business, but first, there must be no notes taken of this meeting, no tape recorders, and if asked, you've never met me. Is that clear?"

I'd had some strange requests in my time, but this was the strangest by far. Time to assert myself. "Well, Professor," I replied tentatively, "if I am to do justice to your case, and represent you at court, I can hardly tell the justices I've never met you before. They'll think me an idiot, and worse still, are bound to question my professional competence. At the very least, Mr. Finnan and I are entitled to an explanation."

"All in good time, young man, but before we begin, I must have your assurances. I'm in mortal danger, and if it gets out you know me, so are you. It's as much for your own protection as mine. Understood?"

Weird or what? Despite my discomfort, it was time to don my wig and gown, figuratively speaking of course. "Well, I'm sure I speak for both of us," I began pompously, glancing at Del, "any conference with a client is in strict confidence and anything said cannot be disclosed to a third party without your consent. However, if I feel I cannot represent you on the instructions you have given me, I shall say so and withdraw from the case. Mr. Finnan will do the same."

"I agree," added Del for good measure.

The professor paused, deep in thought whilst staring intently at us. "Very well," he said at last, "then let's proceed." He leaned forward, speaking in a whisper. "Have you heard of the Circle of Deception?"

"I have," Del chirped up, not exactly capturing the gravity of the occasion, "it's called the M25."

"Is that anything to do with your British Secret Service?" asked the professor in all innocence.

"No, no," replied Del, "it's the London orbital motorway, and once you're on it, there's no getting off," he grinned, "and nobody knows where they're going."

The professor's mouth snapped open, hearing but not believing. I managed to keep a straight face, but only just.

"I'm sorry, Professor," I said, "it's our British sense of humour. Please continue."

"This ain't funny." Del composed himself. There followed an awkward silence.

"OK," he said at last, "but no more wisecracks." He paused. "Now where was I?"

"The Circle of Deception," I replied.

"That's right, but how do you know?"

"You were about to tell us," I said, trying to be helpful. The old fool was losing the plot before he'd even begun.

"That's right. Now have you heard of **N.E.R.D**?"

Del spluttered into his coffee. He'd met quite a few in his time, indeed he'd all but cornered the market in nerds south of the river, so he was eminently qualified to hold forth, but he held his tongue. Very much against his better nature.

"No I haven't," I replied without the trace of a smile.

"And nor should you, as it's top secret. It stands for National Energy Research Development. It's government funded, with headquarters deep in the Mojave Desert. To the select few who know of its existence, and I'm one, we call it the wolf's lair."

Shades of the Führer and Dr. Strangelove. This was getting into the realms of fantasy, and I was struggling to keep a straight face. Del for his part was still spluttering into his coffee, which thankfully the professor chose to ignore.

"Over the past few years, we've been working on an alternative source of energy which, when harnessed, is capable of meeting the entire world's energy needs without reliance on fossil fuels, gas, oil or even nuclear."

I nodded, feigning interest. Best to humour him.

"This source of energy comes from beyond our galaxy, I can't go into details as it's top secret, but it's light years away."

I resisted the temptation to make a quip about energy and light years, as this was not the time, and besides, the professor was warming to his theme.

"Now here's the rub. Details of our work have leaked out, we think it's an insider, and there's a cabal of energy suppliers determined to stop us at all costs, as they will go to the wall, big time, when this new energy source comes on stream." The professor paused for dramatic effect.

"Stands to reason," said Del, bringing himself onside, albeit briefly. That was Del for you, with the attention span of a goldfish, and as far as he was concerned, this conference was going nowhere. Besides, he had a posse of nerds down on his manor waiting to be processed and with only Topsy, his wife and Girl Friday, holding the fort.

The professor ignored the interruption and pressed on. "This cabal is headed by the Ruskies, a corrupt bunch of bastards, and with their enormous reserves of gas and oil, they have the most to lose." Sensing Del's mounting impatience, I nodded whilst surreptitiously glancing at my watch. Time to draw the threads together, as this had nothing to do with the charge of making false claims for disability allowance, but the professor was not to be hurried.

"There's also a smattering of Wogs and Wops and Chinks and Gooks, but the Ruskies are the main players in the cabal." I cringed at this explosion of political incorrectness, but there was no stopping the man. "Now the codename for this cabal is the Circle of Deception…"

"Why's that?" asked Del in a spirit of enquiry.

"Who gives a rat's crap?" the professor snapped back. "Maybe they meet in a circle, and they're all devious bastards, that's for sure."

"Fair enough," replied Del, but taking his courage in both hands, he plunged in. "This is all very interesting, but how does it concern us?"

"If you'll stop interrupting, I was coming to that!" Del was thinking of saying something, but resisted the temptation, at least for the time being. "Now we know the Circle meets here regularly in London Town for two obvious reasons. The place is crawling with Ruskie oligarchs, and your security service is worth diddly squat. You've got an open door policy, come one, come all, and they do, the Wogs, the Wops….."

"Hang on a minute," Del interrupted, "our security service is the envy of the world. We've got James Bond, 007, licence to kill, and all you've got is Felix Bloody Leitner."

Del was a movie buff, and loved action films. His idea of a great night out was three hours at his local Multiplex, then a burger and chips washed down with a pint of lager. Topsy, for her part, preferred a romantic evening out with good food, good wine and good company. As far as good company was concerned, Del was a moveable feast, to be moved as far away from her as possible.

"Yeah, yeah, whatever!" replied the professor, clearly unconvinced. "Now, as I was saying. When the Circle came to our attention, our secret service needed a man on the ground to break into the Circle and report back, and they chose me."

More spluttering from Del. As for me, I couldn't really see Dan D. Lyon as a secret agent, but it takes all sorts. I nodded encouragingly.

"The Circle have limitless funds behind them, at least for now, and they've set up a hit squad to protect themselves and hunt down those who stand in their way." He paused for dramatic effect. "I'm on their hit list."

"That's terrible," I replied, glancing at Del whose shoulders were beginning to shake.

"Too damn right it is!" Another pause. "I've discovered the name of their hit squad – they're called the **Illiterati,** and their leader is called Conan the Destroyer."

"You're not going to tell me the Destroyer is an albino who wears a long cloak and self-flagellates, are you?" I couldn't help myself.

This was more than Del could handle, and he burst out laughing. The professor was not amused.

"What's so goddamn funny? I'm in mortal danger, and you're laughing like a goddamn hyena!" The professor stared at me, his eyes narrowing. "How come you know so much about the Destroyer?" he asked ominously.

"Just a stab in the dark," I replied, trying not to be flippant but failing miserably. "I'm sure Mr. Finnan meant no disrespect, Professor. It's just that this comes as a complete shock to both of us, especially as you're charged with making false claims for benefits, and I can't see how all this fits in."

"That's right," Del had now composed himself.

"It's obvious," he glared back, "the **Illiterati** are hoping to flush me from cover, and once in the open, to terminate me as a real and present danger to their devious schemes."

"So they've reported you to the local Council……."

"And when I appear in court, that's their chance to take me down."

This was either dynamite or a damp squib, and the jury were still out. "I can understand your concern, but what about the American Secret Service?"

"That's right," added Del, as the legal aid payment for this conference had expired at least half an hour ago, "you've told us they're the dog's bollocks, so why can't they protect you?"

"They don't have the manpower." Del scoffed, which the professor ignored. "My court appearance coincides with the official visit to your shores of a delegation of US congressmen who are here on a junkie, so they're double booked."

"But if you're right," I said, "the court clerk must be in on this."

"How so?"

"Well, it can't be pure coincidence that he's fixed your hearing for the very day these congressmen hit town."

The professor took a few moments to absorb the enormity of my suggestion. "Goddamn it, man, you're right. The **Illiterati** are everywhere! They're like the Masons, with their weird handshakes and knobbly knees. You don't know who to trust these days," and with that, he jumped up from his wheelchair and rushed to the window. Carefully drawing back the net curtain a fraction, he peered out.

"Look out, professor," said Del mischievously, "there could be a sniper out there with a bead on you even as we speak."

In one bound, the professor was back in his wheelchair. "Thanks for the warning," he replied, deadly serious. "Now do you see what we're up against?"

I didn't like the 'we' bit, and judging from Del's expression, nor did he. Time to wrap it up.

"The hearing is next Thursday at 2pm," I said. "If you choose to defend the charge, it will be adjourned for trial to some future date, hopefully not to coincide with another official junkie when your secret service will be otherwise engaged. If you plead guilty, it will be dealt with there and then, with a fine and an order to repay the false claims. I assume the US Treasury will cover your costs?" I added. I couldn't help myself.

Del had covered his face with his handkerchief and was visibly shaking.

The professor had other things on his mind. "No problem. Now here's the plan of campaign, which you must follow to the letter." Dear Lord, not more of the same! "You guys will arrive at court at least fifteen minutes before the hearing, to suss out the lie of the land. Keep your eyes and ears open at all times, as our lives could depend on it." I nodded, hoping the end was in sight. "I will make my way to court with Jocky, and we must remain in mobile phone contact at all times. Here's my number," he handed me a piece of paper, "it's been security cleared at the highest level, so memorise it and then eat the paper." No chance, I muttered under my breath. "Now, once you've swept the court, report back to me, and when, and only when, you give me the all clear, Jocky and I will enter court at precisely 2pm. In, out and away before the Destroyer and his hit squad can marshal their forces."

"Good plan," I smiled encouragingly. The fact that in my experience, there would be at least twenty cases listed for hearing that afternoon, called on in no particular order, hadn't escaped me, but now was not the time to throw a spanner into the best laid plans of mice and men. I'd had enough.

Del and I arrived punctually at 1.45pm (we had our marching orders), and our sweeping of the court consisted of us standing by the vending machine slurping undrinkable coffee and wishing we were somewhere else. Thankfully there was no sign of the Destroyer or any suspicious looking characters with bulges under their jackets.

At 2pm precisely, Del's mobile phone rang. He used the theme tune from James Bond as his ring tone. Nice touch, I thought.

"Where are you?" snapped the professor.

"We're in the court assembly area, nothing to report. Where are you?"

"I'm outside down a side alley." He paused. "Have you swept the court?"

Just then the courtroom door was unlocked, and a morose usher walked out. "The court is now in session," he intoned to nobody in particular. "All mobile phones must be switched off." This was the cue for a surge of humanity towards the door.

"We're going in now," Del whispered, doing a passable impression of Rambo, another of his heroes from the celluloid screen, "will report back, over and out." Such an impressionable lad.

We entered court together, like the two amigos, and glanced around. We both saw him at the same time, sitting at the back of the court. He was tall, even when sitting down, with gaunt almost haggard features, and silvery white hair. He had small pinkish and piercing eyes, with a sinewy fit looking body.

"My God," I nudged Del, catching my breath, "it's the Destroyer!" Time for affirmative action.

"Barry," I whispered, reading the usher's name proudly emblazoned on his lapel badge, "do you know the gentleman sitting at the back of the court?" and I nodded in the direction of the Destroyer.

"Who wants to know?" he replied helpfully.

"I am Mr. Potts of Counsel, and this is my solicitor Mr. Finnan."

"Oh my Gawd, Legals," he snorted, "we'll be here all day! Never know when to stop talking!" Barry was obviously not a fan. "That's Ted Dexter and he's with witness support."

"Not the cricketing legend? Former captain of England and all that?"

"Now if I had a pound for every time somebody asked me that, I would've retired years ago." And not before time, miserable git. "So why do you want to know?"

This wasn't going to be easy, but we 'Legals' have a way with words. "Well, Mr. Finnan and I represent a client who has a phobia of tall men with white hair and beady eyes, so we were wondering if Ted could be persuaded to leave." It sounded as lame as it was. I made no mention of Conan the Destroyer, as I thought that was a bridge too far.

Barry gave me a long hard look. "You're pulling my plonker," he retorted as he turned to walk away. Crudely put, but to the point.

"No, Barry, I'm deadly serious," as I hurried after him. "Can't you at least ask him?"

Barry gave me another long hard look. Judging from his expression, I was clearly several sandwiches short of a picnic. Bloody Legals!

"Alright," he said at last, "I'll ask, but this is a public court of law, and if he refuses, there's nothing you or your client can do about it."

"Good man, Barry, and I'll put you on my Christmas card mailing list."

"Now if I had a pound…………." and off he went, chuntering, under our vigilant gaze.

To our collective relief, Ted stood up, my God was he tall, smiled fleetingly in our direction, and left court. Was there a hard edge to his smile, or was it my imagination? Get a grip Toby, I muttered to myself, this is ridiculous.

Del and I followed at a respectful distance behind, trying not to be conspicuous, and watched Ted, or Conan, go through a door marked: Private – Court Staff Only - and out of sight.

Del was quickly on the phone to the professor, giving him the all clear, and within two minutes, he was wheeled into court by Jocky.

The professor, anxious not to draw attention to himself, was sporting an enormous Fedora, a red scarf knotted around his neck, and dark glasses. I thought he bore a passing resemblance to Dr. Strangelove. Spooky or what?

With the coast clear, time to put the second part of the plan into action: in, out and away. Easier said than done. Time to bring on the heavy artillery. I sidled over to the long suffering Barry.

"Barry, my client is old and infirm and in need of constant medication," I lied, but what the Hell, as I was as keen as the professor to be in, out and away. "Any chance of hearing his case first? And in return, I promise to be brevity itself."

That was Manna from Heaven to Barry. "I'll see what I can do," and so saying, he intercepted the Clerk to the Justices as he made his grand entrance, a bit like the Queen of Sheba entering King Solomon's temple, the only thing missing being a blast from Handel's Oratorio and the Heavenly Choirs. They huddled together for a few minutes in animated conversation as Barry worked his charms, such as they were. The Clerk looked over to me, I smiled winningly, and then to the professor, who was now at the back of the court looking suitably pathetic.

Just then the door at the rear of the court swung open. "All rise," boomed Barry, very much his party piece, and no sooner had the justices taken their seats, the Clerk announced: "The case of Lyon will now be heard." Good old Barry, a real trooper.

The professor was wheeled to the well of the court, pleaded guilty, and true to my word, a few well-chosen *bons môts* to brighten the shining hour. As predicted, he was fined and ordered to repay his ill-gotten gains.

As ill-luck would have it, as he was being wheeled out of court, Ted Dexter or Conan the Destroyer chose that very moment to leave the staff room and put in an appearance. He gave the professor one of those enigmatic smiles as he walked past and into court. The colour drained from the professor's face in an instant, and his mouth snapped open in a silent scream.

Belying his years, he leapt from his wheelchair and ran headlong for the exit. Off he went like a long dog, scarf snapping behind him like a bullwhip, with Jocky in hot pursuit, over the hills and far away, never to be seen again.

"*Perchance he for whom this bell tolls may be so ill, as that he knows not it tolls for him; therefore never send to know for whom the bells tolls; it tolls for thee.*"

CHAPTER 4
KNIPHOFIA UVARIA

Just as I was beginning to despair that I would ever climb the greasy pole, along came the case of Thomas Johnson to test my adversarial skills to their limit. The brief came in the name of Nick Ridley, my former pupil master, but when he saw that the trial was to be held in Exeter Crown Court, somewhere in the West Country, he was suddenly double-courted and had to return the brief. With his application for silk soon to be considered by the Lord Chancellor's acolytes, festering in wellie land was not his idea of upward mobility.

Nick had been discreetly following my progress since he cut the umbilical cord, and had been pleased with the feedback from the clerks and chambers' solicitors. There were one or two hiccups along the way, representing the wrong client at Horseferry Road Magistrates' Court was one, but that was to be expected as I was marking out my territory and growing in confidence. Nick put my name forward, and to my delight, the brief was duly returned to me. A shot at the big time, and a chance to shine.

Unlike most of my instructions, which were put together on the back of a fag packet, the solicitors briefing 'PLC', known in the profession as 'Proper London Counsel', had taken the time and trouble to instruct counsel fully. Whether I ranked as PLC remained to be seen, but at least I was Counsel from London, so that was a start.

Will Cutler, one of the partners of Heard Cutler & Corran, used to practise in London and briefed Nick regularly. After pounding the pavements for more years than he cared to remember, he grew tired of the big city life, and when the opportunity arose to buy into a partnership with Heard & Curran in Exeter, he took it and moved lock, stock and barrel down to Devon with his wife and children.

The charge was rape, very serious indeed and to be tried by a judge and jury. At last, a real test of my forensic skills and, more importantly, the chance to wear my wig and gown. The case might even make the local press, something for the Toby Potts scrapbook, which at present was 'work in progress', and very little to show for my Sisyphean efforts to date. As I discovered, the press were a fickle bunch, and after my triumph with Bill Sykes, not even a bi-line in the Slade Green Gazette. Still, as I kept telling myself, it was only a matter of time.

I gingerly opened the backsheet and peered within. Cutler had done a good job, describing in detail the charge, a summary of the evidence against Johnson, and his defence. Johnson was charged with rape, better known in the West Country as 'takin' 'er down', and which he freely admitted. In his defence statement, "she were up for it, and I gave 'er a portion". Basically there were only two defences to a charge of rape: "it wasn't me, guv" or "she were gaggin' for it".

By way of background, the complainant, the honourable Katherine Petrie, with a 'K', was the daughter of Sir Reginald Petrie, baronet and squire of Little Minchelden, a small village near Shagford in the Dartmoor National Park. I wondered if that was a misspelling.

As befitting his status, Sir Reginald lived at Minchelden Manor, an enormous pile of Tudor origins, where he and his ancestors had lived since time immemorial. He ticked all the 'country squire' boxes, hunting, shooting and fishing across his estates, and by all accounts, he was well-respected and a jolly good egg.

Katherine, or Kate to her eclectic circle of friends, was aged twenty three, and after a gap year working in Lesotho hoping to catch Prince Harry's eye, but to no avail, had gone up to a totally nondescript university and, four years' later, had come back down with a totally useless degree in media studies. Exhausted by her intellectual gymnastics, such as they were, she was taking a well-earned vacation at the family pile, where she rode, cavorted with Percy, the local chinless wonder as her father described him, and had a jolly good time.

Tom Johnson was the gardener, as were his father and grandfather before him. He was a horny-handed son of toil, now twenty-five and living with his Mum and Dad in a small tied cottage on the estate. His Dad had been promoted to estate manager, so Tom had expectations. He was a big lusty lad in a bucolic sort of way, with handsome sun-tanned features and an eye for the girls.

As Little Minchelden had absolutely nothing to offer by way of social intercourse, except the church, and he didn't really subscribe to all that mumbo-jumbo, Tom didn't get out much. On high days and holidays, he made the trip into Chagford, I was right, it was a misspelling, where he spent the evening at the Ferret and Trouserleg with other horny-handed sons of toil, ogling the barmaid's tits and getting squiffy on rough cider until it was time to catch the last bus home. Simple pleasures for simple country folk.

Percy Chatterton lived with Ma and Pa in nearby Minchelden Parva. Pa was something in the City, so was away for most of the time, and Ma was best friends with Mr. Martini, shaken not stirred, and was also away in a world of her own for most of the time, so Percy had the place very much to himself.

He was the same age as Kate, and they'd very much grown up together when they weren't away at boarding school or spending long lazy holidays at the Aga Khan's delightful little resort in Sardinia, competitively priced to keep out the riff-raff, or schussing down the black run at St. Moritz.

Percy had lost his cherry to Kate when he was seventeen. They went swimming in the lake at Minchelden Manor, the sun was high and the water inviting. Off came the swimwear in no time at all, one thing led to another, and before he knew it, they were making hot passionate love in the summer house. A day to remember, for him at least, although Kate had been there before. She wasn't exactly promiscuous, but she wasn't backward when coming forward.

This was to be the first of many such encounters, and there was even talk of Percy becoming the future Mr. Kate Petrie. There was no doubt who was the dominant partner in that relationship.

That summer was a rare event in the Mincheldens. It was hot and sunny, long languid days and warm caressing evenings, just like Sardinia without the expense and the all-pervading smell of garlic.

Tom was busy in the garden. Everything that needed to be pricked out had been pricked out, the roses had been sprayed against everything, and the shrubs lightly trimmed. Given the hot weather, he had taken to wearing nothing more than his bucolic shorts, socks and boots. It was a sight for sore eyes.

His main task was to keep the garden well-watered, what with the heat and all, and he plodded round, dragging the hosepipe behind him, watering here and watering there, and sometimes watering himself to cool off.

Tom's manly features didn't escape Kate's notice as she wafted round the grounds in a Diaphanous robe over a bikini that was only just decent by any stretch of the imagination. She suddenly took to showing great interest in the plants, a first for her, although those ridiculous Latin names went right over her head, much like her lectures at university when she could be bothered to turn up.

"Look Tom," she enthused, standing close to his manly sweating body, "aren't those pink flowers an absolute delight?"

"Them be pelargoniums," he replied, as if she were interested.

"And those tall red things at the back, what are they?"

"Them be Kniphofia Uvaria, Miss Kate, better known as red 'ot pokers."

"I like the sound of that, Tom," she giggled, and wafted on down towards the lake. Was it his imagination, or was she giving him the come on? That, members of the jury, is for you to decide, I heard myself saying as I rehearsed my final speech.

Percy was a regular visitor as he came and went, an unfortunate expression in the circumstances. More swims in the lake, the scene of his first conquest, and more torrid tumbles in the summer house. Tom knew more about Kate's dalliances than she cared to admit, and when her folks were away, she did little to hide them. Besides, Tom was staff, and it was none of his business.

On that fateful day, it was hot and sunny again, and Kate was in a particularly flirtatious mood. As Tom was to describe her, she was cock-teasing, and his manly shorts were struggling to hide his excitement. After another suggestive remark about his red hot pokers, she'd forgotten the Latin name, and did it matter, she slipped out of her robe, removed her bikini top and lay out on the sun lounger barely six feet away from him and in full view. This was the cue for Tom to move quickly away and hose himself down from head to toe. After all, he was paid to work, not fornicate, and to be caught pumping Miss Kate by Sir Reginald or Lady Petrie was more than his job was worth. Time for that later.

Reading between the lines, Tom was not much of a reader, he returned that night to the big house, which was in darkness except for a full moon, and ever the romantic, found a ladder and placed it firmly beneath Kate's open bedroom window. Undressing down to his stocking feet, he climbed the ladder and peered in.

To his surprise and delight, Kate sat up, pulled back the sheet to expose her naked body and beckoned him inside. All his dreams came true in that one gesture, as he climbed over the sill and into her bed.

Tom had never been one for foreplay, he couldn't see the point, so he was off and running in no time, with Kate moaning contentedly under his firm and manly body.

They both heard it, just as Tom was reaching a climax. Outside, at the foot of the ladder, came the discordant refrain from The Student Prince:

"Overhead the moon is beaming,
Bright as blossoms on the bough,
Nothing is heard but the song of a bird,
Filling all the air with dreaming".

Kate sat bolt upright, turned on the light and was confronted with Tom's sheepish grin. "Good God, Tom, what on earth are you doing?"

"I'm a pleasuring you, Miss Kate. What did you think I was doing?"

She slapped his face, and pushed him away. "Get out now, before I call the police!"

Percy the Warbler, who had called round in the hope of a nocturnal knock-up, had seen the ladder, took this as an invitation to come on up, and he too had stripped off ready for action. As he was climbing the ladder into the arms of his loved one, he was confronted by the sight of Tom's manly and firm buttocks descending towards him, and he was not best pleased. I mean, a common labourer, it was all too distressing.

Once Tom had decamped the scene, there was the inevitable inquest. With the mood gone, Percy had dressed himself, scaled the ladder, and from his perch on the sill, demanded an explanation.

Percy was not worldly-wise. In his naivety, he had firmly believed he was the one and only to earn Kate's affections, so the idea that she was putting it about wounded him to the quick. Kate's explanation that she mistook him for Tom didn't go down at all well. After all, Percy had breeding and the benefit of a public school education, whereas Tom, as far as he was aware, only had horny hands and a big dick.

Kate's first reaction was to forget all about it, but Percy was having none of it. In a small village, tongues do wag, and if it got about he'd been bested by a gardener, he'd be the laughing stock of the County Set. Kate was also mindful of her reputation, such as it was, so against her better judgment and at Percy's insistence, she made a formal complaint to the police. Statements were taken, Tom was arrested and interviewed, and the CPS reviewing lawyer reviewed the evidence and laughed himself silly. His first reaction was to bin it as a complete waste of public time and precious resources, but those in high places had been contacted by Sir Reginald Petrie, and the dye was cast. As far as Sir Reginald was concerned, his daughter was not an 'honourable' for nothing, and her honour was at stake. Such an innocent! Tom Johnson was duly charged with rape, to await Her Majesty's pleasure. After all, or so it was reasoned, if Kate had consented to sex with Tom in the mistaken belief he was Percy, consent had been obtained by false pretences, and it was no consent at all. Enter Toby Potts Esq, PLC, stage right!

Exeter Crown Court was housed in the city's castle. As far as I could see, the castle and its magnificent cathedral, both with Norman origins, were the only two redeeming features of this otherwise uninspiring provincial backwater.

I had agreed to meet Will Cutler and the client outside court at 9, with the trial listed to start at 10.30. After the usual pleasantries, I spent thirty minutes in conference going through the evidence and explaining to Johnson what would happen. The brief contained a detailed defence statement and Johnson's comments on the statements of Kate and Percy. As it transpired, Percy's statement had been doctored to remove references to his state of undress, and the fact that he was there on the rut, but no matter. Johnson had been fairly interviewed by Plod and given a good account of himself. He was also a man with no previous criminal convictions, something to throw into the balance when the time came.

Will led me along a narrow and dusty corridor and up a flight of steps to the robing room. Whether he had been primed by Nick Ridley to take me under his wing, he was doing a very good job, and as a stranger in these 'ere parts, I welcomed his attentions.

The robing room, in need of a good lick of paint, was occupied by six or more barristers, all munching enormous Cornish Pasties, very much in keeping with the cut and thrust of the provincial Criminal Bar. A reverential hush fell over the Munchkins as Will entered and ushered me in. To the Munchkins, Will was a big-hitter on Circuit with a ready supply of good work, and to be included on his list of approved counsel was a privilege indeed.

With his usual efficiency, Will had already found out that prosecuting counsel was Mark Fisher, in his late forties and big in every sense of the word. He was over six feet tall, with a girth to match, thinning hair and a florid complexion. Will beckoned to him, and detaching the remains of his Pasty from his face, he made his way over. He had a pleasant easy-going manner, but I could tell from his expression that he was far from impressed as he looked me up and down. The Exeter Bar was a close-knit community drawn from home-grown talent, so outsiders were not universally welcomed.

Regular good-quality work was as rare as hen's teeth, so when it came along in the form of a rape trial, they didn't like PLCs horning in on their patch and snatching it from under their Pasties. Most of them had heard of London, but couldn't say they'd been there.

There was little to discuss about the case. We both knew that guilt or innocence would turn on Kate's evidence, and if she gave a convincing account consistent with her witness statement, Johnson would be spending the next few years tending the prison gardens, Kniphofia Uvaria and all.

The trial was listed before His Honour Judge Oliver 'Stogie' Mellors, so-called because of his addiction to gut-wrenching panatelas. As I was to discover, at least three or four times a day, regardless of the state of play and the unfolding of the courtroom drama, up he'd jump without a word of warning and leave court for a ten minute drag.

He was winding down and at the end of his career as barrister and judge. Some wag quipped, and it could have been Fisher, that nobody could remember Mellors ever winding up. He was short and emaciated, with what looked suspiciously like dyed ginger hair, or what was left of it, and the sort of sallow lived-in face that only comes from chomping on too many stogies. He was born in Exeter, joined chambers in Exeter, and was appointed to the Circuit Bench sitting in Exeter. Limited horizons on any view, but by all accounts, he was fair and certainly not an interventionist. That would require him to show some interest in the proceedings, which he never did, and his attention span was as limited as his horizons.

Will, who as a busy practitioner had bigger fish to fry, left me with Archie, a young man on work experience with the firm, a law student from Oxford no less, so I was in agreeable company if nothing else. Will gave me his office phone number, and *in extremis,* could return at a moment's notice.

As we made our way into court, Stogie gave Fisher a welcoming nod and completely ignored me. Word had already reached him that PLC, like Elvis, had entered the building, and even if this particular PLC was nothing more than a callow youth, he was still PLC and the enemy within.

After the preliminary skirmishes, it was time to summon the jury. I had already forewarned Johnson about his right of challenge, which in these enlightened times was to be exercised only if he recognised anybody, and he didn't, so he and I were stuck with the twelve honest men and women true who were called at random.

Four of them, all male and middle-aged, looked like country bumpkins minus their pitchforks, rustic and ruddy-faced. They had a reputation for enjoying seigniorial rights over their livestock, almost a second family, so they could well swing behind Tom, and besides, it was a complete waste of their valuable time when there was work aplenty down on the farm.

Females were well represented, six in all. Four of them were of matronly age, and from their expression and demeanour, looked as if they were determined to take their virginity with them to the grave. They would probably go with the prosecution. The other two females were younger, and one in particular caught my eye as she smiled winningly at me, or so I thought. A real looker, and very much a rose amongst thorns. I put them both down as floating voters, but open to persuasion.

Of the remaining two, both male, one looked about Archie's age, probably a student at the university, earnest-looking and attentive. He'd even brought his own notepad and pen. What a geek! I put him on the back burner.

Finally, a loose cannon on deck in the form of a dishevelled forty something with wild staring eyes and a nervous twitch, who looked as if he'd just escaped from somewhere, or the medication hadn't yet kicked in, or both. He was Hannibal Lector personified.

He could go either way or completely over the top, so I decided to give him a wide berth.

Once the jury had settled down and, like empty vessels waiting to be filled, gazed around at their unfamiliar surroundings, up jumped Stogie and shot out for another drag. They must have thought it was part of the arcane ritual, knowing no better, and as they waited patiently, a few struck up a conversation in low hushed tones, mainly about what was happening, or more to the point, what was *not* happening.

Suddenly, and without warning, Hannibal jumped up and marched towards the door. The jury bailiff, otherwise known as Sheila from Admin, also jumped up.

"Excuse me, the court is in session. You can't leave without the judge's permission."

Hannibal totally ignored her and marched out. Maybe it was time for his medication. Sheila looked over to Fisher, who shrugged his shoulders. This wasn't in his remit, and he certainly wasn't going to tackle Hannibal single-handed.

"Best wait for the judge," he said, passing the buck.

Ten minutes later, Stogie returned, sat down, and nodded to Fisher. "You may now open the case for the prosecution."

"Er, Your Honour, we are one juror short."

Stogie glanced over at the jury box and the vacant seat. "The call of nature, perhaps, but he should have asked first." A somewhat absurd suggestion in the circumstances. "Let's wait for his return."

And wait we did. Five, ten, fifteen minutes passed, and still no sign of Hannibal. Stogie, who was beginning to feel the effects of nicotine starvation, jumped up again. "Mr. Fisher, I shall rise whilst enquiries are made within the common parts. However," he added as a precaution, "if the juror is indeed incommoded, best to handle it sensitively. Don't just burst in on him unannounced."

A search party was sent out, with Sheila in the vanguard, and Hannibal was found in the car park, dragging on something that smelled suspiciously like weed, but nobody sought fit to challenge him. He was eventually persuaded to return to court.

"Members of the jury," it was time for Stogie to assert his authority, "you are gathered here today to perform your civic duty and to return a verdict in due course in accordance with your oath." Choosing his words carefully for fear of being hoist on his own petard, he continued. "This means that you must remain in court until you are given permission to leave." Hannibal was giving Stogie the evil eye, not a pretty sight. Time for oil on troubled waters. "However," he continued, "if any of your number wants a break at any time, you only have to ask." Stogie smiled reassuringly as Hannibal twitched malevolently. "Now, Mr. Fisher, we have wasted enough time. Pray continue."

Fisher rose to begin his opening address. "Er, Your Honour, one of the jurors has his hand in the air." It was one of the country bumpkins on the back row.

"Yes?" snapped Stogie irritably.

"May I have a break please?"

"What, already?!? We've barely begun!"

Bumpkin was not to be brow-beaten. "Your Honour just told us all we had to do was ask, so I'm asking. Either you meant what you said or you didn't." There were mutterings of support from his fellow bumpkins. Mutiny in the ranks, to be handled carefully.

"Very well," said Stogie, "the court will rise for ten minutes. I suggest you all take advantage of the time allowed for a comfort break, so that when we resume, we can continue uninterrupted." The court rose.

Ten minutes later, refreshed and as receptive as they were ever likely to get, the jury settled down, Stogie returned, and Fisher finally got to open the case for the prosecution. There were chortles from the back row as Fisher described the events of that night, and especially the bit where Tom was having it away. Stogie shot them a disapproving glance. No levity was allowed in his court without his permission.

Finally, the *moment de verité* as Kate was called to give evidence. This was make or break time.

As befits a member of the minor aristocracy, she took the oath in a firm voice with a hint of arrogance as she turned to face Fisher. A tough nut to crack.

After her evidence in chief, which she delivered word-perfect, it was my turn to cross-examine. In conference with Will, we had identified two obvious weaknesses in Tom's case that I was determined to avoid at all costs. Firstly, he had been employed by Sir Reginald for seven years, and not once had Kate shown any interest in him or his lusty ways until that long hot summer. Secondly, the ladder and his discarded shorts, which were his Achilles heel. It suggested to me, and possibly to the jury, that he had only one thing on his mind, and according to the prosecution, would have pressed his suit regardless, as Fisher had put it somewhat pompously in his opening speech. As the country bumpkins had never had a suit, pressed or otherwise, in their entire lives, this went right over their heads.

"As we all remember, last year was an exceptionally long and hot summer," I began, trying to keep Kate on side for as long as possible.

"It was."

"And you decided to spend the summer at home in Minchelden Manor."

"I had," she replied.

"Doing what?" I asked.

"As little as possible." That didn't go down at all well with the back row, and it showed. They had no time for the idle rich and their idle ways.

"And did that include Percy Chatterton?" No point beating about the bush or the Kniphofia Uvaria for that matter.

"Sometimes."

"And did that include having sex with him?"

"That's none of your business," she snapped.

Stogie cleared his throat and looked disapprovingly at Kate. "Miss Petrie, counsel is entitled to put questions to you as part of his case, and you are obliged to answer them. If counsel puts an improper question to you, I shall intervene. Do you understand?" Kate nodded reluctantly. "So what is the answer to counsel's question?"

"Yes," she replied after a pause. The Matrons clicked their teeth in disgust, but the bumpkins were showing a lively interest and nudging each other. The student was scribbling furiously, and that last answer was heavily underlined. Hannibal's nervous twitch was becoming more and more pronounced. Time perhaps for another drag on his medicinal weed.

I pressed on before he asked for another break. "So you knew Percy intimately?"

Another pause. "I suppose so," she replied reluctantly. This was not playing well to the gallery. Thank God Mama and Papa were not in court to witness her washing her dirty laundry in public. Like many parents, they thought she was Snow White, and to hear that she had drifted would be a bitter pill to swallow on the dinner party circuit.

"And not only did you know Percy intimately, you had seen him naked many times?"

Another long pause. "I don't agree I'd seen him naked many times, but yes, I had seen him naked." More nudges and winks from the bumpkins and audible gasps from the Matrons.

"Enough times to know what he looked like?"

"Yes."

I felt I'd done enough to lay the groundwork. Time to move on to more difficult territory.

"Tom the gardener," I continued cautiously, "you'd also seen him half-naked during that long hot summer, gardening in just a pair of shorts?"

"I have no recollection of seeing him at all," she replied haughtily. "After all, he's staff." That went down like a lead balloon with the jury, and any sympathy they might have had evaporated like the early morning mist. Very much an own goal, but now was not the time to gloat.

"That's simply not right, is it? In the week leading up to the incident in your bedroom," I continued, "you saw him and spoke to him on a daily basis."

"As I said, I have no recollection of seeing him at all." She was not prepared to give ground.

"And you expressed interest in his plants, and in particular, his Kniphofia Uvaria."

"You'll have to enlighten me, and I dare say the jury, Mr. Potts," interrupted Stogie.

"Certainly, Your Honour. They are better known as red hot pokers, long and stiff with a prominent red tip." There were audible guffaws from the back row.

"That's disgusting!" she shot back.

"And during these conversations which you deny ever having with Tom," I pressed on, "you were dressed in a see-though robe and a tiny, tiny bikini."

"Well, yes, I wore a bikini, it was hot."

"And it wasn't just the weather that was hot, was it Miss Petrie?"

"I don't know what you mean." Yes she did, but she wasn't about to admit it.

"When you were in the garden chatting to Tom, you were sexually aroused."

A moment's hesitation, but was it enough? "No I was not."

Like Stogie, it was time to wind down.

"When Tom appeared at your window that night, you knew perfectly well who it was."

"No I did not. I thought it was Percy."

"Couldn't you see? There was a full moon, as bright as blossom on the bough." A nice touch, I thought, and a nod towards Percy the Warbler.

"I'd had the best part of a bottle of bubbly," that wouldn't play well to the back row, "and besides, the thought of having sex with Tom never entered my head. I mean…" Her voice trailed off.

"Because he was a common gardener, is that what you were about to say?"

"Well, er, no," she replied unconvincingly.

"No further questions." I sat down. As Nick Ridley had taught me, leave the jury wanting more, and leave unanswered questions hanging in the air. I felt I'd sown the seeds of doubt in the jury's minds, and if I were right, Johnson should be acquitted. That said, and again as Nick had taught me, the high point for the defence is at the end of the prosecution case, and after that, it was all downhill.

With the court clock nudging half past twelve, Stogie addressed the jury.

"Members of the jury, we will now adjourn until half past two," and so saying, up he jumped and left court at a gallop. As I was to discover, a two hour lunch break was *de rigueur* for Stogie to recharge his batteries. I was making my way to the robing room when Fisher and the Munchkins swept past, to be joined by Stogie loitering with intent outside and billowing smoke from his panatela, and off they went down the hill at a lively pace to their favourite watering-hole. I was not invited.

Will, attentive to my every need, met me at the court steps and offered to buy me lunch, an offer too good to refuse. Archie was sent off to fend for himself.

"There's quite a good restaurant close to the court, it's called the Wine Library, and popular with the Bar and Bench. I recommend it."

We descended some narrow steps into a large panelled room which gave every appearance of a gentleman's club without the gentlemen. There was a good selection of cold meats and salads, but no Cornish Pasties, and an even better selection of wines. Fisher was first in the queue and scooping enormous helpings of food onto his plate when he caught Will's eye and came over.

"Hello Mark, how's the trial going?" asked Will.

"Passably well, thanks Will," he replied, looking embarrassed.

"I don't know if you've met Toby Potts," continued Will mischievously, nodding towards me.

Fisher coloured visibly. "I would have invited you to join us Toby," he blurted out, "but I assumed you'd made other arrangements." It sounded as feeble an excuse as it was.

"No matter," I replied graciously, "another time perhaps."

Fisher went back to rejoin the Munchkins, and for a moment, all eyes turned on us as they counted the cost of their discourtesy.

"A very provincial Bar," said Will dismissively, "almost incestuous and much to learn. So how is Nick?" he asked, changing the subject.

For the next half hour we chatted about life in London, not exactly at the sharp end where he'd left it, but he still had contacts in the Big Smoke and memories of happy times. Will was about to order an expensive bottle of claret when I stopped him.

"If you don't mind, I'll stick to mineral water," I said. What a creep, but Will was impressed, and it showed, the more so as the Munchkins were swilling down copious quantities of the house wine and braying loudly. Not an edifying sight, and duly noted.

Promptly at a quarter to three, the trial resumed. After Tom's interview with the police had been read to the jury, and his good character duly noted, Fisher closed the case for the prosecution, and it was time for Tom to step up to the plate and start swinging.

He gave his evidence well enough, in quiet and measured tones. This contrasted well with Kate's offhand arrogance, and I felt it struck a chord with most of the jury.

"Turning to the day in question," I continued, "what happened?"

"Well," he replied, "Miss Kate had been giving me the eye all week."

"Meaning?"

"Just little things, showing an interest in the garden for the first time in her life, and especially my Kniphofia Uvaria, standing real close to me in her next-to-nothings, and then, before I could say Pelargonium Multiflorum, she laid out on the sun lounger and stripped off, as close what I am to the jury 'ere. Mark you," he added with a chuckle, "it were a beautiful sight to see, there's no denying that."

"And what did you think?" I asked.

"She were giving me the 'come on', that's what I thought, so like any red-blooded male, I thought I'd oblige. It would've been rude not to, what with 'er being the master's daughter an' all."

"Quite so," I said.

"That's a comment," muttered Fisher through his post-prandial haze.

"So what happened that night?" I continued.

"I got the ladder from the garden shed and put it up to Miss Kate's window, the 'ouse were in darkness," he added, "but there were a full moon. I took me kit off, up I went, she gave me the 'come on' just what I expected, so I came on."

"Now there's no dispute you had sexual intercourse with Miss Kate. What happened next?"

"Well, Miss Kate and I were 'aving a gay old time, when we 'eard Mr. Percy outside the window singing, enough to put any man off 'is stride, and that were it. 'e can't sing to save 'is life," Tom added for good measure, much to the jury's amusement.

"And how did it end?"

"Well, as soon as Miss Kate 'eard Mr. Percy, she come over all hoity-toity, slapped me face and told me to get out, so I did."

"Go on."

"As I were leaving to go 'ome, I 'eard 'em 'aving a right old barney. 'e were accusing 'er of being unfaithful, she were saying it were all a mistake, and that's all I 'eard."

"And what was the next you heard of this?" I asked.

"It were about two day later, the Polliss came to arrest me, said I'd raped Miss Kate. I told 'em they'd got the wrong end of the stick. They seemed to believe me, but told me it weren't their decision, summat about a reviewing lawyer. Anyway, 'bout two week later, they charged me, and 'ere I am."

Fisher rose unsteadily to his feet to cross-examine.

"How long had you been working for Sir Reginald?" he began.

"About seven year," Tom replied.

"And in all that time, had Miss Kate ever 'come on' to you, as you somewhat crudely put it?"

"Not once," replied Tom. Oh dear, not what I wanted to hear. "But then, this were the first really 'ot summer for many a long year, and the 'eat can do strange things to the body. It gets the sap rising." Good on you Tom, one in the eye for Fisher.

"You clearly knew what you were going to do that night, didn't you?" he continued.

"Of course," Tom replied, "it weren't a social visit." Titters from the jury. Stogie was well out of it, snoozing fitfully.

"So why the ladder? If Miss Kate was up for it, why not knock on the door, or call up to her from below her open window?"

"It's the romantic in me, sir," said Tom without a moment's hesitation. "The girls love it."

"You mean to tell this jury," Fisher said with heavy irony, "that you've used a ladder before?"

"I 'ave indeed, sir. Some bring flowers and bubbly, I bring me ladder. It's never let me down yet," he grinned. "Only the week before, I'd been courting sweet Molly Malone from the village, up and in I went, and she didn't slap me or shout rape."

"And I suppose you're going to tell this jury that you stripped down to your stocking feet to woo sweet Molly Malone?" he asked sarcastically.

"I did indeed, sir. I always do. It adds to the excitement."

The rest of Fisher's cross-examination was putting his case to Tom, who denied each and every suggestion. It was lacklustre performance and added nothing as he went through the routine. Eventually, he slumped back in his seat, having earned his brief fee but no more.

Stogie shook himself from his torpor. "Members of the jury, we will now adjourn for the day, and meet again tomorrow promptly at ten thirty. You will then hear counsels' final speeches and I shall sum up, after which you will retire to consider your verdict."

Will was outside court to meet me and invite me to dinner, and invitation I politely declined. "If you'll forgive me, I shall have a light supper, work on my final speech and then early to bed." Again the creep, but regardless of the verdict, I wanted Nick to feel he'd made the right decision in recommending me to his friend, and hopefully, a good report from Will as to my sobriety if nothing else.

The next morning, promptly at eleven, Fisher rose to deliver his final speech. I listened intently, waiting for the killer blow, but it never came. His mind was elsewhere, probably the headlong rush down to the Wine Library.

Then it was my turn to dazzle and captivate in equal measure. I had decided to keep my speech short and to the point, as there was only one point to consider. The one word "consent" loomed large. It was the elephant in the room, or more precisely, the elephant in the bedroom.

I had kept a discreet watch on the jury, as advised by Nick, to gauge their reactions during the evidence for tell-tale signs. I felt that the bumpkins were on board, the matrons remained sour-faced throughout, which left the floating voters and Hannibal, who had shown no obvious interest from the moment he took the oath. Miss Rose smiled a lot, but then she smiled a lot all the time, so I had no idea which way she would go.

I started with a review of Tom's character, a gentle hard-working man, good at his job, reliable and dependable.He was a red-blooded male, of course, but would he risk his good name, and his job, by forcing himself on an unwilling girl, and, more to the point, the daughter of his employer? It was wholly out of character. I got a few receptive nods.

I made light of the ladder and Tom's nakedness, as he had given me sufficient ammunition when describing his romantic encounter with the fragrant Molly Malone, and I turned it to his advantage. I stressed the moonlit night, and the difference between Percy's and Tom's naked form when Kate invited him in. Even with the best part of a bottle of bubbly inside her, she could not have been mistaken as she now claims.

"Finally, and it gives me no pleasure to say so, Kate lied to Percy when he caught them red-handed, she lied to her parents to save what they believed to be her honour, she lied to the police, and she has lied to you, members of the jury." It was a nettle, or as Tom would have it, an Urtica Urticaceae, that had to be grasped, and there was no shying away from it.

"She has told you," I continued, "in her abrupt and somewhat haughty manner, that she, the Honourable Katherine Petrie of Minchelden Manor, and a member of the minor aristocracy, has the right to be believed over the word of Tom Johnson, who is nothing but a common gardener." I paused for dramatic effect. "It is a sad and misguided world indeed where some believe they are more equal than others. That may have been the case in days gone by, but in these enlightened times, we are all equal under the law and more importantly, all equal in the eyes of you, members of the jury. I invite you to find Tom Johnson not guilty of rape."

I sat down, drained of all emotion. I felt I had done enough, but only time would tell.

Stogie took his usual ten minute break, and then he summed up. He gave the jury the necessary directions on the law, together with a brief summary of the facts. I suspected that his brevity may have had something to do with the whiff of the Wine Library in his nostrils, as the clock nudged towards twelve thirty and watering time.

The court rose, with a direction that, ready or not, there would be no verdict taken before two thirty. Fisher hesitated briefly at the door of the court, wondering perhaps if he should invite me to join Stogie and the Munchkins, but the moment passed. Old habits die hard, and booted and spurred, they were off down the hill without so much as a glance behind them. To be honest, I was quite relieved.

Will, solicitous as ever, was there to meet me, and together with Archie, we avoided the Wine Library in favour of an agreeable Bistro overlooking the cathedral close. As before, I stuck to mineral water. If the verdict went against Tom, I would have to mitigate on his behalf before sentence was passed, so I needed a clear head.

Archie was good company, obviously hand-picked by Will from the scores of applicants seeking work experience with such a prestigious firm. When asked, he gave an incisive summary of the trial, and he was full of praise for my adversarial skills. He was also firmly of the opinion that Tom should never have been charged. Amen to that!

Will went back to the office, and I returned to court with thirty minutes to spare. Archie, sensibly, left me to my own devices. I found a conference room to make some notes if I was required to mitigate, but whatever I said would be nothing more than window-dressing. The law was clear – a convicted rapist went to prison, and the only issue was the length of the sentence. According to my trusty Archbold, Tom should expect a sentence of five years, which, with good behaviour and jumping through the sex offender's hoops and a promise to behave himself in the future, could see him released in two years' time.

Even if he were acquitted, Tom faced an uncertain future. Sir Reginald had put him on 'gardening leave', very apt in the circumstances, full pay of course. As a pillar of the community, Sir Reginald didn't want an unfair dismissal claim hitting his doormat, but Tom couldn't stay on at the Manor. Such a pity, as good gardeners at slave-labour wages were hard to come by.

Tom was no fool, and he had put out feelers with Little Minchelden District Council, Parks and Gardens Department. Some of the councillors had already seen Tom's handiwork up at the Manor, when Sir Reginald threw open the gardens for the benefit of local worthy charities. They had missed out three years' running on the best-kept village award, in fact they hadn't even reached the finals, so with Tom's green fingers working miracles, it would put them firmly back on the map, and one in the eye for Minchelden Parva, last year's winners.

Time and enough for all that as I made my way to court. It was two thirty by the court clock, and no sign of life. I caught Sheila's eye, sitting as she was outside the jury retiring room door, like Cerberus at the Gates of Hell, charged with the heavy responsibility of preventing entry to unauthorised persons, or in the case of Hannibal, preventing him from escaping. I looked enquiringly. She shook her head.

Promptly at two fifty-six, Stogie, Fisher and the Munchkins came barrelling up the hill, well-fed and watered and fit for nothing. Thirty minutes later, the court reassembled.

Stogie addressed us both. "Gentlemen, the jury have been de-liberating for three hours, and have not yet reached a verdict. As you know, after two hours have elapsed, I am allowed to accept a verdict on which at least ten are agreed. I shall bring them back into court and give them a majority direction," and so saying, he nodded towards Sheila.

The jury filed back into court, and the geek identified himself as the foreman, a reward no doubt, for all those copious notes and flowcharts. I watched them carefully as they were asked if they had reached a unanimous verdict. They had not.

From their expressions, it was difficult to tell if just one or two were holding out. I'd been there before at the Bailey when Santa Claus had been triumphantly acquitted on a majority verdict, with the transvestite marching to a different tune.

"Members of the jury," intoned Stogie, "if you cannot agree on a unanimous verdict, the law allows me to accept a verdict on which at least ten of you are agreed. Please retire and continue your deliberations."

Off they went, back into their retiring room. Stogie was not best pleased. It was his invariable practice to draw stumps no later than three forty five at the latest, and the thought of sitting into the twilight hours depressed him no end.

Thirty minutes later, Stogie came back into court with a face like thunder. "Bring back the jury," he snapped at Sheila.

With the jury back in court, Stogie addressed them with a hint of impatience in his voice. "Members of the jury, have you reached a verdict on which at least ten of you agree?"

"No we have not," replied the Geek.

"Very well," continued Stogie, "if I give you further time, is there any reasonable prospect of reaching a majority verdict?" Dear God, he prayed, please say no.

"No, Your Honour, we are hopelessly divided."

Hallelujah, there is God in Heaven. Stogie addressed us. "Gentlemen, unless you seek to persuade me to the contrary, I shall discharge the jury from returning a verdict." It was not so much an enquiry as a statement of intent.

"No Your Honour," we replied in unison.

"Very well." He turned to the jury. "Thank you for the care and attention you have given to this most unusual case, and I shall now discharge you. You may leave court."

Hannibal was off like a rat up a drainpipe, with the others following him out in dribs and drabs. Four hours without a drag on his medicinal weed had left him with severe withdrawal symptoms.

To my surprise, Stogie addressed Fisher, who rose heavily. "Mr. Fisher, as the jury have failed to reach a majority verdict, I do not believe a retrial is in the interests of justice. I shall rise whilst you take instructions."

Fisher did as he was bidden, and fifteen minutes later, he returned to court.

"Your Honour, the prosecution do not seek a retrial in this case, and offer no further evidence."

"Thank you Mr. Fisher, and for the record, I agree." Stogie turned to Tom. "Stand up. You have heard what Mr. Fisher has said. I shall therefore enter a formal verdict of not guilty. You are free to go."

Tom was over the moon, bright as blossom on the bough. He thanked me profusely, and then he was gone.

I had already checked out of my lodgings, but Will was having none of it. He had been alerted by Archie, and by the time I had changed, he was there to meet me.

"Well done indeed, Toby, I'm sure Tom Johnson is absolutely delighted, as am I. Many congratulations."

"Thanks in great measure to your excellent instructions and your support," I replied. "Now, if I hurry, I can catch the six o'clock train back to London."

"No you will not," he replied firmly. "You deserve a celebration. I've already spoken to your clerks, they are keeping you free for tomorrow, so tonight Archie and I will wine and dine you, and you can return to London in the morning. I've booked a room for you at the Stanhope, at my expense of course, and we will meet you in the bar promptly at seven thirty."

I didn't know what to say. I had checked the prices at the Stanhope when booking overnight accommodation, they were way beyond my budget, especially as legal aid didn't cover my expenses, so I savoured that rare moment when I began to believe it was all worthwhile, that I had arrived, and the only way was up.

Tomorrow would be another day, but today was for living and dreaming the dream. As Percy the Warbler would have put it:

> *"Nothing is heard but the song of a bird,*
> *Filling all the air with dreaming."*

CHAPTER 5
THE ROTTEN APPLE

B ack to earth with a bump.

After the euphoria surrounding my great forensic triumph, I had been wined and dined by Will, slept like a baby in an enormous double bed at the Stanhope, and after breakfast, had been driven to the station by Archie in Will's top-of-the-range Range Rover. I felt like royalty, or minor aristocracy at the very least. Toby Potts had arrived.

Given the lateness of the hour when the jury were discharged and Tom gloriously acquitted, the local newshound had long since departed to put the paper to bed. Instead of holding the front page for breaking news, the Exeter Enquirer led with the proposed extension to the ring road. No pithy statement on the steps of the court from eminent PLC, that justice had been done and had been seen to be done, with Will and Archie smiling appreciatively in the background but far enough in the background not to steal my thunder, and worse still, no photo opportunities.

Of course if Tom had been convicted, that would have been different. I could see the headlines now: "Toff's daughter taken down by randy gardener", with a prominent colour photograph of his Kniphofia Uvaria. Acquittals didn't make headlines, and certainly not in the West Country.

I arrived back in Chambers by late afternoon, and I had to admit, there was a certain swagger to my gait. No point hiding my light under a bushel, I thought. Will had already phoned Nick singing my praises, so Nick was well pleased, and the news had filtered down to the clerks' room. My star couldn't have shone brighter.

I wandered in at six, ready for my next challenge, and looked expectantly at Michael, the first junior clerk.

"A good result by all accounts down Exeter way Mr. Potts," he said with no visible enthusiasm. "I've heard of it, but can't say I've ever been there."

"A treat in store for you Michael," I replied cheerfully, "and they do a very good line in home-made Pasties."

"Quite so. Now tomorrow, I've got a pre-trial review at Snaresbrook for the CPS, and if you play your cards right, I'll put your name forward for the trial."

I smiled weakly, took the dog-eared brief, and resisting the temptation to tell Mike where he could shove it, headed home. Back to earth with a bump.

The case was not without interest, which made a change. According to the reviewing lawyer's review, the defendant was charged with the theft of a car, not just any car, but a brand-new BMW worth £70,000 of anybody's money, from the forecourt of Carrs Auto Traders in Chingford. Some weeks' later, that same car was clocked doing eighty through Chingford town centre, and pulled over by Plod. The innocent purchaser for value, as we lawyers would say, was mortified to learn that he had bought a ringer. The defendant, who denied all knowledge, had been traced through a small ad he had placed in the Chingford Chimes. He was duly charged and bailed to appear at Snaresbrook Crown Court.

As I entered the robing room, I spotted a familiar face, and groaned inwardly. It was Noel Cantwell from Twilight Chambers, who caught my eye and came over.

"Potts," he smirked, "the jewel in the Crown Prosecution Service. I gather you're instructed to prosecute my client. A bit out of your depth on this one, aren't you?"

"Cantwell," I replied, ignoring the slight, "charming as ever, and always a pleasure to lock antlers with such a formidable adversary," I lied. I didn't like the man and his oleaginous ways, and it was not without good reason that his chambers were nicknamed 'twilight'. He trod a fine line between the straight and narrow and the downright crooked, such was his reputation, and if self-importance had anything to do with professional advancement, he'd be Lord Chief Justice by now. "Now let me guess," I continued. You'll offer me a bind-over if I offer no evidence?" This was Cantwell's invariable opening gambit, regardless of whether his client was charged with murder most foul or shoplifting.

"Got it in one, Potts," he said, "after all, better a glass half-full than half-empty."

"I will take instructions, but I can give you the answer right now. No way!"

"So be it, see you in court!"

The case was listed 'promptly' at ten before His Honour Judge 'Bonkers' Clarke, the resident judge, who reserved all preliminary matters to himself. Mine was therefore one of twelve cases all listed 'promptly' at ten, somewhere near the bottom. As a result, there was a lot of hanging around at the court door waiting to be called on, as 'Bonkers' applied the principle of random selection which bore little resemblance to the order in which the cases had been listed. We were cannon fodder, as befitting our status of non-essential court users, a term applied to any counsel who had the temerity to try and park in the car park.

I sat down away from the madding crowd but within earshot as I watched an increasingly nervous Cantwell pacing up and down and looking in vain for his client. As it transpired, it was a fruitless exercise, as his client hadn't turned up. What a hoot!

It was now ten-thirty, and only two cases disposed of. It was going to be a long morning, and with no payment for time waiting, very much a loss-leader. My mood of self-pity was interrupted by a well-dressed and distinguished man in his mid-forties, looking pale and worried as he approached me.

"Excuse me," he said in a cultivated voice, "and forgive the intrusion as we haven't met before, but I wonder if you can help me."

I stood up. "I will if I can," I replied, "what seems to be the problem?"

"My name is Richard Anstruther-Browne, and my son Hugo was arrested two days' ago." I nodded. "He's been charged with possession with intent to supply Class A drugs. He appeared before the Magistrates yesterday, who refused bail, and he's now renewing his application before His Honour Judge Clarke."

"So how can I help?" I asked, not fancying his chances.

"I engaged the services of a local solicitor who specialises in crime, and who undertook to brief experienced counsel with Chambers in the Temple. We arranged to meet outside court at nine-thirty, but by ten, and with no sign of him, I phoned the solicitor. He apologised profusely, it had apparently slipped his mind."

"That's outrageous," I said. Probably one of Cantwell's cronies.

"My sentiments precisely," he replied. "The solicitor advised me to speak to the court listing officer, which I have done, and I am told that if the application is to be adjourned, the earliest the court can hear it will be in seven days' time."

"I'm afraid that's the court service for you," I said, "they don't like thinking on their feet."

He paused. "I know it's a fearful imposition, but I wonder if you could represent him this morning? Seven days is a very long time for a young man when you're languishing in Brixton Prison."

Good Lord, I thought to myself, a dock brief, harking back to the bad old days when prisoners appeared in court unloved and unrepresented, and with leave of the judge, which was given sparingly and usually reserved for hanging offences, they could pick a barrister at random seated in the well of the court. It was a way for junior barristers to gain useful court experience at bargain-basement rates, but I had a feeling the tradition had long since been abolished.

Anstruther-Browne sensed my unease. "I shall of course pay you for your services," he said, "will two hundred pounds be sufficient?"

I gasped. "That's far too much," I heard myself saying and never thought I would, "the going rate is twenty-five pounds." Shut up, you fool! "But first things first," I continued, "there is an experienced local barrister here at court," I nodded towards Cantwell, still searching frantically for his client, "you may be in safer hands with him."

"Yes, I noticed him," he replied dismissively, "but I consider myself a good judge of character, which is the reason I approached you and not him." Praise indeed. "You may appear young and inexperienced," I groaned inwardly, as it had been going swimmingly well, "but I like your manner and the way you hold yourself." That's better, I thought. After all, he was addressing the Lion of Exeter and the toast of the West Country.

"Is your son here?" I asked.

"No, the Prison Service have declined to produce him." A law unto themselves, and anyway, all that form-filling and pencil-licking and arranging transport to drive a no-hoper across London, only to have his application refused in short order by Bonkers, it wasn't worth the candle. "However, I am sufficiently acquainted with the facts to give you as much information as you might require."

"In which case, please give me a few minutes. I have a case in Court One that requires my attention," I didn't want my new-found friend to think I was just hanging about for the sheer hell of it, "and then I need to make a phone call."

After what seemed like an eternity, the pre-trial review of Cantwell's absent client was called on. I made the usual application for an arrest warrant, Cantwell huffed and puffed but to no avail, warrant granted, and it was back to the robing room to make that all-important phone call.

"Del? It's Toby."

"Hello Tobes, where are you?"

"At Snaresbrook Crown Court..."

"You poor lamb, what have you done to deserve that?"

"A question I frequently ask myself, but I need a favour." I explained what had happened. "So I need you to instruct me. I can't promise the brief will come our way, as the client has in mind more experienced counsel, but I said I'd help out."

"Consider it done, Tobes. I'll send one of my special 'one liner' backsheets into Chambers." I laughed. Del's instructions were notorious for being brief and to the point. "Good luck."

"Thanks Del, much appreciated."

Del was about to ring off. "I forgot to ask, what's the client's name?"

"Hugo Anstruther-Browne."

"Sounds very grand, but then so does Toby Potts. Speak soon."

Fortunately, Bonkers was going at a snail's pace, so I had time to take instructions and get a reasonable picture of Hugo and the charge against him. On the positive side, he had no previous convictions, but against him, and I could hear Bonkers barking, this is a serious charge which, if proved, carries with it a substantial sentence of imprisonment. He would add for good measure that any time spent in custody awaiting trial would be time served behind bars, so the sooner he makes a start, the sooner he'll be released. Application refused.

The application was eventually called on, and as I entered court, Bonkers nodded briefly. I ushered Anstruther-Browne to the seat behind me.

"The application of Browne will now be heard," announced the usher. "The defendant does not attend."

Bonkers was reading the prosecution summary as the CPS in-house lawyer rose to his feet. "This bail application is opposed, Your Honour. The charge is a serious one, and as Your Honour sees from the summary, the defendant was arrested in the early hours of the morning in possession of forty Class A amphetamine tablets, better known as Speed, with a street value of £1000. It is the Crown's case that this quantity was not for personal use, and the defendant was in possession of them with intent to supply."

"A self-evident fact, Mr. Newman," snapped Bonkers.

"Quite so, Your Honour, and after arrest, he made a full and frank confession."

"On tape?" asked Bonkers.

"Er, no Your Honour, but duly noted in the interviewing officer's pocket book."

"In this day and age, as you should know, Mr. Newman, that doesn't amount to a row of beans."

Newman paused, duly chastened. "If convicted," he continued, "the defendant faces a lengthy sentence of imprisonment, and if granted bail, it is the Crown's submission that he will abscond."

Bonkers read on. "No previous convictions and aged eighteen. Where does he live?"

"He shares rented accommodation in Finchley. It's a property let out to students."

"Very well. Is that all?"

"The defendant was refused bail by the Magistrates Court, and renews his application before Your Honour."

"I'd rather worked that out for myself, Mr. Newman, and irrelevant. This application is *de novo* as you should know." He glowered at Newman, and then glowered at me.

"So Mr. Potts, another hopeless application, and you've drawn the short straw." Bonkers pushed his chair back and threw down his pen. "Possession with intent to supply Class A drugs, the most serious category as laid down by the Misuse of Drugs Act, carries with it only one possible sentence."

"May I begin where I know Your Honour would want me to begin," I started, trying to compose myself, "bail is of right, and any order interfering with the liberty of the subject can only be made if there are compelling reasons for doing so."

"I'm aware if that," he retorted, "and you've heard them."

"With respect, Your Honour, I have heard nothing of the sort. I have heard that the defendant faces a serious charge, but so do many who appear before Your Honour and are admitted to bail. To do otherwise would be to prejudge the outcome of the trial, and the defendant is innocent of the charge unless and until he is convicted on admissible and compelling evidence." Bonkers was about to interrupt, but I pressed on. "Your Honour has already and rightly commented on the so-called police station confession which, in the past, was capable of misleading judge and jury alike, and there were many instances of miscarriages of justice resulting from it. Thankfully no more, as any confession must now be taped, and as Mr. Newman has told you, it was not. So to adopt Your Honour's words, it doesn't amount to a row of beans. I also add for completeness that the defendant was denied access to a solicitor, which again is a gross abuse of his rights."

"Was he indeed? What do you say about that, Mr. Newman?"

Newman stood up. "My instructions are that the defendant was offered a solicitor but declined."

Bonkers cleared his throat loudly. "Moving on, and assuming what you say is right, that still doesn't account for the large quantity of drugs found on him when he was arrested."

"They were not his, and the first time he saw them was when the interviewing officer produced them at the police station."

Bonkers' eyebrows shot up. "So the defence is that the police planted these drugs on a wholly innocent young man? A serious allegation."

"Your Honour is correct, and if I may add, a wholly innocent young man who has never been in trouble before."

"Yes, yes, I've made a note of that."

"Thank you Your Honour. The Crown submit that if admitted to bail, the defendant will abscond. If this is a real, rather than a fanciful, concern, Your Honour has the power to grant bail with suitable conditions, such as residence and curfew, and his father, who sits behind me, is willing to stand as surety. With Your Honour's leave, I would like to call him."

Bonkers looked pointedly at the court clock, hardly able to hide his impatience. "Very well," he said at last, "but I don't have all day."

Anstruther-Browne took the oath.

"Please give your full name and address to the court," I began.

"Richard Maxwell Anstruther-Browne, and I live at Number Ten Chester Street Belgravia." Bonkers looked impressed, but there was a long way to go.

"And are you the defendant's father?"

"I am."

"And what is your occupation?" I asked.

"I am a solicitor," he replied.

"I don't believe we've met before, Mr. Anstruther-Browne," interrupted Bonkers, "do you practise locally?"

"No Your Honour, I am a senior partner in Farringtons, with offices in the City."

Bonkers' mouth snapped open. "Do you mean Farringtons, the Queen's solicitors?" he asked in awe.

"That's correct, Your Honour, but we do have other clients," he added with a smile.

I felt weak at the knees, and I was not alone. Should I bow, or curtsy, or drop to one knee?

From then on it was plain sailing. There was no way Bonkers was about to refuse bail to the son of the Queen's Solicitor, it was more than his pension was worth. In no time at all, Hugo had been granted bail, with the condition that he reside with his father and not at that grotty student house in Finchley, and he was made the subject of a curfew. With the hearing over, Bonkers rose, bowed low, not to me but to Anstruther-Browne, and adjourned to catch his breath. If it had been permitted under the rules, he would have invited him to coffee and biscuits in his private quarters. As for me, and on my subsequent visits to Snaresbrook, Bonkers accorded me a respect that had been singularly lacking since I first appeared before him. After all, this twerp Potts must have something about him if he hob-nobs with the Queen's solicitor.

Outside court, Anstruther-Browne was effusive in his praise of my advocacy skills, an effusion I was happy to encourage, although if the truth be told, I doubt if I would have succeeded without his seismic contribution. He asked for my professional card, which I didn't have, as I had no professional services to hand out to justify the printing costs. I blustered in the best traditions of experienced counsel, and gave him my details on a scrap of paper. He shook my hand warmly, I wished his son Hugo good luck, and with that, he went on his way. Another photo opportunity missed on the steps of the court.

On my return to chambers, I mentioned picking up the additional work, as I had to account to the clerks for everything I did, but modesty prevented me from disclosing the identity of my benefactor.

Two days' later, a cheque for £200 plus VAT arrived in the post, with a penned note of thanks. The clerks pounced on it like a dog on a rat, and by the time they had deducted their commission (for doing nothing) and chambers rent and VAT and travel and tax, I had about £100 for the Toby Potts Piggy Bank. Still, better than nothing.

Later that afternoon, as I was whiling away my time in the room I shared with Nick Ridley and trying to look busy, the phone rang. It was Paul.

"I've got a Mr. Somebody-Browne on the phone," he grunted, "wants to speak to you."

I wasn't sure why the great man was phoning me. Perhaps there'd been cock-up with bail, it had been known before, and Hugo was still languishing in Brixton Prison, or worse still, he wanted his money back.

"Put him through, Paul," I said, feeling apprehensive.

"Mr. Potts?" I immediately recognised his cultivated voice. "Forgive me for bothering you again, but I wonder if you would consider representing my son at his trial?"

I gulped, my mouth went dry and my hands started shaking.

"I was exceedingly impressed with the way you handled yourself before Judge Clarke. I had never met the man before, or even heard of him, so I had one of our interns run a check on him, and by all accounts, he has a reputation for being difficult, self-opinionated and bombastic."

"And those are just some of his better qualities," I added, "but you didn't hear that from me."

Anstruther-Browne laughed. "Turning to Hugo's case," he said, "I feel confident that in your hands, he will receive the best possible representation." He paused. "Without wishing to cause offence again," he continued in measured tones, "you will be alive to my position as Hugo's father, and the effect this had on Judge Clarke."

"I am indeed," I replied, wondering where this was leading, but I had a sneaking suspicion.

"Given the seriousness of the charge, I was tempted to instruct Queen's Counsel, but if I did, there is a chance the press and media could get hold of it, and this might damage my reputation." Oh dear, I thought uncharitably, no more tea and biscuits with Her Majesty in the Chinese drawing room. "Hugo and I feel that a barrister with a more modest profile would be in both our best interests, hence this phone call."

I'd been here before, when I represented the Earl of Brockenhurst. He too wanted a barrister with a low profile, and I fitted the bill rather well, though I say it myself. And what thanks did I get? Not so much as a postcard, or an invitation to join him and his party at Henley, or Ascot, or the Glorious Twelfth.

I also wondered how far Hugo had been consulted in this decision, if at all, and whether this was a face-saving exercise entirely for his father's benefit.

I was also not best pleased with the unintended slight about my youth and inexperience, but it was my week for coming back to earth with a bump. Perhaps it was to be my lot in life, always the bridesmaid, never the bride.

"Yesterday I contacted that numbskull of a solicitor and withdrew my instructions on Hugo's behalf. If you care to recommend a solicitor to instruct you, I will have the papers transferred without delay. Needless to say," he added for good measure, "I shall be responsible for paying your fees." Music to my ears, a privately-paying client.

I needed time to think, as there was a good deal at stake, not just for Hugo and his Dad, but for me and my professional reputation. I had to be upfront. I promised to phone back the next afternoon with my decision, and thanked him for his confidence in me, such as it was.

Fortunately, Nick Ridley was in chambers that evening, and I explained what had happened. "So what do you think I should do?" I asked.

"In my experience, these 'planting' defences are pretty hopeless, it's like ploughing a lone furrow. You say he did, he says he didn't, and unless the police officer looks like he's just crawled out from under a stone, which is unlikely, your client will sink without trace." Pretty depressing. "However, I'm sure you can handle it, so no worries there." I smiled in appreciation. "Anstruther-Browne was clearly impressed with the way you handled the bail application, even if his rank and title swung it in your favour, and you have rightly earned his confidence. I can't say I know the man, and let's face it, for us criminal hacks, the chances of representing the Queen on a charge of exceeding the speed limit on her way to open Parliament are few and far between."

I laughed. Nick paused and leaned back in his chair. "However, there's a real risk Anstruther-Browne will want to make the running, possibly for selfish reasons, but he's not your client, and he's not the one facing a lengthy sentence of imprisonment."

"Duly noted," I replied.

"To start with, I suggest you speak to Del Finnan. He's not everybody's cup of tea, but he's honest, hard-working, and above all, he really cares for his clients. He helped you out at court, so he's entitled to first refusal. If he's happy to take over the file and instruct you, then you should arrange to see Hugo in conference as soon as possible. But a strong word of advice. Make sure his father does *not* attend. You need to take instructions from your client without his father looking over your shoulder."

With these words of wisdom ringing in my ears, I immediately phoned Del, who was up for it. The next afternoon I phoned Anstruther-Browne, on his direct line no less and normally reserved for royalty, and the brief was transferred from the numbskull in Snaresbrook before his feet could touch the ground. In no time at all, Toby Potts PLC was duly instructed to represent Hugo at his forthcoming trial.

A conference was arranged the following week, and in the meantime, my adversarial skills were kept keenly honed on a succession of high-profile cases that included dangerous cycling on the pavement, shoplifting, and a rematch with Cantwell at Snaresbrook after his errant client had been nicked driving a brand-new Mercedes, and he was asking for bail! Normally the CPS in-house lawyer would have handled it, but the clerks still wanted to put my name forward for the trial, so I was bundled off to wave the flag and make myself visible. Bonkers refused bail without breaking stride and described the application as a waste of public time and money. At least I was treated to a welcoming smile, much to Cantwell's irritation.

Promptly at four-thirty, Del arrived with Hugo in tow. He seemed a personable lad, tall, handsome, with piercing blue eyes and tousled blond hair, a bit like Lenny DiCaprio but without the acne. He had an easy manner about him, and was convention-ally dressed in a T-shirt, blue jeans and trainers. Not quite the outfit I would have chosen for my first meeting with PLC, but no matter.

After the introductions, it was time to review the evidence. Del had provided me with a broad outline of the prosecution case, and as Nick had predicted, on the face of it there were very few nuggets to pan as far as his defence was concerned.

On the night in question, Hugo and seven mates had piled into a dilapidated Volkswagen campervan and headed to the Dive Bar in Chingford. Not my idea of a night out, but then I was so much older and wiser. Apparently it was *the* place for cheap booze, totty and music so loud it shot the wax out of your ears. As he told Del, there were plenty of drugs around, it went with the territory, but he didn't use them, and he certainly didn't push them. He admit-ted to smoking the occasional joint, but that was it.

It was about three in the morning when Hugo stepped outside for a breath of fresh air and a drag on a rollup. He'd been drinking, but wasn't drunk. Just then the boys in blue cruised past, and as it was a quiet night in Chingford, they stopped and went over. After all, a collar for possession of cannabis would show they were earning their keep, even if it was small beer. Chingford and small beer went together like peaches and cream.

Reading between the lines, Hugo didn't handle it well. I suspected there was a hint of arrogance in the Anstruther-Browne genes, and a tendency to talk down to the plebs. When asked what he was smoking, Hugo told them it was none of their business. When pressed, he told them to shove off. The boys in blue insisted on a body search, there was a struggle, and before he knew it, he was cuffed, nicked and bundled into the police car.

Once at Chingford Police Station, Hugo was strip-searched, he didn't have any choice in the matter, and then to the cells to await the arrival of DC. 'Ding-Dong' Bell, the duty CID officer from the Drug Squad.

It was past ten when Bell put in an appearance, and Hugo was brought from his cell to the interview room. According to his account given to Del, there was no tape recorder, and nobody else present.

Bell came straight to the point. Wearing protective gloves, he produced the bag of Speed and dropped it on the table between them. "Ever seen this before?" he asked.

"Of course not," replied Hugo. "What do you take me for?"

"An arrogant little shit and a pusher," snapped Bell. "Does that answer your question?"

Hugo was slowly beginning to appreciate the seriousness of the situation. "If you're suggesting these are mine, I want a solicitor," he said.

Bell snorted with derision. "In your dreams Sunshine! Time-wasting jerkoffs, that's what they are. You'll get a solicitor when I'm good and ready."

There followed a long silence as Bell glared at Hugo malevolently. "Take a long hard look at the bag," Bell continued, "you might recognise it."

"I don't need to. I've already told you, it's not mine."

Suddenly Bell reached out across the table, grabbed Hugo's hand and pushed it onto the bag. "So how do you account for the fact that your fingerprints are on it?"

Hugo was horrified. "This is police corruption," he shouted, "it's a stitch-up."

"You better believe it, Sunshine!" he smirked. Another long pause. "I'll tell you what, seeing you're a nice boy, and I want to help you." Bell placed the drugs in a tamper-proof bag and removed his gloves. "I'm making an entry in my pocket book here," and as he wrote, he read out loud: "Suspect admits the drugs are his, and he had them to sell." Bell looked up to admire his handiwork. Hugo was speechless. "So here's the deal. You sign here, and I'll tell the custody sergeant to release you on bail. But if you don't," he continued menacingly, "you'll be banged up with the hard cases in Brixton, who like a tight young arse, and who knows when you'll see the light of day again."

Hugo was appalled, but refused to be intimidated. He leant forward across the table and looked Bell straight in the eye. "To use your own expression, in your dreams Sunshine!"

For a moment, Bell's fists clenched as he thought about giving Hugo a fucking good spanking, but the moment passed. He pushed his chair back and stood up. "Wrong call," he said as he left the interview room.

I looked up and caught Hugo's eye.

"So what do you think, Toby?" he asked. "You don't mind me calling you Toby, do you?" he added, "after all, we're much the same age."

I could see why Bell considered giving him a fucking good spanking. "Whatever makes you feel comfortable," I replied with a rictus grin.

I turned to Del. "It's the bad old days all over again, Del, when the police were a law to themselves. I thought we'd seen the last of them." Del nodded.

"So what do you think?" Hugo repeated.

"To put it bluntly," I replied, "it's Bell's word against yours, and it all boils down to which of the two of you gives the more convincing account. Bell is a seasoned pro, so he knows all the traps and pitfalls, and he must have given evidence scores of times." I paused. "You're not a pro by any stretch of the imagination, and a good prosecutor could have a field day."

"Meaning what?" he asked.

"Well, it's not just about what happened at the police station. If I were prosecuting, I'd be asking why you refused to be searched outside the Dive Bar, and the obvious explanation being that you had the drugs on you and didn't want the arresting officers to find them."

"Yeah, you're right. I wasn't particularly proud of my behaviour that night, but I'd been drinking."

"Did you call them fucking plebs?" I asked.

"I might have done, I can't remember." Hugo looked at me. "So what are my chances?" he asked.

"You're no fool, Hugo, what do you think?"

There was a long silence as I exchanged glances with Del.

"So I might as well plead guilty and get it over with," he said in a tone of resignation.

Absolutely not," I replied firmly, surprising even myself, "you have a complete defence to the charge. But I can only do so much, the rest is down to you."

There was another long silence. Time to move on, I thought.

"I met your father at Snaresbrook," I said, "when he asked me to make a bail application on your behalf."

"Yeah, he told me you stepped in at the last minute," replied Hugo, "he also told me you did a brilliant job. Thanks for that."

"I'll take that as a vote of confidence," I smiled. "When I made the application," I continued, "I was told that you were living in student accommodation in Finchley. Why's that?"

"You've met my old man," Hugo replied, "very grand and all that, but not exactly a barrel of laughs. I'm in my gap year, and I'd rather spend it with my mates." I nodded. "I'd put my name forward to spend the year in Lesotho, working with Prince Harry, you may have heard of his work with the orphanage," I had, "but no luck. Seems like half my college had put their names down," he added.

"Fair enough. One other thing," I added, "your father gave his name to the court as Anstruther-Browne, yet you were charged as Browne." I looked up.

"I dropped the double-barrelled name when I left school. Is that a problem?"

"No problem at all, but it might come out. Your father is certainly keen to play a low profile, perhaps for obvious reasons."

Hugo nodded. "No surprises there," he replied.

"Right," I said, trying to sound masterful, "unless there's anything else you want to ask me, Mr. Finnan and I have work to do to prepare your defence. Do we have a date yet for the pre-trial hearing?"

"Yes," replied Del, "next Thursday. As I'm fully committed, I'll send somebody to sit behind you, and needless to say, I'll be there at the trial."

"Good." I looked up at Hugo. "This is a preliminary hearing, when you will be asked to enter your plea of not guilty, and hopefully, the court will set a date for the trial." Hugo nodded. "A word to the wise, Hugo. You will be appearing before the senior judge, who is old-fashioned and a stickler for convention. I suggest you dress appropriately, jacket and tie, not the one with the dancing condoms, no jeans and T-shirt if you catch my drift, and definitely no trainers." I was beginning to sound like his father, old before my time.

Hugo smiled. "Got it."

"I'll see you on Thursday." We shook hands. "Try and stay positive."

After Hugo had left, I had a brief chat with Del. "I'd like a copy of the custody record, it might show something, but I'm not holding my breath."

"Consider it done," replied Del.

"This CID officer, DC. Bell, ever heard of him before?" I asked.

"Only gossip on the grapevine. A hard bastard by all accounts, cuts corners, but he gets results. If our client is telling the truth, he cut all the corners in the book."

"Anyway, Hugo has one thing going for him."

"What's that?"

"Snaresbrook juries don't like the police, bent or otherwise, so he may get a sympathy vote. That said, if Bonkers is the trial judge, he'll get no sympathy at all." I glanced down at Hugo's CV. "I see he went to Eton. Heard of it of course, but can't say I've been there." I looked up. "How about you, Del? Are you an OE?" I added mischievously.

Del put his head back and roared with laughter. "I went to the school of hard knocks," he replied, "Camberwell Green Comprehensive. Survive that and you'll survive anything. Mark you, it has its compensations," he added with a grin, "most of the old boys are now my clients." He stood up. "Right, Tobes, good to see you again, but we humble solicitors have work to do," I laughed, "and thanks for putting my name forward. Gawd forbid, if word gets out on the Green I'm representing an Old Etonian, I'll never live it down!"

Hugo arrived promptly at nine, and as instructed, looked the picture of innocence and as smart as paint. I parked him in the public waiting area whilst I went off to robe, and minutes later Potts the Toreador, wigged and caped, emerged ready to do battle. Just as well, because across the hall, advancing towards me, head down and ready to charge, was none other than Bootsy Farmer. My first thought was to intercept him before he got to Hugo. He had enough to worry about without Bootsy twisting his arm to cop a plea of guilty.

"Mr. Farmer," I said, trying to look pleased, "we meet again."

"We do indeed, Mr. Potts, and always a pleasure," he replied. "You've got your work cut out with this one," he continued, stating the obvious. "I suppose you've told him about time off for an early plea? No point delaying the inevitable."

"Helpful as ever, Mr. Farmer. Have you read the file?" I asked.

"I had a quick look on the way here. He's a bit of a toff is our lad, but that won't help him."

"What will help him, Mr. Farmer, is you and me working together to secure his acquittal, an irresistible combination if I may say so," I replied firmly. "I have seen the client in conference, he will enter a plea of not guilty and take his chances with the jury."

"Well, if you want my opinion…….."

I didn't. "Time to introduce you," I said, escorting him over to Hugo. Hugo stood up and shook hands. "A pleasure to meet you sir."

Bootsy couldn't remember the last time anybody called him 'sir', if ever. His chest puffed out and I could see he'd taken an immediate liking to this fine upstanding young man. For the first time in years, Bootsy felt loved and needed, and in no time at all, they were chatting away like best mates.

Leaving the two of them together for a bonding session, I checked the court lists, and contrary to my expectations, Hugo's case had been listed before His Honour Judge 'Branston' Pickles, a recent appointment from 'oop North', and wishing he were still there. According to robing room gossip, it was a sentiment shared by most who appeared in his court. He was a judge who spoke his mind in a broad Yorkshire dialect, but he was fair and, as he kept reminding one and all, blessed with an abundance of common sense.

The pre-trial hearing was uneventful. Hugo, addressed as Browne by the court clerk, duly entered his plea of not guilty, with Bootsy smiling encouragingly from behind me. As required, Newman for the prosecution handed up his witness list, which included the arresting officers and DC. Bell. I indicated I would not be calling any witnesses other than Hugo. I had discussed with Del the possibility of taking statements from Hugo's mates, but I couldn't see the point. They were all more or less bladdered, and not one was outside when Hugo was arrested.

We then came to points of law. Newman had none, but I raised the possibility of several breaches of the codes of practice which the police are obliged to follow on arrest and subsequent detention.

"It will be my submission, Your Honour, and taking these codes of practice at their highest, they were more honoured in the breach than the observance."

Branston perked up, clearly excited. "The King doth wake tonight and takes his rouse, keeps wassail and the swaggering upspring reels, and as he drains his draughts of Rhenish down, the kettle-drum and trumpet thus bray out the triumph of his pledge."

"Ay, marry is't," I replied, "but to my mind, though I am native here and to the manner born, it is a custom more honoured in the breach than the observance." Thank God for a classical education, I thought, even if it was honed at Rougemont College for the sons of Gentlefolk and not on the playing fields of Eton.

"Well spoken, Mr. Potts, and here I was, thinking Snaresbrook to be a cultural wilderness." Not far off the mark, I muttered under my breath. "Now if you want culture, Yorkshire is the place."

"I agreed, Your Honour," I was on a roll, "and with the Stephen Joseph Theatre in Scarborough, Yorkshire boasts one of the cultural centres of the country."

"You know it?" asked Branston, clearly impressed.

"I do indeed, Your Honour, when I had a student job in Ravenscar. I visited the theatre several times, and I remember in particular a stunning performance of Absurd Person Singular."

"By heck," he said, "one of my all-time favourites, by the great Alan Ayckbourn." Branston dabbed his eyes as he wandered down memory lane, loving every minute of it. Then, with an effort, he brought himself back to the matter in hand.

"As for your submissions," he said, "with an abundance of common sense, they seem your only line of defence. If what the defendant says is true, and that's a matter for the jury, not me, he'll be acquitted, but these are serious allegations." I nodded. "We don't have this sort of behaviour oop North, I can tell you that Mr. Potts. It wouldn't be tolerated."

"With this in mind, Your Honour," I said, "my instructing solicitor has asked for a copy of the custody record, but I have yet to see it."

"What do you say about that, Mr. Newman? With an abundance of common sense, the defence are entitled to a copy, and so am I. We all need to know what went on at the police station, and the custody record should tell us."

"I asked for it two weeks' ago Your Honour," replied Newman, "and like my learned friend, I have yet to see it. I will ensure it is available in good time for the trial."

"You'll need to get a wiggle on, Mr. Newman," replied Branston, "as this case will be listed for trial before me on Monday with a time estimate of two days. I hope I shall have the pleasure of your company again, Mr. Potts?" He smiled warmly, then looked across to Hugo. "Bail as before. Call on the next case."

That went well enough, I thought, as I said goodbye to Hugo. I was about to say the same to Bootsy when he took me firmly by my arm. "May I buy you a cup of coffee, Mr. Potts?"

"That's very kind of you, Mr. Farmer," I replied, trying to hide my surprise, as we made our way to the canteen.

Settling down to two steaming cups of coloured water that passed for coffee, Bootsy looked at me intently.

"We haven't always seen eye to eye," he said in measured terms, "but I respect you as an advocate, even if you're young and inexperienced." I took that as a back-handed compliment, and I smiled. "I've taken a liking to Browne, he seems a good lad, and I don't want him going down for something he hasn't done."

My eyebrows shot up. Was this the Bootsy I knew when we first met at Wormwood Scrubs in the case of Tosser Willis? I remembered it well. Acting on Bootsy's 'advice', Tosser copped a plea before I'd even sat down, and ever since, I'd given Bootsy a wide berth. I might have misjudged him, but I regarded him as the enemy within. I sipped the brown water and waited for him to continue.

"I know Bell, we worked together at Paddington Green before he was moved sideways. He was bent then, and he's bent now." I could hardly believe my ears. "He's been turned down for promotion at least five times to my certain knowledge, sailing too close to the wind if you know what I mean, but he's just managed to stay one step ahead of the Independent Police Complaints Commission, mainly because they're a bunch of tosspots."

Bootsy was on a roll, and I wasn't about to stop him.

"About two years ago, the powers that be moved him to Chingford, hoping to see the back of him. Chingford's known as the graveyard slot, where nothing's supposed to happen." I nodded. "Anyway, hearing the case against Browne, it has Bell's grubby finger marks all over it. It's a complete stitch-up, and the lads at Chingford don't have the balls to stand up to him. He can be very intimidating," Bootsy added for good measure.

"I suspected as much," I replied, "and I agree with you. Hugo's not a pusher, but knowing he's been stitched up and proving it are two different things. As you've told me before," I added, "the Met stick together, so who's going to break ranks?"

"I'll bet my pension that come Monday morning, the custody record will have gone missing, because it's been shredded by Bell. Now you'll make your submissions about being denied a fair trial and all that, after all, that's what you're paid to do, but there's no guarantee the judge will agree, so it's Bell's word against Browne's, and Browne may be a lot of things, but he ain't street-wise."

"You're right there," I replied, "but I'll give it my best shot."

"Of course you will, Mr. Potts, and I have every confidence in your powers of persuasion," said Bootsy, lacking somewhat in sincerity, "let's hope it's enough. As Churchill was fond of saying, tomorrow's another day." There were times, I thought, when Churchill and Bootsy were joined at the hip. "Good luck."

≈‡ ‡≈

The following evening, I was just leaving chambers when the phone rang. It was Del.

"Are you sitting down, Tobes?" Del was almost breathless.

"I am now. What's happening?"

"I've just returned from court, and waiting for me was a plain manila envelope with DC. Bell's internal disciplinary record inside."

"Good God!" was all I could think of saying in reply.

"Good God is right, Tobes, and excuse the language, it's fucking dynamite! It goes back five years, and for the discerning defence advocate, it's pure gold!" I gasped in astonishment. "By the way, that's you, in case you were wondering," he added with a chuckle.

"So who left it?" I asked.

"No idea. Topsy was at the hairdresser's all afternoon, so there was nobody minding the shop. Any ideas?"

"No," I replied, although I had a sneaking suspicion. "I need to see it, Del, the sooner the better."

"Say no more, Tobes, it's on its way by courier, even as I speak. It should be with you in about thirty minutes. Are you around this weekend?"

"I'm around most weekends," I replied. "In case you've forgotten, I'm a grass widower, with my fiancée in darkest Africa having a ball, and me in darkest Earls Court feeling unloved."

Del laughed. "The path of true love and all that." He paused. "Why not come round to my place for Sunday lunch? Topsy's a fair cook, and we can go through Bell's record and plan our line of attack. Take a cab, and I'll put it on Anstruther-Browne's account."

"Good idea, and thanks for the invite. I thought for a minute you were going to suggest Chez Alphonse, where you and Topsy had such a memorable meal!"

"I remember it well," he spluttered, "and it wasn't just the food that was out of this world! A month's earnings, minimum! See you about twelve."

With Topsy rattling the pots and pans in the kitchen, Del and I settled down in his backroom to go through Bell's record. Del was right, it was dynamite.

"I've made a list of relevant entries over the past five years," I said, handing Del a copy. "In summary, three convictions quashed by the Court of Appeal where Bell gave evidence. I've checked the court transcripts, and their lordships were very critical of his flagrant breaches of the codes of practice, so that should go well for us." Del looked at my list and nodded. "There's also three cases where the prosecution offered no evidence for much the same reasons."

"That's a turn-up for the books," Del interrupted, "it must have been pretty serious for the CPS to jack it in."

"I agree, but here are the real nuggets," I continued. "Over the past two years, Bell has secured four convictions for possession with intent to supply, and here's the best bit, in each case the poor sods were charged with possession of a bag containing forty amphetamine tablets!"

There was a gasp of astonishment as Del absorbed the enormity of this disclosure.

"Jesus Christ, Tobes, he's using the same bag of drugs!"

"My thoughts precisely, Del, and you remember the fingerprint evidence against Hugo? There were several unidentified sets of prints besides Hugo's found on the bag."

"So how do you want to play this tomorrow?" asked Del.

"There's only one way," I replied. "I'll have to give a copy to Newman and ask him to confirm it's a genuine record. He'll huff and puff and rush around like a headless chicken, that's what he's paid to do, and he'll demand to know how we got it." Del nodded in agreement. "As you know, the court frowns on 'ambushing' witnesses, and if I produce it like a rabbit from a hat when cross-examining Bell, the judge may rule it inadmissible, so we've got to be upfront."

"Fair enough," replied Del.

"Then all we can do is stand back and wait for the shit to hit the fan," I said. "I intend showing it to the judge and asking him to stop the trial. As things stand, he's onside. We have Hamlet and Scarborough in common."

"Yeah, Bootsy told me you were quoting Churchill," and we both laughed.

"Lunch is ready," Topsy called from the kitchen.

As Del promised, she was indeed a 'fair cook', and waiting to be uncorked was a very drinkable bottle of Côtes de Rhone.

"Jesus Murphy, Topsy," said Del, eyeing the label, "how much did this set me back?"

"There are times, Del, when you can be such a tight-wad," Topsy retorted, "I swear there's moths inside your wallet."

Del, duly chastened, poured the wine. "I wonder if I can put it on Anstruther-Browne's account," he muttered.

Monday dawned grey and dreary as I rattled my way to Snaresbrook on the central line, a journey I had taken more times than I cared to remember. I had absolutely no idea how the case would pan out. Judge 'Branston' Pickles was an unknown quantity, and whilst we'd hit it off, with his abundance of common sense he might be tempted to leave the case to the jury. I knew how Newman would react if he'd briefed himself for the trial, and even if he hadn't, he'd still have the last word. It was written in counsel's instructions, in bold type: **Counsel is instructed to refer all matters requiring a decision to the reviewing lawyer.**

The one unknown quantity and the loose cannon on deck was DC. 'Ding Dong' Bell. After all, if things went against him, it wasn't just his reputation at stake, such as it was, it was his entire future in the Metropolitan Police. As Bootsy had put it several times, the finest bunch of lads you'd never wish to meet, or I think that's what he said.

And what of Bootsy and that strange conversation over a cup of undrinkable coffee? Was he trying to tell me something, or just sounding off in support of his new-found friend?

And finally, who had provided Del with that damning record? I didn't think it could be Bootsy. For as long as I'd known him, it was "one for all and all for one" when it came to the Met, and I didn't see him breaking ranks. The prime suspect was Hugo's father, the high and mighty Richard Anstruther-Browne. He had the connections and the means, there was no doubt about that, and he'd run Bonkers through the system with the flick of a switch before deciding to brief me. But since Del came on board, he'd said nothing and done nothing to show any interest in Hugo's fate. His only interest was keeping his name out of the papers.

And why me? After all, with his connections, he could have had the pick of the crop, and I didn't buy that bullshit about keeping a low profile and briefing a young and inexperienced barrister. If I were Hugo's father, with my innocent son facing a lengthy term of imprisonment, I'd move heaven and earth to secure his acquittal, and though it pained me to say so, I wouldn't be my first choice.

Perhaps Hugo wasn't his son, but his wife's love-child, and his real father was a Russian oligarch, or a media tycoon, or even royalty, it had happened before. I vaguely remembered the story of Queen Victoria having an affair with her gillie, and his name was Browne, and this was Anstruther-Browne's devilish plot to put Hugo away for a few years so he could claim the boy's rightful inheritance. Mark you, that was pretty far-fetched, as it happened a hundred and fifty years ago, but blood is thicker than water. Any why had Hugo dropped the Anstruther part of his surname? This had Barbara Cartland stamped all over it.

I was shaken out of my reverie as the train came into the station, and I walked the short distance to the court. It was high noon, and time to face down the Clanton brothers.

As I approached the main door, Hugo was waiting for me. We exchanged the usual pleasantries, and I explained there would be some preliminary legal discussions before the trial started over the admissibility of evidence. I didn't tell him what about, as I didn't want to raise his hopes in case they were dashed.

"Have you seen Mr. Finnan yet?" I asked.

"He's here, and waiting for you in the main hall," he replied. "Is it alright if I wait here?"

"Of course, and we know where to find you if we need you." I smiled encouragingly and made my way inside.

"Right, Del," I said, "time to put the cat amongst the pigeons. Is DC. Bell here yet?"

"I can't be sure," replied Del, "but there's a bloke hovering around the CPS office that fits the bill."

Very apt," I replied with a grin.

"Big, stocky, with a pugilist's face that looks like it's been on the receiving end of a few knocks in its time. Not a pleasant sight."

"I'll go and see Newman, deliver our bombshell, and see you in the canteen," I said.

I made my way the length of the hall to the CPS office, and as I was about to go in, I turned to the big, stocky bloke with a pugilist's face standing outside. "It's DC. Bell, I presume?"

"Who wants to know?" His manner was hostile and confrontational.

"I'm Toby Potts, and I represent Hugo Browne."

"Do you indeed?" he retorted. "Then good luck to the both of you, you're going to need it," and with that, he turned away.

I found Newman, looking busy but with little to show for it.

"Good morning," I said, "I just popped in to collect my copy of the custody record."

"Ah," he replied without the hint of an apology, "there's a problem. It's gone missing, very regrettable of course, but these things happen, so we'll have to proceed without it."

"Very regrettable indeed," I said, "have you asked DC. Bell for an explanation? After all, he's the officer in the case."

"Don't tell me how to conduct the prosecution, Mr. Potts, it illbehoves you." His manner was brusque. "And you should know, as you yourself prosecute here from time to time," a veiled threat if ever there was, "any discussions I have with the officer in the case are privileged."

"Quite so," I replied, "but the judge will ask for an explanation…"

"And I shall deal with that in open court in the usual way. Now if that's all?"

"Thank you for your co-operation." I made as if to leave. "Oh, by the way," I added, turning back, "I have a document here that might interest you. With His Honour's leave, I intend putting into evidence. You may wish to take instructions, and in the meantime, my solicitor and I can be found in the canteen." I duly handed over Bell's disciplinary record and left with a flourish.

I had barely reached the end of the corridor when I heard Newman beckoning furiously to Bell, and they both went inside.

I settled down with Del to await Newman's response, which came barely ten minutes later. He flew through the door, and like the Assyrian of old, bore down on us like a wolf on the fold. But we were well prepared, our cohorts were gleaming in purple and gold, and the sheen of our spears was like stars on the sea.

"We need to talk immediately, and in private," he almost spat out the words.

I looked at Del, who had a mischievous twinkle in his eye. "Have you met my solicitor Mr. Finnan?" I asked, enjoying the moment.

"No I have not," Newman gave Del a perfunctory nod.

"If you've finished your coffee, Mr. Finnan," I continued, "shall we join the prosecutor in conference?"

"Good idea," said Del, "before the coffee finishes me."

We found a room and sat down.

"What's the meaning of this?" Newman could barely control his temper.

"I should have thought it was obvious," I replied calmly, "this trial will turn on the credibility of DC. Bell as a witness of truth. This document shows he's a disgrace to the Metropolitan Police, and the sooner you both accept it, the better for the proper administration of justice." Pompous, I thought, but effective.

"This is outrageous!" Newman blurted out.

"I agree," I replied.

"That's not what I meant, and you know it. If you think this is a good career move, Mr. Potts, you're sadly mistaken, and your youth and inexperience won't save you."

I was appalled. "Is that a threat, Mr. Newman?" I asked pointedly.

"It's not a threat, it's a promise. You can forget about prosecuting at Snaresbrook for as long as I'm in charge!" he almost shouted. "In fact, you can forget about prosecuting anywhere, full stop!"

"Mr. Finnan," I turned to Del, "are you making a note of this?"

"A full note, Mr. Potts," replied Del, glaring at Newman, "and in all my years of practice, I have never witnessed such disgraceful behaviour."

Newman, too late, realised he'd overstepped the mark by some distance. Pulling himself together, he tried a conciliatory smile. "I apologise for my outburst, Mr. Potts, and I retract what I have just said."

"Thank you, Mr. Newman," I replied graciously, "and apology accepted. Now if you will calm down, I am entitled to know if the document I showed you is genuine. Does DC. Bell accept it's an accurate record of disciplinary findings against him? I assume you've taken instructions?"

"As I said before," Newman was back on the defensive, "my discussions with DC. Bell are confidential."

"No they are not!" I snapped. "You prosecute here from time to time," I continued sarcastically, "and you should know that your first duty is to the court, not to the CPS or some bent copper!"

"Don't lecture me, Mr. Potts!" he snapped back.

"Somebody needs to," I replied. "When we go into court, I shall show the document to the judge. He and I will want to know if you, on behalf of DC. Bell, accept it as genuine. So what's the answer? And remember, Mr. Finnan is taking a careful note of this conference."

There was a long and uncomfortable pause as Newman glared defiantly at me. He knew he was a beaten man, but years of ignoring the obvious made it a bitter pill to swallow. "Very well," he replied at last, "it's a genuine document."

It was a Moses moment, as the Red Sea parted.

However, he was down but not out. "I shall still object to you using it in evidence in the strongest terms until you satisfy me, I mean the court, that it was not improperly obtained." Again he glared defiantly at me. "So how did you get it?"

"To adopt your own Mantra, any discussions between me and Mr. Finnan are confidential and therefore privileged," I replied.

"Don't give me that claptrap!" he retorted.

"It's your claptrap, Mr. Newman," I shot back. "You can't have it both ways." Again the awkward silence. "Answer this if you will," I continued, "if I had asked you under the normal rules of disclosure to produce this document, would you have done so, or would it have disappeared into the ether like the custody record?"

Newman stood up. "I have nothing more to say. The trial will proceed and you and the defendant must take your chances with the jury." He left, slamming the door behind him.

"I don't know how you can put up with this, Tobes," said Del. "I know the CPS are blinkered morons, but this guy's in a league of his own. That said," he added, "I'll support you of course if he tries to scupper your prosecution practice, but take my advice, walk away."

Thanks Del," I replied, "maybe it's time for a career change anyway. I don't get this bullshit from you or any other defence solicitors, it's insulting. I may be young and inexperienced, but when I make a decision, you back me to the hilt, and I respect that. With the CPS, their Mantra is "buy a dog and bark yourself", and what do you get? Dogs!"

"Well said."

"OK, Del, time to touch base with Hugo, and then it's down to the judge. I shall ask him to stop the trial and enter a verdict of not guilty. If he's against me, then I'll use Bell's disciplinary record to discredit him, and hope that's enough."

Branston, with his abundance of common sense, needed little persuasion. Newman's submission that the document was inadmissible received very short shrift.

"I am not here to decide how this document came into the possession of the defence. If you believe there has been chicanery, you are free to pursue your own inquiries, but that is a matter for you. You have confirmed this is a genuine document, and I therefore rule it admissible and relevant in the trial, and Mr. Potts may cross-examine Detective Constable Bell on it if he chooses to do so."

"Very well, Your Honour," replied Newman, but he wasn't going down without a fight.

"So in a nutshell, Mr. Newman, and I hope you agree," he said, "the sole issue for the jury to decide is whether they believe DC. Bell or the defendant."

"That's correct, Your Honour," replied Newman, with DC. Bell sitting grim-faced behind him. "And with respect to my learned friend, it is for the jury, not Your Honour, to decide."

"Under normal circumstances I'd agree, but these are far from normal circumstances. If Detective Constable Bell's disciplinary record was uncontroversial, it would indeed be a matter for the jury. After all, it is not uncommon in my experience for complaints to be made against serving officers, it goes with the territory, and in that regard, they are easy targets." Bell nodded vigorously. "But taken as a whole, Constable Bell's record is nothing short of a disgrace." Bell stopped nodding vigorously.

"I disagree, Your Honour," replied Newman, trying to shore up the sinking ship. "DC. Bell has the right to be heard, and if the jury accept his evidence, they may well convict the defendant."

"What? On tainted evidence? I think that most unlikely," said Branston, "and may I remind you that you are supposed to act as a minister of the Crown. You are not here to seek a conviction at any price, and if you are, you're in the wrong job."

Touché!

"So it boils down to this. If you insist on presenting your case to the jury and calling Detective Constable Bell, and if, at the end of your case, Mr. Potts makes a submission I cannot possibly refuse, what have you achieved?" Newman was about to reply, but Branston waved him down. "That then leaves the question of defence costs to be considered." It was the one word that had the CPS running for cover. It was the final insult to add to injury as far as they were concerned. The colour drained from Newman's face at this ultimate indignity, as it would go down on his record, never to be expunged.

Branston turned to me. "Can you give me an estimate of defence costs to date, Mr. Potts?"

"The defendant is paying privately for my services and those of my instructing solicitor," I replied, "so I would put his costs in the region of £5000." No point selling myself short.

"Well, Mr. Newman, there you have it. Do you need time to reconsider your position?"

"Er, yes please Your Honour," although Newman, as the reviewing lawyer, had only himself to refer to, in bold type of course.

"Take as long as you need, Mr. Newman," said Branston rising, "and I shall return in exactly ten minutes."

Newman bustled out of court, closely followed by Bell muttering darkly about a stitch-up. That was pretty rich, coming from him.

Ten minutes later, Newman bustled back into court, this time without Bell in tow, and barely gave me a second glance.

Branston returned and addressed Newman. "What is your decision, Mr. Newman?"

"It has not been an easy decision, Your Honour," Branston raised his eyebrows, "and the prosecution have a strong case." I groaned inwardly. Stubborn to the last, Newman was going down with the ship, and taking all hands with him. "However, I have carefully reviewed Your Honour's helpful comments, even though I don't agree with them," Branston raised his eyebrows even higher, "and in the circumstances, the prosecution propose leaving this charge on the file, not to be proceeded with without leave of the court or the Court of Appeal."

This was a way of avoiding a trial where the prosecution believe there is evidence to proceed but choose not to do so for a variety of reasons. It also prevents the judge from entering a verdict of not guilty.

"Mr. Potts," Branston looked at me, "do you have anything to add?"

"I do indeed, Your Honour," I replied. "As I understand the law, this proposal is not open to the prosecution, as the defendant has not pleaded guilty to any part of the indictment, and as Mr. Newman should know, there is only one count. The prosecution in this case has only two options: proceed to trial or offer no evidence. May I refer Your Honour to the relevant passage in Archbold?"

"There is no need, Mr. Potts. You are absolutely right. Really, Mr. Newman, if you are to prosecute in my court, a basic understanding of the law is the very least I can expect. You have wasted enough valuable court time as it is, and my patience is exhausted. I shall enter a verdict of not guilty, and the defendant may leave the dock. If you want to appeal my decision, feel free to do so. Finally, Mr. Newman," continued Branston icily, "in the short time I have been sitting in Snaresbrook, you have appeared before me as the trial advocate on several occasions. I can only surmise, in the Greater London area there must be a substantial pool of able and talented advocates such as Mr. Potts, drawn from the independent Bar, and I stress the word 'independent', who can and should be briefed in cases as serious as this one, and who can give you the benefit of their advice if you are prepared to follow it. As we say oop North, an advocate who briefs himself has a fool for a client."

This was heady stuff, and I'd never heard a judge so forthright in his criticisms, not even Bonkers. Newman had no choice but to stand there, mute of malice.

"So if you won't take advice from counsel, take some advice from me. Know your limitations, and in future, if you appear before me as the trial advocate, you will need to persuade me it's in the interests of justice to do so, and on present form, I shall need some persuading. Do I make myself clear?"

"Abundantly clear, Your Honour," replied Newman through clenched teeth.

"Very well. Now to the other matters in hand," continued Branston purposefully, "I shall place Detective Constable Bell's disciplinary record under the seal of this court, as frankly, I cannot trust the prosecution not to mislay it." This was getting better by the minute. "It will be forwarded to the Director of Public Prosecutions with a full report of these proceedings. Mr. Potts," I rose, "I delegate to your instructing solicitor the task of drafting the report, copy to me and the prosecution by 4pm Friday, and you, Mr. Newman, will have seven days thereafter to make representations. Before doing so, you may wish to take advice from senior counsel. The cost of drafting the report will be borne by the CPS, not to exceed £1000 plus VAT."

Newman gasped. This was his worst nightmare, being lectured by some interloper from oop North. The sooner he went back to Ilkla Moor baht 'at, the better all round.

"Now where are the drugs?" asked Branston.

"I have them here, Your Honour, in a tamper-proof bag."

Branston scoffed. "A case of shutting the stable door after the horse has bolted, but no matter. Hand them up." Newman did as he was told. "These drugs will also be kept in a safe place, and forwarded to the DPP at the same time. Mr. Potts," I rose again, "and at the risk of imposing further upon the good offices of your instructing solicitor, he may be willing to contact the solicitors of the four defendants convicted of possession of the same quantity of drugs allegedly planted on his client, as they may wish to refer these convictions to the Criminal Cases Review Commission and thereafter to the Court of Appeal."

"I am sure my instructing solicitor will oblige," I replied, turning to Del who nodded his agreement.

"Thank you, and his reasonable costs will be paid by the CPS, not to exceed £500 plus VAT."

Newman's worst nightmare just got worse.

"Finally, as for defence costs in the case, I am making no order. Whatever else, your client behaved foolishly that night and brought this prosecution on himself. It may have been the drink, or possibly the exuberance of youth…"

"Which, according to Oscar Wilde, is lost on the young, Your Honour," I added.

Branston chuckled. "Well said, Mr. Potts. Good day to you," and so saying, he rose and left court, clutching Bell's disciplinary record and the bag of drugs.

Newman beat a hasty retreat to lick his wounds before reviewing himself favourably and blaming this disaster on a hostile judge and the sharp practices of young and inexperienced counsel. He was heading for a fall, make no mistake about that!

We found a room, and as soon as Hugo sat down, he put his head in his hands and sobbed uncontrollably. After a minute, he composed himself and looked up, tearful and red-eyed.

"I can't begin to thank you enough Mr. Potts, you were absolutely brilliant." I smiled at the ultimate accolade, as a grateful client was a rare event. "And thank you so much Mr. Finnan for everything." Del looked well pleased, as he should.

"We're delighted it turned out so well," I replied, "but I'd give the Dive Bar a wide berth for a while. The police, like elephants, have long memories. Good luck with the rest of your life, and in the nicest possible way, I hope I don't see you again." He laughed. "Now, just in case DC. Bell is still lurking around and nursing a grudge, I'm sure your father will pay for a cab to take you and Mr. Finnan home."

"Good idea Tobes," replied Del, "a good result. Well done." He looked at Hugo. "We're not abandoning the hero of the hour to fend for himself, are we Hugo?"

Hugo shook his head and grinned. "No way!"

"I'll whistle up a cab," said Del, "and we'll all leave together."

Ten minutes later, as we drove away, I took one last lingering look at the court that had been so much a part of my life. I was proud of what I'd done to secure Hugo's acquittal, but Newman would never forgive me. He would hold me personally responsible for his public humiliation, and the stinging attack on his professional competence would rankle with him for years to come. Goodbye Potts, the Hammer of the Ungodly!

The clerks would have to find me work at other court centres, after all, that's what they'd paid to do, so time to pull their fingers out, but I'd have to put it more diplomatically if I was to continue my climb up the greasy pole to fame and fortune.

When I arrived back in chambers, I explained to Nick what had happened. He was appalled, and immediately consulted senior members of chambers and Fred, the senior clerk. Del produced his notes of the conference, and Fred was delegated to make a formal complaint to the DPP about Newman's behaviour. Some time later, I learned that Newman had been relieved of all his duties at Snaresbrook and, with delicious irony, had been posted oop North, a fate worse than death. However, it was a pyrrhic victory, as the wounds ran too deep to forgive and forget, and the CPS were a tight-knit clan with a siege mentality. For my part, I could live with the disappointment of never locking antlers with Cantwell and Bonkers again, and I moved on to fresh pastures and new challenges.

I never found out who delivered that incriminating document to Del. It was like "Deep Throat" in the Watergate scandal that eventually brought down Nixon. When I next saw Bootsy, he made no mention of it, and I didn't ask.

Bootsy told me that 'Ding Dong' Bell's offer to resign was accepted with immediate effect, and he was last seen scouring the 'wanted' ads to top up his pension. Dear Lord, I hope he doesn't become a solicitor's outdoor clerk! The thought of him sitting behind me in court, seething with pent-up hostility, was more than I could bear.

Two weeks' later, I received a cheque in chambers from Anstruther-Browne that exceeded my wildest expectations. I also received a case of Veuve Clicquot champagne with a hand-written note: "Dear Mr. Potts, I realise by convention that counsel cannot accept monetary gifts as a reward for services rendered, but I hope this case of champagne will go some way to expressing Hugo's and my gratitude for all you have done."

As Bootsy would say, quoting Churchill: "What goes around, comes around."

Food for thought.

CHAPTER 6
ALMA MATER

I wasn't really the model old boy. I'd bought the old school tie, and that was about it. I went back once in the year after I'd left Rougemont for Founder's Day, just to show off my natty new sports jacket and touch base with a few familiar faces, but Founder's Day was really for the parents, past, present and future.

It had all the usual ingredients. A gymnastics display in the Sports Hall by the fifth form, the First XI cricket team taking on a team of veterans, various art exhibitions and tea and scones on the Headmaster's lawn. That same night there was a black-tie dinner in the Assembly Hall, followed by a well-rehearsed speech from the Headmaster telling us how privileged we were to have been a part of life at one of the most prestigious public schools in the country, which, frankly, was gilding the lily, and speeches from a former MP who had lost his seat at the last election, and some old buffer who'd received a knighthood for services to farming. There were the usual rallying cries to give generously to the College Foundation, and that was about it.

Rougemont College was rooted firmly in the third division, but as the Headmaster was the first to admit, in private at least, it offered a sound education to the local community at fees they could afford. And for the most part, it did. With a rural catchment area, many of the old boys went on to a career in farming, others into land management and estate agency, and a handful into accountancy. Very few went into the law.

Sitting in chambers one evening, I got a phone call that brought memories of my years at Rougemont flooding back.

"Mr. Potts?" It was Mike, the first junior clerk. "I've got a Mr. Harris on the line, wants to speak to you personally, but won't say what it's about. He says he's a solicitor."

"Thanks, Mike, put him through."

"Is that you, Potts?"

Somewhat abrupt, I thought. "Speaking."

"It's Charles Harris. You remember me of course." I didn't. "We were at Rougemont together, Wellington House, although I was three years' your senior."

Suddenly the penny dropped. It was 'Flogger' Harris, so-called because he couldn't leave himself alone. I never liked the chap, but I had little to do with him.

"Good Lord," I replied, "a real blast from the past. I don't think we've met since you left. How are you?"

"Passably well, thanks."

"So how can I help?" I asked.

"I'm now a solicitor in a small firm in Lewes, Bennett & Co, you may have heard of us?" I hadn't. "Anyway," he continued, "there's been a spot of bother at the Alma Mater, and HM has been in touch to see if I can help."

"What sort of bother?"

"Well, in a nutshell, there's been a spate of petty thefts in the changing room at Wellington, but nobody could nail the thieving little bastard. So Old 'Tripod' Biddle, you remember him of course?"

"I do indeed," I replied, "Head of Chemistry and erstwhile Careers Master."

"That's the man. Mark you, bloody useless as a Careers Master, suggested I went into farming! I mean, seriously, could you see me as a farmer?" He guffawed.

From what I remembered of 'Flogger', I couldn't see him as a solicitor either, but it takes all sorts.

"Anyway, Tripod came up with the super wheeze of treating a ten pound note with invisible ink, and once touched, the ink sticks to the hand like shit to a barn door. Are you with me so far?"

"I am indeed," I replied. He should have taken Tripod's advice and gone into farming.

"Good. Now there was a whole holiday coming up, you remember the form, where we were all supposed to jump on our bikes to meander along the leafy lanes, plenty of fresh air and vigorous exercise and communing with nature."

I had a vivid picture of Flogger exercising vigorously.

"For those of us in our senior years, we used to cycle to the nearest pub, down copious quantities of beer and crisps, and cycle back again."

I laughed. "I remember it well."

"Anyway, to cut a long story short, after the boys had left, the tenner had gone, so when they returned, Bill Cooke the Housemaster had an inspection, and a third former by the name of Nigel Onslow was caught green-handed." He paused. "That was the colour of the ink," he added helpfully.

Tripod was right, he really should have gone into farming.

"So bang to rights, as we say in our profession," I replied.

"Do we indeed?" said Flogger, "I haven't heard that one before."

Tripod was right, he should definitely have gone into farming.

"So how can I help?" I asked, trying to move forward.

"Well, as you can imagine, Onslow was paraded before HM, who contacted his folks. He told them he would report the theft to the police if they didn't remove the boy from College forthwith.

They did so that very night, and drove the thieving little tyke home in disgrace."

"Understood." I waited for Flogger to continue, as there must be a point to all this.

"However, they contacted my firm in pretty short order, as we have a significant presence in the area." I found that hard to believe. "Apparently the boy has denied any involvement in the theft, and they are insisting on HM referring the matter to a full meeting of the College Governors. HM is wetting himself, I mean if it got into the press and all that, but he has no choice."

"Quite so," I replied, trying to sound helpful.

"The boy's folks want him represented at the hearing, which is fair enough, but our firm doesn't do advocacy, not much call for it in these parts, we tend to specialise in boundary disputes and farm tenancy agreements if you follow my drift."

"I do."

"Quite so. So I trawled through the Old Boys' membership list in search of suitable counsel to keep it in-house so to speak, and I'm not exactly spoilt for choice. There are a couple of big hitters, but HM and the parents want to keep it low-key, and your name popped up." He paused. "You're still practising, I presume? Haven't jacked it in to become a plumber?"

"No, Charles, I'm still at the coalface."

"Good," he replied. "By the by, I don't remember seeing you at any of our recent fund-raising events. I'm secretary of the Old Boys Association, as you probably know," I didn't, "and I like to keep an eye on lapsed members."

"Yes, sorry about that, pressure of work," I lied, "but I have every intention of attending your next event."

"Splendid, I knew I could count on you. I assume you'll help out with the Onslow case, what's your hourly rate?"

I didn't have a clue. "Can I transfer you to my clerk, and he can discuss the details."

"OK, I'll send you a full brief, and the hearing's next Thursday. I've arranged a conference with the boy and his parents Wednesday afternoon five o'clock my office. See you then," and without further ado, I transferred him to Mike.

⊨⊰⊹⊱⊨

I knew that part of East Sussex well from my schooldays, so I found Flogger's office without difficulty. Flogger was on hand to greet me, and after coffee and a wander down memory lane, it was time to meet the boy and his parents, but not before he'd sold me a ticket to the next fund-raising event. As it was to be held in London, I had no excuses.

Onslow's parents were understandably worried about their son and the disgrace he could bring on the family name if this gross calumny was not expunged from the record as soon as possible. Dad, with his jaw jutting out belligerently, was clearly spoiling for a fight, and would need careful handling. I suspected it was more at his insistence that the matter had been referred to the Board of Governors, as Nigel seemed bored and disinterested. He was small for a fourteen-year old, rather mousy-looking, with poor eye contact, but then, I was PLC, and I could be intimidating. Best to put the lad at his ease.

"So," I began, trying to sound avuncular and reassuring, "as Mr. Harris will have explained to you, the hearing tomorrow before the Board of Governors will re-examine the evidence against you to decide if you were guilty of the theft. It's not a court of law, but it will follow very much the same procedure, with the Headmaster acting on behalf of the College, and I will be acting for you. OK so far?"

"Yes sir," replied Nigel.

"And what are the options, Mr. Potts?" asked Mum nervously.

"In brief, Mrs. Onslow," I said, "if the Board finds Nigel guilty, then the Headmaster's decision to remove him will be confirmed, and sadly you will have to find him another school. If there is a doubt as to Nigel's guilt, it should be resolved in his favour, and he will be invited to return, probably at the start of next term. There will no doubt be an adjustment in the fees to compensate for his enforced absence." Mr. Onslow grunted, expecting no less.

"I see," replied Mum, "and thank you for that."

"What I want to know," Dad interjected, "is what are Nigel's chances?"

"Well," I replied cautiously, "as you know, the evidence against Nigel is strong."

"Not in my book it isn't!" Dad snapped, "Nigel has assured us he's not guilty, and that's good enough for us, so we expect him to be exonerated. After all, that's why we're paying you."

"Quite so, Mr. Onslow," I treated him to one of my most winning smiles, "but success doesn't depend on the payment of my fees." Best to prepare him for the worst, just in case.

"Well...."

Time to take command, as this was getting us nowhere. "I suggest we start with a review of the evidence, and then Nigel can fill in the blanks." I looked down at my instructions. "We know that Mr. Biddle planted a ten-pound note in the changing room which he had treated with green invisible ink, and when touched, the ink stained the hand."

"Yes, yes," Dad retorted, "we know all that."

"Calm down dear," said Mum, "Mr. Potts is only trying to help." She smiled encouragingly at me.

"Thank you Mrs. Onslow. Now unless the rules have changed since my day, boys are not supposed to go into other boys' houses without permission. Is that right, Nigel?"

"Yes sir," he replied.

"So the Board will assume that if Nigel didn't take the money, it must have been taken by another boy in his house," I said with compelling logic, one of my many forensic skills.

"So where does that leave us?" asked Flogger, trying to be supportive to justify his retainer.

"Well, if Nigel didn't take the money...."

"He most certainly did not!" interrupted Dad in high dudgeon.

"Just a moment please, Mr. Onslow," I replied firmly, "as this is crucial to Nigel's case, and simply saying he's innocent won't work. If Nigel didn't take the money, he clearly handled it some time that day, otherwise how do you account for the green stains?" I pressed on before Dad could interrupt again. "It therefore follows, as night the day, that the thief handed the ten-pound note to Nigel, which is curious. I mean, why on earth would he want to do that?"

"Nigel's explained all that to the Headmaster and Mr. Harris, hasn't he?" Dad looked over to Flogger.

"That's right, Mr. Onslow," replied Flogger, "but Counsel needs to explore with Nigel the exact train of events." Good for you, Flogger, I thought. Buying that ticket to the next fund-raising event was already paying dividends.

"Let's look at your explanation, Nigel. You rode alone to the nearby village of Barcombe Cross, which is about five miles from College." Nigel nodded. Very much Nigel-No-Mates as far as I could tell. "You met an older boy from your House in the village, a chance encounter you said, he too was alone, you got chatting, and he offered to buy you a Coke and a packet of crisps, as older boys sometimes do."

Nigel nodded again, but this was more than Dad could bear. "What are you suggesting, Mr. Potts?!? That something improper went on?"

"Good Lord, no, Mr. Onslow," I replied hastily, as Flogger's shoulders began to shake. So many memories came flooding back, but now was *not* the time to relive them. "However, it's well-known that in single-sex schools, older boys do sometimes befriend younger boys. There doesn't have to be a sinister motive, but it helps to explain why Nigel is reluctant to tell us about it."

Dad was not convinced, but held his peace, much as Flogger did all those years ago.

"So continuing the narrative," I pressed on, "he gave you the ten-pound note, off you went to the shop, and when you returned, gave him back the change. Is that right?"

"Yes sir."

"And then the older boy mounted…"

"This is intolerable!" Dad was incandescent.

"Mounted his bicycle and cycled off into the middle distance, never to be seen again that day." Dad had a very vivid imagination.

"Yes sir," replied Nigel-no-mates.

"Turning to the green ink," I continued, "did you see any green ink on the older boy's hands whilst you were in each other's company?"

"No sir, I wasn't really looking."

I decided against asking what the older boy was doing with his hands, as this could tip Dad over the edge. I also decided against asking Nigel what he was doing with *his* hands, as this could tip Flogger over the edge.

"So when did you first notice the green ink on your hands?"

"When I got back to House later that afternoon," replied Nigel. "Mr. Cooke was inspecting our hands, took one look at mine, and marched me off to the Headmaster's study."

A glimmer of light at the end of the tunnel perhaps. If Cooke had stopped inspecting hands once he'd found the culprit, or so he thought, then the older boy could have returned unnoticed.

"And what of the older boy, do you know if he returned to House before or after you?" I asked.

"I can't say sir, but I didn't see him."

"Going on from there," I continued, choosing my words with care, and with Dad ready to jump down my throat, "we have this problem. When you were asked by Mr. Cooke, and the Headmaster, and presumably your parents, to name the older boy, you refused to do so, and as I understand it, you still refuse to do so. Why is that?"

"I don't want to sneak on him," replied Nigel.

"Shades of *Casabianca*," I observed dryly.

"Great film," said Flogger brightly. "I mean, that final scene between Humphrey Bogart and Ingrid Bergmann, real tear-jerking stuff." Flogger should definitely have gone into farming.

"Actually," I replied, "I was thinking of the epic poem by Felicia Hemans:

The boy stood on the burning deck
Whence all but he had fled;
The flame that lit the battle's wreck
Shone round him o'er the dead.
Yet beautiful and bright he stood,
As born to rule the storm;
A creature of heroic blood,
A proud though childlike form.

There was a deathly silence, as there must have been on the good ship *Orient* just before it exploded. Dad, for the first time in the conference, was speechless.

"Oh, that Casablanca," said Flogger, mired in ignorance, "great poem."

"That's lovely," said Mrs. Onslow, "and so tragic."

"Yes, yes, my dear," Dad snapped impatiently, "all very lovely, but I'm paying Mr. Potts here to represent our son, and all he's doing is spouting poetry. Where's this getting us?"

"In a nutshell, Mr. Onslow," I replied, stung by the rebuke of this literary pygmy, "Nigel is at risk of going down with the sinking ship."

Dad was not amused, and it showed. "So what are you telling me?" he demanded.

"On the instructions I've been given by Mr. Harris," time to call up the cavalry, "Nigel was the only boy found with green dye on his hands." I paused, choosing my words carefully. "Given the passage of time, even if Nigel were now prepared to name the older boy as the probable thief, there is no corroborative evidence as we lawyers would put it. So unless the older boy is willing to confess to the theft and throw himself on his sword, so to speak, then it's his word against Nigel's. The Board of Governors may well conclude that Nigel is trying to shift the blame to save his own skin." I looked over to Flogger. "Is there anything you wish to add, Mr. Harris?"

Flogger, who'd accepted a sizeable retainer, now had to tread a fine line between supporting me and humouring the Onslows. He chose to flannel.

"Mr. Potts has summarised the position very well," he replied cautiously. "However," he continued," as Dad Onslow glowered menacingly, "we are all quite convinced of Nigel's innocence, and I'm confident Mr. Potts will do his utmost to restore his good name."

Hang on, I thought, was this the same Flogger who described Nigel as a thieving little tyke when we first spoke? Time to call it a day.

"Well," I concluded, "I think that's as far as we can go, so unless there are any other questions," Dear Lord, no more questions, "we'll meet again tomorrow morning at ten. The hearing takes place in the College library."

Flogger had booked a room for me at the local hostelry, and after a wash and brush-up, we met in the bar for a pint or three. He was agreeable company in a blustering sort of way. The last thing he wanted to talk about was the thieving little tyke, which suited me, so we talked about the old times at Rougemont, which didn't take long, and life at the sharp end as up and coming lawyers. As Flogger didn't have a sharp end, that didn't take long either. He couldn't see the point of practising at the Bar, too precarious, and too many mice chasing the same piece of cheese. He wasn't far off the mark in that regard.

"Right," he said, looking at his watch, "I'm off for a curry. Can I interest you?"

"No thanks," I replied, "I'm not really a curry person. It always looks like something you tread in during a country ramble."

He laughed. "Nonsense," he replied, "you don't know what you're missing. Bloody good food, and as cheap as chips. Have a good evening, and I'll see you tomorrow."

⭅┼┼⭆

We assembled outside the library at half-past nine. Nigel had scrubbed up well, I thought, as had his folks. Flogger looked decidedly green round the gills, a powerful vindaloo taking the edge off his blustering bonhomie.

Shortly before ten, HM arrived, leading the panel of Governors like cows into the milking parlour. He paused as he passed us, and nodded towards Flogger.

"Morning Charles," he enthused, "good to see you again. Nasty business this."

"Quite so," replied Flogger, and then, turning towards me, "you remember Toby Potts, Headmaster?"

HM inspected me briefly. "Can't say I do," he replied, "but with so many boys in College, I only remember the high-flyers," and with that, he swept on past me and into the library. Pompous jackass!

The Chairman of the Board of Governors introduced himself and his four colleagues. I didn't know any of them, and why should I, but they were the usual pillars of society, male, grey, earnest and self-important, very much like the Headmaster.

HM opened the proceedings. "Gentlemen," he began, "we are here this morning to review the decision I took some weeks ago to exclude young Plimsoll from College after he had been caught stealing a ten-pound note."

Time to start earning my fee. "Forgive the interruption," HM didn't, "but the boy's name is Onslow. Is the Headmaster telling us that he excluded a boy from College whose name he didn't even know? Perhaps he wasn't a high-flyer." I couldn't resist it.

"Hear, Hear," muttered Dad, nodding vigorously. He wanted a fight to the bitter end, and no more poetry.

HM reddened and glowered at me. "A simple slip of the tongue, and of no consequence," he replied.

"It *is* for the boy," I shot back, "and many a miscarriage of justice has resulted from a simple slip of the tongue. Remember Bentley and Craig?"

"Actually I don't," replied HM, "when were they here?"

I thought about saying something, but decided against it, and besides, Flogger's rumbling stomach was becoming a serious distraction.

The Chairman intervened. "Have no fear, Mr. Potts, we are fully familiar with the case and Nigel Onslow as the aggrieved boy." He smiled reassuringly. "Now, Headmaster, what evidence do you wish us to hear?"

"Thank you Chairman," replied HM, "to assist the boy and his parents, I propose asking Mr. Biddle to tell us about the treated ten-pound note, and then Mr. Cooke, the boy's Housemaster, who discovered the incriminating stains on the boy's hands." He called out to the back of the room. "Mr. Biddle, will you step forward please?"

Tripod was much as I remembered him when, as Careers Master, he advised me that if I couldn't find a proper job, to go into the law. Whether that was good advice remained to be seen, and the jury were still out. He was older, with a stoop acquired after years of bending over Bunsen burners, certainly greyer, but the same fleshy features and the same pronounced strawberry nose.

After introducing himself, he described what he had done. "It's a clear solution, invisible to the naked eye, but once it comes into contact with the warm hand, it becomes an indelible dye."

"And how long would you expect it to remain on the hand?" I asked.

"That depends on a number of factors, such as scrubbing vigorously with pumice stone and repeated washing with an astringent, but I would expect traces to remain for up to three days." Not the answer I wanted, but it was my fault. As Nick Ridley used to impress on me, never ask a question to which you don't know the answer. I wasn't about to ask him the chemical constituents of the solution, as I'd rather dozed off at the back of his class when I was at College. There were certain areas of chemistry that interested me, like boy meets girl and all that, but that's as far as it went.

"Of course Mr. Biddle, you'd agree that some astringents are more effective than others," I continued cautiously.

HM was getting twitchy, and with new parents booked in for the full tour promptly at eleven, he was anxious to get on. "Potts," he interrupted as if I were still in the lower sixth, "this is a waste of the Board's time, and more to the point, a waste of my time. The Board knows that Plimsoll's hands were stained with green dye when he returned to House, so what's astringent got to do with it?"

"The case for Nigel Onslow," I replied, "is that he was handed the ten-pound note by another older boy, presumably the thief, and that's how the dye got onto his hands."

"A bit far-fetched, isn't it?"

"With respect, Headmaster, that's for the Board to decide."

There was an awkward silence, as HM looked pointedly at his watch, a gift from the grateful Governors and parents after twenty years of unstinting service. I decided to press on, as this was my only line of defence.

"So can you help, Mr. Biddle?" I asked.

"I'm sorry, I've forgotten your question." I repeated it. "Ah, yes, astringents, you're quite right, some are more effective than others, but that's self-evident."

"How about acetone?" I asked, having done my researches.

"Yes, acetone is a very strong astringent," he replied, "but not readily available."

"How about nail varnish remover, readily available in most chemists' shops?"

Tripod paused before answering. "Yes," he replied guardedly, "but as you'll remember from my Chemistry classes if you were paying attention, it can cause severe reddening and blistering of the hands. I wouldn't recommend it."

I felt I'd sown the seeds of doubt. "Thank you for your help, Mr. Biddle."

As Bill Cooke was making his way forward, Flogger leaned over and whispered. "Back in a jiffy, the call of nature," and off he hurried to the vindaloo. Serves him right. Dad Onslow glowered at his receding back, singularly unimpressed. Flogger was like that kid on the burning deck. The idiot should have gone into farming.

"You were there, on the Headmaster's instructions, to inspect the boys' hands when they returned to the House," I began, "and in particular, green dye."

"That's correct, but the Board already knows this."

Cue for HM to look pointedly at his watch again as he cleared his throat noisily. I ignored him.

"All boys were required to be back in House by six o'clock at the latest?"

"Correct."

"And what time did Onslow return?"

"If my memory serves me, about five."

"And how many boys had returned before him?"

"I can't be precise, but about half, mostly juniors. The more senior boys tended to leave it to the last minute," he chuckled.

"Quite so. Now when you saw Onslow's hands, you marched him straight off to the Headmaster?"

"That's correct."

"So what about the other boys who returned to House after Onslow? From what you tell us, nobody inspected their hands."

"I never considered the possibility that another boy was involved in the theft," he replied. "I didn't regard it as feasible then, and I don't now, regardless of what you are insinuating. And besides," there was no stopping him, "if Onslow was handed the note by another boy, why didn't he tell us there and then? That would have been an ideal opportunity for a further hand check to lend some credence to this absurd flight of fancy."

"You know the system as well as anybody, Mr. Cooke," I replied. "If a junior boy such as Onslow sneaked on an older boy, or on any boy for that matter, his life would be made a living hell!"

Cooke paused just long enough for my purposes. "I disagree," he replied, but to my mind, his answer lacked conviction.

I felt I had done enough, and if this were a jury trial, I'd be submitting there was a reasonable doubt. I needed a short break to speak to Nigel and his parents, and to track down the absent Flogger. After all, this was supposed to be a team effort. The Board graciously gave me ten minutes, much to HM's displeasure.

I found Flogger in the vindaloo, lost in a noxious green fog.

"Are you going to be much longer, Charles?" I asked, with my handkerchief clamped firmly to my face.

"Bit of a stomach upset, I'm afraid Potts," came the voice from the fog, "can you manage without me?"

Nigel was adamant. He was not going to give evidence under any circumstances. I understood his predicament, and I didn't try to change his mind.

We filed back into the library, I made my submissions, succinct and to the point, or so I hoped, and the Board then asked us all to leave again whilst they deliberated. Ten minutes later we were called back in.

The Chairman delivered their verdict.

"We have listened carefully to the evidence, and we have taken into account Mr. Potts's able and well-reasoned submissions. If Nigel Onslow is to be believed, he was handed the stolen ten-pound note by the thief, an older boy whom he met by chance and whom, for his own good reasons no doubt, he has consistently and persistently refused to identify. However, there is not a shred of independent evidence to support his claim, and we therefor reject it. We find that Mr. Cooke and the Headmaster behaved perfectly properly, indeed they couldn't have done otherwise, faced as they were with overwhelming evidence of Onslow's guilt, and the Headmaster was fully justified in expelling the boy. That concludes our deliberations."

It was like the Court of Appeal, there to support the trial judge with a few well-chosen and acerbic phrases. I could hear their lordships now: "We have listened carefully to Counsel's able submissions, but we are not persuaded. Appeal dismissed."

The Board rose as one and filed out, followed by HM with a self-satisfied smirk. No chance of tea and scones on his lawn for the foreseeable future. That left me and the Onslows, still minus Flogger, to conduct the post-mortem.

"Well, that was a waste of money!" growled Dad, appreciative to the last.

"Don't be so unpleasant, Tom," Mum came to my rescue, "I thought Mr. Potts did all he could in difficult circumstances, and we should be very grateful." Good old Mum.

Dad was not persuaded. "So where do we go from here?" he demanded, jaw jutting out.

"The Governors are here to support the Headmaster," I said, "so it's hardly surprising they chose to do so. If they reached a conclusion that was simply not open to them on the evidence, then you can appeal to the Secretary of State for Education for yet another review."

"More wasted money, and more wasted time," Dad retorted.

"In my professional opinion," I continued in measured tones, "it's unlikely the Inspector will overturn the Governors' decision, so as you say, why waste more money and time?"

"So what do you advise?"

"Even if Nigel was allowed back into College, he'd be damaged goods so to speak, and I doubt if he'd have a happy time for the next four years with this cloud hanging over him."

To my surprise, Dad nodded in agreement. "That may well be right."

"As loving and caring parents," I continued, laying it on with a trowel, "you want what is best for Nigel."

"Of course," replied Mum, giving Nigel's hand a comforting squeeze.

"There are a number of good private schools in the area, and dare I say it, some with a better reputation than Rougemont."

Dad nodded. "Hear, hear." At last, Dad was coming onside.

"Any one of those schools would welcome Nigel as a fee-paying pupil, and you and he can put this unfortunate business behind you."

"But what about the stigma of being expelled?" Dad asked. "How do we live that down?"

"That's simple enough to explain," I replied. "If you take my advice, when asked about it, tell them the truth."

Dad's eyebrows shot up. "I can't see how that will help."

"Oh do shut up Tom," said Mum, losing her patience, "and listen to what Mr. Potts has to say. Please go on," she smiled encouragingly.

"If they ask, and they might not, you tell Nigel's new school that he was falsely accused of theft, an accusation he strenuously denied, and you were so appalled at the way he was treated, you removed him forthwith."

Dad stroked his jaw, deep in thought. "Excellent suggestion," he said at last, "and if I may say so, Mr. Potts, you show wisdom beyond your years. That's what we'll do."

At last, gratitude from the most unlikely source.

We said our farewells, and the three of them drove away with a cheery wave, or what I took to be a cheery wave, in the direction of HM, who was plodding around the College with new parents in tow. I couldn't face another trip to the vindaloo, where Flogger was still incommoded, so I walked the short distance to the station and took the first train back to London.

That was the last I saw of Flogger. Unfortunately I was unable to attend the Old Boys' dinner, pressure of work, it's the price to pay for the busy practitioner, so I was deprived of the pleasure of renewing my acquaintance with Flogger and HM. It was a disappointment I bore with commendable fortitude, even though I say it myself.

CHAPTER 7

ALLAHU AKBAR

Snaresbrook was becoming but a distant memory after my spat with Newman, and I had to admit, I wasn't missing the cut-and-thrust of prosecuting low-grade crime, the bone-shaking journey, locking antlers with the oleaginous Cantwell, and suffering the slings and arrows of outrageous misfortune at the hands of Bonkers.

The clerks, in that skewed way of thinking they had made their own, and to show they were earning their commission, had sought fresh pastures to plug the gap in my practice, and as Mike told me one morning, they were getting a positive feedback from the CPS in Croydon.

"This could play well, Mr. Potts," he enthused, "and by all accounts, there's plenty of work to be had."

I smiled weakly and groaned inwardly. The fact that Croydon was as far from my flat in Earls Court as it was possible to imagine, even farther than Snaresbrook, meant another bone-shaking journey, and the prospect of honing my adversarial skills on yet more low-grade crime filled me with dread. After all, I was up and coming, not down and out. But as the clerks were fond of reminding me, you've got to start somewhere, work was work, and it paid the bills. Actually, it didn't, as there was no travel allowance, no waiting allowance, and if the trial didn't proceed, no brief fee. I should have gone into farming.

My early days as the Croydon Crusader were very much a mixed bag. There were the usual 'no-hopers' that fell by the wayside almost before they'd begun, and where "counsel's evaluation" damned me with faint praise. But then, as I kept reminding myself, give me the tools and I'll finish the job. Bootsy would have been proud of me. There were one or two minor successes where the defendant had offered a plea of guilty to a lesser offence, and after much soul-searching by the reviewing lawyer, accepted with ill-grace.

As chance would have it, I had one minor triumph when I prosecuted to conviction a man charged with illegal trading, selling hooky goods that looked as if they'd fallen off the back of a lorry. On closer inspection, you could almost see the tyre marks. Emboldened by this triumph, Mike put me forward to prosecute Amjad Mohammed Khan, charged with the grave and weighty offence of assisting unlawful immigration, and I was given the nod.

My instructions, as ever, were short on the facts and long on counsel's duties, which included the usual prohibitions about taking any decisions whatsoever, as these were the sole preserve of the reviewing lawyer.

I had rapidly discovered that Croydon had absolutely nothing to commend it. Clinging to the skirts of South London, it was a dormitory town in every sense of the word, full of office blocks taking advantage of the lower rents yet within easy commuting distance of central London. The commuters arrived at 8.30, went inside their egg boxes, emerged at 5.30 and went home. By all accounts, night-time was no better. There were a few wine bars, pubs and clubs, but not exactly jumping, and low-grade crime consisting of drunk and disorderly, urinating in public, and for real excitement, arriving legless at King Khan's Balti Restaurant and throwing up.

Croydon had one redeeming feature. It was within a stone's throw of Gatwick, London's second airport, so for those in need of relief from the daily grind, and there were many, it was a short hop, skip and jump onto a plane and off into the blue beyond, or at least as far as the Costa Brava, with sun, sea, sand, sunburn, sex and sangria, and as Flogger Harris would have put it, as cheap as chips.

But Gatwick wasn't just one-way traffic, and passing the Costa Bravans on the way out were planeloads of immigrants from the Hindu Kush on the way in, courtesy of PIA, known as Pak-em-In Airlines, searching for a better life in Brick Lane, Leicester, Birmingham, Bradford and all ports between.

For the Immigration Service, this was their worst nightmare, as a sea of brown faces reeking of curry washed towards them, jostling and jabbering in a foreign tongue and hardly a word of English amongst them. It didn't help that they all looked the same. The menfolk, and a few of the womenfolk, sported big bushy beards, and they all had the same name. To a man they were Mohammed Khan, hundreds of them, with only their first name to distinguish them from their compatriots. There was Benares Mohammed Khan, Ali Mohammed Khan, Sidique Mohammed Khan, and so on and so forth until the last syllable of recorded time, and all clutching addresses of their nearest and dearest in Brick Lane, Leicester, Birmingham, Bradford and all ports between.

There were the usual rejects. Those who didn't have any documentation, but with Pak-em-in Airlines in the business of making money, they were allowed to board regardless. Then there were those whose documentation didn't tick the right boxes, or in some cases, didn't tick any of the boxes, so they were all herded together and collectively bussed to the nearest holding pen in Crawley, otherwise known as a detention centre.

Time for the immigration lawyers, like circling vultures, to work their magic. They too were bussed into Crawley, with legal aid forms at the ready. First there was the inevitable hearing before the Immigration Tribunal, conveniently located in Crawley. Next stop was the Immigration Appeal Tribunal, followed in the fullness of time by the House of Lords and thence to the European Court of Human Rights. The gravy train was pakked fit to bursting, just like the good old days in the Hindu Kush, so let them wagons roll! Eight years' later, when all appeal avenues had been exhausted, it was time to start all over again.

As chance would have it, an eagle-eyed Immigration officer processing the Khans spotted a pattern to some of the documents that aroused his suspicions. The forged visa stamps all bore the same hallmark, and all appeared to have originated from the British High Commission in Peshawar. However, following painstaking inquiries taking several months with the Pakistani Police, it was established that the forged visas were coming from a post office box in Croydon.

The matter was duly reported to Plod, and in the fullness of time, a team was put together headed by DCI. Dougie Sanders to investigate possible violations of the Immigration Act. A round-the-clock surveillance was set up, and in the course of the next two weeks, a man wearing pyjamas, a colourful waistcoat and a funny little hat and sporting a bushy black beard, was observed coming and going on a daily basis. Dougie, sharp as a sausage, thought he could be a Paki. Dougie was not politically correct.

The suspect was followed back to King Khan's Balti Restaurant, and with Dougie spearheading the operation from an unmarked police car across the road, the order to go in was given.

"Go! Go! Go!" shouted Dougie into his two-way radio. It was just like the movies.

The team went, went, went, and as they burst into the Restaurant, they reeled back from the overpowering smell of stale vomit and an evil-looking balti of the day, simmering away in the fly-blown kitchen. Dougie made a mental note to contact Health and Safety at Croydon Town Hall.

The suspect was identified as Amjad Mohammed Khan, and according to his entry visa, which looked decidedly dodgy, he was a native of Peshawar. Dougie concluded this was somewhere over there. In his possession were several envelopes, all addressed to Amjad Mohammed Khan, and containing sweaty wodges of money, all in rupees. When converted into sterling, they amounted to ten thousand pounds. Better than slopping out the restaurant on a daily basis and serving the sort of food even Flogger Harris might have difficulty digesting.

Amjad was nicked and taken into custody on suspicion of assisting unlawful immigration, which he denied. Although he had been in Croydon for over ten years, he still insisted on having an interpreter and a solicitor present when he was interviewed. His native language, he was to tell Dougie, was Urdu.

Fortunately, Croydon had more than its fair share of Urdu-speaking interpreters, some better than others, and solicitors specialising in immigration law were ten-a-penny.

On any view, the interview was not a success. The interpreter's first and only language was Urdu, with a smattering of English coming a very distant second. The solicitor introduced himself as Fazil Mohammed Khan, who had a better command of English, but the interview had barely begun when the three of them were jabbering away like best mates. This was not how it was supposed to go.

Dougie, as befitting a high-ranking detective, did his best to assert his authority, but it was like swimming in treacle. It didn't stop him from trying. Speaking slowly and loudly, a habit he had picked up when addressing waiters on the Costa Brava, he pressed on.

"When you were arrested, you had the equivalent of ten thousand pounds in rupees, which as I understand it, is the currency of Pakistan." Dougie had done his homework. "Two thousand pounds in five separate envelopes, and each postmarked Peshawar. So what's your explanation?"

There then followed several minutes of jabbering. When at last they stopped, Dougie waited expectantly for the answer. He looked at them, and they looked at him.

"So what's the answer?" asked Dougie.

"I am not prepared to disclose what my client is saying to me," replied Fazil with a straight face. "Any communications between a client and his solicitor are privileged and confidential, as you should be knowing."

Dougie's mouth fell open. In all his years on the force, he thought he'd heard it all. "If you know anything about the law, Mr. Khan," he snapped irritably, "and I doubt it, you'll know I'm entitled to ask questions. Your client can refuse to answer them, that's his right, but where he chooses to answer, I'm entitled to know what he said."

"No you are not."

"Yes I am."

They glowered at each other.

"I am resenting your suggestion that I am knowing nothing about the law," said Fazil, breaking the awkward silence. "I am having a diploma in law from Croydon Polytechnic."

"Well there's a load off!" retorted Dougie, beginning to lose his composure, "we can all sleep easy in our beds tonight!"

"I am resenting your hostile tone, officer, as is my client."

"How do you know? Have you asked him?"

This was the cue for more jabbering, as Dougie sat stony-faced, drumming his fingers on the table.

"My client is resenting your hostile tone, officer," said Fazil at last, "and on my advice, will not be answering any more of your questions."

"He hasn't answered *any* of my questions you moron!" Dougie had lost his composure. "And you," he glared at the interpreter, "you're supposed to be interpreting and all you're doing is sitting there like a nodding dog. So what do *you* say?"

The interpreter smiled inanely, nodding all the time. Cue for more jabbering.

"The interpreter is resenting your hostile tone, officer," replied Fazil, "and will not be interpreting any more of your questions."

That was the final straw. "I am now terminating this interview, and for the benefit of the tape, the suspect refuses to answer any questions on the advice of his solicitor, and the interpreter doesn't speak a word of English." Dougie stormed out, slamming the door behind him. Cue for more jabbering.

Amjad was bailed to return to the police station in twenty-eight days' time, and the file was submitted to the reviewing lawyer from the CPS to review the evidence.

Jason Alcock, known in the service as Alcock and No Balls, was the reviewing lawyer for the Croydon area. In his considered opinion, there was a strong circumstantial case against Amjad. However, whilst there was evidence linking the forged visas to Amjad's post office box, there was no evidence linking him directly to the forgeries. His restaurant had been thoroughly searched, and his flat above. The search was hampered by the presence of a dozen or more relatives, wives and cousins and uncles and aunts, all claiming kinship to Amjad, and all jabbering away like a cartload of monkeys.

'No Balls' reasoned that the visas were being forged elsewhere in Croydon, and brought into the restaurant by 'mules' posing as diners, in return for a gut-wrenching balti and a share of the action.

'No Balls' also had an ace up his sleeve. With that forward thinking that had marked him out for rapid promotion, he had engaged the services of a competent interpreter to listen to the taped interview and provide a verbatim account of what was said. This turned out to be an inspired decision, as Amjad had admitted to Fazil that the money collected from the post office box was in payment for entry documents into the United Kingdom, although he denied any knowledge of forged visas. Pull the other one, Kushty, it's got bells on it!

Amjad was duly charged with assisting unlawful immigration, and bailed to appear at Croydon Crown Court on a date to be fixed.

Dougie's further inquiries met a brick wall. Word in the community had got out as soon as Amjad had been arrested. There were no more envelopes in his post office box, no more forged visas finding their way to Peshawar, and diners at his restaurant had dwindled to a trickle, with only the lager-louts keeping it open for the usual balti of the day and a good old-fashioned chunder.

No pre-trial conference had been arranged. There were budgetary constraints, and besides, with the reviewing lawyer's firm hand on the tiller, counsel's role was to put up and shut up, and be grateful for the work.

I arrived in good time for the trial, listed for three days. An extra day had been allowed for the evidence to be interpreted, a treat in store. The trial judge was His Honour Judge "The Glums" Clutterbuck, recently retired, and the self-same judge who had presided over one of my earlier forensic triumphs at Middlesex Crown Court in the porn trial of Larry King. I was sure he'd remember me with affection. Croydon, being Croydon, boasted no resident judge, and let's face it, who in their right mind would want to be resident judge at Croydon, so Her Majesty's business was conducted by itinerant judges, most of whom had recently retired, and rather wishing they had kept it that way.

Wigged and gowned, I presented myself outside Court One to await the arrival of the CPS law clerk, who would sit behind me, fill in 'counsel's evaluation form' and generally look busy. Across the hall I noticed a huddle of three, one whom I assumed was the defendant, dressed in pyjamas, the second, also dressed in pyjamas but with an air of authority befitting a graduate of Croydon Polytechnic, and the third, more soberly dressed and sporting a brand-new wig and gown, whom I took to be my opponent. I nodded briefly towards them. They ignored me. As far as they were concerned, I was the infidel.

Shirley the CPS law clerk hove into sight with three minutes to go. She was short and stocky, clearly the wrong side of forty by several years, with dyed hair of indeterminate colour and a down-turned mouth. She looked disinterested, as she contemplated three days of holding the line between an inexperienced prosecutor and a bunch of Kushties. It would take a charm offensive of Sisyphean proportions to win her over, but I was determined to give it my best shot, and with a glowing evaluation from this raddled harridan, who could say what the future might hold?

I smiled winningly, which she ignored as she swept into court. It was my day for being ignored. I followed respectfully a few paces behind as she settled down for the ordeal ahead and, pen poised, opened her counsel evaluation form.

I ascertained from the usher that my opponent was Khalid Mohammed Khan, with a busy immigration practice and strong community ties. He entered stage left with his client and solicitor, followed by a dozen or more interested spectators, all male, and judging from their pyjamas and bushy black beards, all from the Hindu Kush. Not a female in sight, as this was a male-dominated culture which had been planted, lock, stock and barrel, into the leafy suburbs of outer Croydon, and what was good enough for the Hindu Kush was good enough for Croydon.

"All rise," announced the usher as The Glums made his way into court. We rose, he nodded briefly towards counsel's bench, and we all sat down.

"Mr. Khan," he began, at which point Khalid, Fazil and Amjad rose as one, followed in short order by the entire public gallery. This took The Glums by surprise. "Actually," he continued, waving at the assembled multitude, "I was addressing Mr. Mohammed Khan of counsel. The rest of you can sit back down." With much clattering, they did so. "Are you ready to proceed?" Silly question as it turned out.

"No, My Honour," replied Khalid, "this is not what I am wanting."

"Pray tell me why."

"My Honour, there are matters of law I am wishing to submit."

The Glums looked bemused. "Very well, but first the interpreter should be sworn."

The interpreter took the oath, just, and turned to the court. "My name is Ahmed Mohammed Khan, and the language of interpretation is Urdu."

"Splendid. Please take a seat next to the defendant in the dock."

Ahmed stared blankly back. "What is this you are saying to me?" he asked.

The Glums looked even more bemused. "Please take a seat next to the defendant in the dock," he repeated, speaking slowly and loudly.   Another blank stare.

Khalid rose. "Perhaps I can be helping, My Honour." He turned to the interpreter, jabbered away, presumably in Urdu, and the interpreter sloped off to the dock. This was not going well. Time for judicial intervention.

"I ask in a spirit of enquiry, Mr. Khan, is the interpreter fluent in English?"

Khalid turned once more to the interpreter, with more jabbering away. "He is telling me My Honour that he is most definitely fluent in English."

There was a long pause. "Very well," said The Glums at last, "on your assurance as the defendant's counsel, let us proceed. Now what matters of law do you wish to submit?"

"Has My Honour seen the record of interview?"

"I have indeed, and most interesting reading it is."

"I am submitting that the interview should be ruled inadmissible."

"Why so, Mr. Khan?"

"The conversations between the defendant and my instructing solicitor are most definitely privileged, and cannot be given in evidence. In addition, where the officer is calling my instructing solicitor a moron, this is a gross abuse of executive power."

The Glums permitted himself the flicker of a smile. "It may well have been an infelicitous remark in the heat of the moment," he replied, "and unless there are objections from Mr. Potts, I am content that this remark be excised from the record."

"No objections, Your Honour." It may have been true, but it wasn't important. Oh Lord, I suddenly remembered, I was supposed to consult the reviewing lawyer before taking any decisions. I turned round quickly just as Shirley's pen was poised for action. "Do you agree?" I asked in a stage-whisper. Too little, too late, as Shirley was already scribbling furiously.

There were ructions from the dock affording a welcome distraction from Shirley's blank stare. The Glums looked up. "Is there a problem, Mr. Khan?"

Khalid looked round. More jabbering. "The interpreter is saying that he is not understanding 'infelicitous' or 'excised', so he is not being able to translate them. And speaking for myself, I too am not understanding them."

The Glums and I exchanged glances. The time estimate of three days was rapidly turning into three weeks, and with no end in sight.

The Glums addressed the defendant. "The remark that your solicitor is a moron will be crossed out," he all but shouted.

"Now let's get on." He paused to compose himself. "As to your submission that the conversations between the defendant and your instructing solicitor are privileged and therefore inadmissible, I am against you. Anything said by the defendant in the course of a recorded interview can be adduced...I mean given in evidence. Now if there is nothing else, I suggest we empanel the jury."

"Before we are doing that, My Honour, will My Honour be giving me a certificate?"

The Glums' mouth dropped open. "A certificate of what?" he asked testily.

"A certificate of public importance."

Rather like DCI. Sanders, The Glums thought he had heard it all, but this was in a league of its own. "If you mean a certificate that my ruling raises a point of general public importance, it can only be granted on conviction, and the defendant has not *yet* been convicted. In addition, a certificate can only be granted by the Court of Appeal for consideration by the House of Lords." The Glums had had enough. Waving Khalid down, he turned to the usher. "Summon the jury-in-waiting."

Twenty would-be jurors filed into court, from whom twelve would be selected at random. After the court clerk advised the defendant of his right to challenge, twelve names were called out, and twelve filed into the jury box. There were eight men, three of whom were wearing pyjamas and sporting bushy black beards, and four women. *A recipe for a hung jury*, I thought to myself, but there was nothing I could do about it.

The first juror, a woman, was about to take the oath, when up popped Khalid again.

"My Honour, the defendant is objecting to this person."

"On what grounds, Mr. Khan?" asked The Glums wearily.

"She is a woman."

"Yes, I can see that. What of it?"

"In the defendant's culture, nurtured in the Hindu Kush," replied Khalid, "women are never permitted to sit in judgment on their menfolk."

The judge's knuckles whitened as he fought to control his temper. "In our culture, Mr. Khan, as you should know, men and women are equal. The Hindu Kush plays no part in the proper administration of English justice. Objection overruled."

"I am disappointing, My Honour…"

"You are indeed, Mr. Khan, but for the time being, there is nothing either of us can do about it."

The next six jurors duly took the oath, despite mutterings from Khalid, and then the first of the pyjama party was handed the book. I rose magisterially.

"Before this prospective juror takes the oath, Your Honour, it might be prudent to enquire if he is fluent in English and if he knows the defendant. As I understand it, there is a close-knit Asian community here in Croydon."

"Good point," nodded The Glums approvingly, but Khalid was up on his feet like a jackrabbit.

"This is discrimination of the highest order, My Honour," he fumed, "and up with which I will not be putting."

"Calm down, Mr. Khan. Counsel's request is perfectly proper. This trial is estimated to last three days, although on present form, it could last an eternity. There is an interpreter of sorts, but his duty is to the defendant, and he cannot be expected to interpret for the benefit of the jury. If this juror, or any juror, cannot understand English, the defendant will be denied a fair trial, and I'm sure you wouldn't want that." A nice touch, I thought. The Glums addressed the juror, checking the name cards handed to him by the usher. "Mr. Ammar Mohammed Khan," the juror nodded vigorously, "do you speak English?"

"Most excellently well, thank you Your Majesty," replied Ammar, beaming from ear to ear.

"And how long have you lived in England?"

"Two years Your Majesty, here in Croydon, a most excellent town, but I am not liking your weather."

"And I am not liking our weather either, Mr. Khan," chuckled The Glums. "Now to the matter in hand, do you know the defendant Mr. Amjad Mohammed Khan?" and he pointed to the dock.

"I am most certainly knowing Amjad," replied Ammar, still grinning from ear to ear. "He is a most excellent gentleman. We are all knowing him," he added for good measure, looking at his two cousins, who nodded enthusiastically in agreement.

There were stirrings on counsel's bench as Khalid turned round and began a fevered conversation with Fazil.

"And how well do you know him?"

That was the cue for Khalid to pop up again in a state of visible panic. "My Honour, I am becoming increasingly concerned about My Honour's cross-examination of this juror, and I am objecting in the strongest terms. It is most irregular, and a breach of his human rights." If in doubt, throw in human rights, I thought uncharitably.

"And which particular human right am I breaching, Mr. Khan?"

"The defendant's right not to be subjected to inhuman and degrading treatment," replied Khalid in all seriousness.

With a supreme effort, The Glums managed to control himself. "Thank you Mr. Khan, your objection is duly noted." He turned back to Ammar. "How well do you know Amjad Mohammed Khan?" he repeated.

"Amjad is our cousin, Your Majesty. We are paying him to provide us with most excellent visas," he replied, "so that we may be coming to your most excellent country."

You could hear a pin drop as Ammar's bombshell silently exploded. Even Shirley stopped scribbling. Khalid was on his way up again, but The Glums waved him back down.

"Mr. Potts," I rose, "the trial cannot proceed with this jury, as they are now privy to information that could prejudice them against this defendant. In the circumstances, I have no option but to discharge them." I nodded. "Usher, escort the three jurors into a private room, where they will remain until further order. Those who instruct you may wish to make DCI. Sanders available to interview all three here at court, separately of course and under caution. Once the interviews have been completed, I am to be informed. I shall adjourn the trial until ten tomorrow when a new jury panel can be summoned."

More in hope than expectation, I returned at nine the next morning to be met by Dougie Sanders. Shirley, predictably, was nowhere to be seen, as her body-clock was programmed to activate at nine-forty-five, and not a minute earlier. We found a room and I read through the transcripts of the three interviews.

"All three confirm what Ammar said in open court," said Dougie. "Their evidence could be crucial."

"I agree. Where are they now?" I asked.

"Downstairs in the cells," replied Dougie. "After he had read the transcripts, the judge remanded them in custody overnight."

I nodded. "And what about the defence, have they received copies?"

"Yesterday evening. There was a lot of muttering about human rights and the House of Lords, so get ready for more of the same." Dougie flicked through his file. "I've photocopied a genuine visa issued by the British High Commission in Peshawar, and the visas produced to me by the three suspects." He pushed the photocopies across the table. "They're pretty good forgeries, enough to fool the Immigration Service unless they're particularly vigilant, and we both know they're not. See if you can spot the difference."

I could, as I was PLC, and hugely intelligent. "On the forgeries, Comission is spelt incorrectly every time," I replied, feeling pleased with myself.

"Got it in one, Mr. Potts," said Dougie, clearly impressed, and so he should be. "So what happens now?"

"I'm the organ-grinder's monkey, Inspector, I do as I'm told. What does Mr. Alcock say about all this?"

"Haven't a clue, Mr. Potts. By the time we'd finished transcribing the interviews, he'd gone home. Bloody clock-punchers," he added with feeling.

"Time to find out, I suppose." I checked my watch. It was nine-thirty. "Let's go and shake him and see what falls out." Dougie chuckled.

We waited impatiently outside the CPS office for a further ten minutes until No Balls finally put in an appearance, sauntering along the hall without a care in the world. Dozy bugger, I heard Dougie mutter under his breath. I agree, I muttered back.

Once he'd settled down with his coffee and gingernut biscuits, No Balls started thumbing through the transcripts.

"I'm going to need more time to consider this lot," he said, slurping his coffee. "We'll have to tell the judge."

"Mr. Potts and I were here at nine," retorted Dougie on a short fuse, "and where were *you?* What a way to run a service! If you want more time, *you* tell the judge you only tipped up at nine-forty, and spent the first five minutes drinking coffee and munching biscuits! And where's that useless law clerk?"

Just then, Shirley, the useless law clerk, popped her head round the door. It was nine-forty-five, and her body clock had activated.

"Is there a problem, Jason?" she asked.

No Balls wasn't used to being spoken to in such a way, but DCI. Sanders was a high-ranking officer and needed careful handling.

"There's no need to be offensive, officer, we're all working together as a team..."

"Then start working for Chrissake!" he snapped. "If you want my advice, and you do," he glared at No Balls, "Mr. Potts here knows the score, so let him do what you're paying him to do, which is to prosecute. He gets my vote," he added for good measure.

Praise indeed from the most unexpected source. Whatever else, Dougie was now firmly on my Christmas card mailing list.

There was a long awkward silence. No Balls was being asked to think outside the box, something he'd never done in all his years with the Service. This Potts lad seemed competent enough, but he was young and inexperienced, and if it went 'tits up', No Balls would have to carry the can. On the other hand, he had the luxury of reviewing himself favourably, which he always did, so it was a 'win win' situation.

"Very well," he said at last, and with five minutes to go, "you have the confidence of the officer in the case, which is good enough for me," he lied, "so proceed as you think fit."

I wished I had a tape of that remark. It was a seminal moment, and unlikely ever to be repeated. Dougie and I hurried to court, with the useless Shirley following in our wake.

The Glums entered court promptly at ten, with no sign of Khan, Khan, Khan and Khan. The remaining Khans were already packing the public gallery, ready for the courtroom drama to unfold.

"Can you help, Mr. Potts?"

"I have not seen them at court this morning, Your Honour."

The Glums turned to the usher. "Please tannoy them to attend court immediately."

We sat patiently, and five minutes' later, they appeared, looking hot, bothered and flustered.

"I am sorry for keeping My Honour waiting, but we were in conference," said Khalid.

"Conferences normally take place outside court hours, Mr. Khan," replied The Glums acidly. "Now Mr. Potts, where do we stand?"

"I know Your Honour has been provided with transcripts of the three interviews, and they make for informative reading."

"They do indeed."

"I have considered whether the three jurors should be charged with an offence under section 24A of the Immigration Act 1971, as there is evidence that they obtained leave to enter the United Kingdom by deception. The section can be found at page 2264 in the current edition of Archbold." I had done my homework.

"Give me a moment," said The Glums as he leafed through his copy. "Yes, I have it."

"However, in my submission, the interests of justice would be better served if these three gave evidence for the Crown." The Glums nodded approvingly. "Whilst they may have acted naively, they appear to be witnesses of truth and therefore worthy of belief."

"I agree."

"With this in mind, and with Your Honour's leave, I shall ask DCI. Sanders, whose help has been invaluable," might as well return the compliment, "to take short statements from each, simply adopting their transcripts as their evidence-in-chief, and assuming there are now sufficient jurors to form a fresh jury, we can proceed without further delay."

"This seems an eminently sensible approach, Mr. Potts. How long do you need?"

"Thirty minutes please, Your Honour."

The Glums nodded. "I shall rise."

As soon as The Glums had left court, there was a general hubbub and a lot of jabbering as Dougie went off to take statements from the three jurors. Khan, Khan, Khan and Khan repaired to their interview room for further discussions, followed swiftly by the entire public gallery, streaming out into the street, never to be seen again. With Amjad's dodgy visas doing the rounds, it was time to cut and run.

Thirty minutes' later, with the statements duly signed, the court reassembled. As before, there was no sign of the Khans. Perhaps they too had cut and run. Another tannoy, and another five minute wait before they returned to court.

"Yes Mr. Potts?" asked the Glums.

Before I could answer, up popped Khalid.

"Before My Honour is hearing from my learned Potts," he said, "I am asking for the charge against Amjad Mohammed Khan to be put again."

"So be it."

The court clerk rose. "Stand up. You are charged with assisting unlawful immigration. How do you plead, guilty or not guilty?"

"Guilty," replied Amjad.

"Very well. The Defendant will be remanded in custody to await sentence in three weeks' time, and I shall want a full background report. Mr. Potts," I rose, "it is a matter for you, but DCI. Sanders may wish to alert the Immigration Service so that they can make their own inquiries."

"I am sure that will be done, Your Honour."

"The court is obliged to you both for your assistance in this matter. I shall rise."

"Before My Honour is rising," said Khalid, "and with the defendant now pleading guilty, I am asking for my certificate."

The Glums had had enough. "Application refused," he snapped, and without breaking stride, left court.

Dougie pumped me warmly by the hand. "An excellent result, Mr. Potts, and a masterful performance if I may say so."

"You're very kind, Inspector. Now, I suggest we report to the Gruppenführer for a debriefing. But first things first, coffee and gingernut biscuits." We exchanged knowing glances. Shirley, still smarting from being described as useless, chose not to join us, and with her down-turned mouth, lumbered off to submit her own report.

It turned out to be a pyrrhic victory. Although I hadn't initiated the confrontation with No Balls, I had been a witness to it. He was not a man to forgive and forget, and he didn't. I was a constant reminder of his incompetence, and he didn't like to be reminded. Petty vindictiveness seemed to run with the job, and in due course, Croydon, like Snaresbrook, became a 'no-go' area for my nascent prosecution practice. Another challenge for the clerks, I thought, but I wouldn't miss Croydon. Potts of the Bailey perhaps? Only time would tell.

CHAPTER 8

BIRD OVER

After my experiences in Snaresbrook and Croydon, I was beginning to feel that I wasn't cut out for prosecuting. I felt I could hold my own, even against the likes of Cantwell, but it needed a mind-set I didn't possess. Worshipping at the shrine of the reviewing lawyer didn't sit comfortably with me, and all this nonsense of buying a dog *and* barking yourself made for an uneasy relationship. Either I was good enough to carry the can, or I wasn't, and to be constantly playing second fiddle to the likes of Newman and No Balls, slurping his coffee and munching his biscuits, was a major irritant. What was the point of an independent Bar if I was never independent?

I didn't have this trouble with my defence practice, such as it was. Most of the time I was left to my own devices, aided and abetted by the likes of Bootsy Farmer and Churchill, an irresistible combination, but it seemed to work. On the rare occasions when a grown-up solicitor put in an appearance, such as Will Cutler down Exeter way, it was a team effort. I welcomed his input of course, but he never sought to interfere or question my judgment when decisions had to be made.

These and other thoughts were occupying my mind when a received a phone call in chambers from Peter Simkins. The name didn't ring an immediate bell.

"Mr. Potts? You may not remember me, but I instructed you on behalf of Lord Brockenhurst."

The bell rang. After all, it wasn't every day I was instructed on behalf of the aristocracy, and this was Aristocracy with a capital 'A'. A belted Earl no less, tracing his lineage back to William the Conqueror, and whom I had represented to a triumphant acquittal at Little Hampden Magistrates' Court. That's the Earl, not William the Conqueror.

"Yes indeed," I replied, "a pleasure to hear from you again." Perhaps he was phoning to invite me to join his lordship for a long weekend at the family seat, and not before time.

"I would like to instruct you in a case involving one of his lordship's gamekeepers, one Taffy Williams. He's Welsh," he added helpfully, as if that mattered. "I have discussed the matter with his lordship, he was singularly impressed with the way you handled his minor contretemps with the hunt saboteurs."

"Yes, I remember the case well," I replied.

"This is altogether more serious, I'm afraid." He paused. "The charge is one of attempted murder."

My mouth went dry. "Very serious indeed," was all I could think of saying.

"His lordship doesn't want it splashed all over the tabloids, so would prefer to keep it low-key, if you follow my meaning. No offence intended," Simkins added hastily.

"And none taken, Mr. Simkins," replied low-key Potts.

"Splendid, I knew you'd understand. I've spoken to your senior clerk, I forget his name.."

"Fred."

"Quite so. He's booked a conference in chambers at four-thirty on Thursday, and the brief will be with you tomorrow. I will be sending one of my junior associates to assist you."

"Thank you."

"Given the seriousness of the charge, Williams has been committed to stand trial at the Bailey." I felt a frisson of nervous excitement. "Very tiresome, and despite my best efforts to have it tried locally."

"I wouldn't be too concerned, Mr. Simkins," I replied, as if the highest criminal court in the land were my second home. "After all, murder and attempted murder are daily fare at the Bailey, so less likely to be picked up and splashed all over the tabloids."

Simkins paused. "I hadn't thought of that, Mr. Potts. You're absolutely right." He sounded reassured, and brownie points for me. "If any matters arise following your conference, do not hesitate to contact me."

It took a few minutes to sink in. Potts of the Bailey! It had a certain ring to it, and I liked what I was hearing. I hadn't been back since my one and only triumph with Santa Claus, presided over by old Sourpuss himself, so it was time to get back in the saddle and hit the ground running.

No sooner had Simkins rung off, Fred was on the phone.

"Another feather in your wig, Mr. Potts," he enthused. "Mr. Simkins has told me all about it, so I'm keeping you out of court tomorrow so you can get up to speed. It's a big step-up for you, and we mustn't disappoint the noble Earl."

"Quite so, Fred." I wondered if he was phoning me on his knees.

"Mike had put you forward on a committal for sentence in Croydon, mending fences and all that, but I've returned it, and the CPS will cover it themselves."

Thank God for small mercies. The Glums would be thrilled to bits! 'No Balls' and Shirley standing shoulder to shoulder, and putting the world to rights. I hadn't been invited back for the sentencing of Amjad, no surprises there, but I later learned that he had been sentenced to two years, with a recommendation for deportation. More work for Khalid, with appeal after appeal, and thence to the House of Lords, clutching his certificate, or so he hoped. I suspected the House of Lords might tell him where to stick it.

⊨╫╪⊨

I was in chambers promptly by nine the next morning. The brief had arrived, and I took it to my room to "get up to speed" as Fred had put it. I began by reading the background statement.

Taffy had been in service for over ten years. Nobody was 'employed' by the Earl, they were all in service, shades of yesteryear when the peasants knew their place and tugged their forelocks a lot as their lords and masters rode by. His duties were to keep an eye on the game birds, reared in their thousands to be blasted out of the sky during the shooting season, and keep down the vermin. This included foxes, deer, badgers, rabbits, indeed anything that moved and had the temerity to be where it shouldn't be in the great scheme of things. Taffy, like his lordship, liked everything neat and tidy.

On the day in question, with his trusty twelve bore, he was walking the lower forty, rough ground and woodland in the heart of the shoot, when he was disturbed by something moving in the bushes ahead. Whatever it was, it was where it shouldn't be, so in the best traditions of John Wayne, shoot now and ask questions later, he let off a shot. There was a yelp of pain, and out staggered 'Randy' Andy Chisholm, his backside peppered with birdshot. That was plain for all to see, as his trousers were round his ankles at the time. Also staggering out and also in a state of undress, but mercifully unpeppered, was Blodwen Williams, Taffy's wife and faithful companion till death them do part. An unfortunate expression in the circumstances.

Despite his injuries, Andy was off like a long dog, leaving Blodwen to explain the unexplainable. She failed miserably, and in very short order, she was packed off to her mother's in Cardigan

156

Bay to await the inevitable inquest. By law, she couldn't be compelled to give evidence against her husband, and wisely chose not to do so.

Andy summoned help, and an ambulance took him to his local hospital. It wasn't his idea to press charges, for obvious reasons, but the hospital staff were obliged to report non-accidental injuries to the police, and they did.

After the usual navel-gazing, the CPS elected to charge Taffy with attempted murder. They were influenced in this decision by statements taken from the landlord of the Brockenhurst Arms and a clutch of hardened drinkers, who had overheard Andy bragging about his dalliances with the fragrant Blodwen. He fancied himself as a ladies' man, especially after he'd bought that bottle of splash-it-on-all-over Brut which, according to the label, made him irresistible. It had the added bonus of keeping the flies away during the hot summer months.

It's not surprising how alcohol loosens the tongue, and there were plenty of loose tongues a wagging in the Brockenhurst Arms. It wasn't long before word reached Taffy, and one night, there was an ugly confrontation in the public bar. After a heated exchange of words, Taffy, a big man, pulled Andy towards him by his shirt front and shouted into his face: "You come within a country mile of my Blodwen, and I'll fucking kill you!"

When interviewed by Plod, Taffy admitted making the threat, but it was in the heat of the moment, and of course he didn't mean it. He stuck to his story that he thought it was probably a deer in the thicket, and fired more to scare it off than kill it. Whilst there may have been rutting going on, he had no idea it was Randy and Blodwen.

He made a good point, which I underlined in red, when he told the interviewing officer that if he had deliberately fired at Andy in mid-rut, he could've injured Blodwen, and whatever else, he wouldn't harm a hair on her head. Was it worth taking a statement from her, and calling her as a witness? Something to think about.

━╪ ╪━

The conference that Thursday was a morale-boosting exercise, as Simkins had covered all the main issues in his instructions. Williams was indeed a big man, six-foot-six in his enormous stocking feet, and big rough hands. His weather-beaten face sported a two-day stubble, not sure if it was coming or going, big brown eyes and a mop of brown curly hair. Joy, Simkins' associate, and known to one and all in the office as 'What A', was very easy on the eye, she reminded me of my dear-departed Susie, especially when she crossed her legs, and a welcome change from the likes of Bootsy.

"Mr. Simkins has asked me to tell you that the trial will be in the court warned list as of Monday, so it could be listed at any time during the next two weeks," she said, opening the proceedings. "He hopes you will be available at short notice to represent Mr. Williams, knowing as he does how busy you are."

If only, I thought. "Thank you, and I shall certainly make myself available." As his lordship was paying for my professional services privately, it was the very least I could do. I turned to Taffy.

"Now Mr. Williams, your defence to this serious charge is accident. You fired towards the bushes, thinking it was vermin you were shooting at…"

"And it was vermin I shot!" he retorted. "I wasn't aiming at the randy little sod, look you, but he got what was coming to him." Spoken with feeling, but not helpful. "Anyway, he were trespassing, so he got what he deserved."

"A word of advice, Mr. Williams. Do *not* say that to the jury! It could be taken the wrong way and used against you. And besides, unless I've missed a trick, you are not permitted to shoot trespassers."

"More's the pity!"

158

For such a big man, he had a remarkably sing-song voice. I suppose it harked back to the valleys, and the days when Dafydd Ap Leuan and his merry men would sing to the enemy from the battlements of Harlech Castle. Some would turn and run, others would stand and fight. Whatever else, it made for a tuneful engagement. And who could possibly understand a language where vowels were as rare as hen's teeth?

Time to change tack. "I don't know if you've seen the forensic scientist's report..."

"Yes I have."

"Good. Now I can't claim to be an expert on firearms. If I fancy a pheasant, I buy one from the butcher's." If the noble earl had invited me to join him on the Glorious Twelfth, the first day of the shooting season north of the border, I might have grasped some of the basics, but with a gillie at my shoulder holding my hand, gun and hipflask, not necessarily in that order, why bother?

Taffy snorted in derision. "A bit of a townie, are we, Mr. Potts?" That put me firmly in my place. "Still, you're not alone, look you. Half of his lordship's weekend guests don't know one end of a shotgun from the other," he laughed, "and they're paying five thousand pounds for the privilege. Plain daft if you ask me."

Taffy was right, look you, but not my place to comment. Time to move on.

"As I understand it," I had done some research, "you were using Number Four shot, which is shot with a diameter of 3.3 mm, and each cartridge containing no more than fifty lead pellets. It is sometimes referred to as birdshot, and used predominantly on small birds such as quail, snipe and partridge." Taffy nodded approvingly. He was impressed and back on side. "The medical report tells us that 15 pellets were removed from Chisholm's ample posterior, leaving the remaining pellets scattered to the four winds."

"I take back what I said about you being a townie, Mr. Potts. You obviously know your stuff, look you."

Praise indeed as my chest swelled, and Joy smiled engagingly, a smile I returned in full measure. Perhaps a rousing rendition of "Men of Harlech" to round off the conference, or as Taffy would have it: *"Rhyfelgyrch Gwŷr Harlech"*.

"One final matter. Given the size and spread of the shot, can you give me some idea of the distance between you and Andy when you fired in his direction?"

"I'd say about eighty yards," replied Taffy.

Ten days later, the call to arms came suddenly and unexpectedly when Fred phoned me in my room. "I have some good news and some bad news," he said. "The good news is that the case of Williams is listed tomorrow, clear start at ten-thirty. It was due to be heard by Judge Duckworth, but his trial has overrun."

"And what's the bad news, Fred?"

"It's now been listed at short notice before Mr. Justice Boniface."

There was a deathly silence as I absorbed the enormity of that statement. Mr. Justice Boniface, known to one and all at the Bar as "Old Sourpuss", was a judge who didn't suffer fools gladly and who spoke his mind. If you weren't marching to his tune, you were a fool. I remembered vividly the grilling handed out to Ronald Berger, my first pupil master, who was sent packing in very short order in the case of Browne. If Berger hadn't possessed the hide of a rhinoceros, it could have set him back years.

On the positive side, with the exception of a few minor hiccups along the way, he had treated me fairly during my first trial by jury, when I successfully defended Santa Claus. Perhaps he was just being kind to a new boy, but I was soon to find out. Kindness was not a virtue for which he was generally known.

"All rise," intoned the court usher, "the Honourable Mr. Justice Boniface presiding."

Sourpuss, belying his years, strode into court and assumed the throne of judgment. He glowered at both of us, making it clear he would rather be somewhere else. If it hadn't been for that idiot Duckworth and his overrunning trial, he would have enjoyed a leisurely breakfast with his copy of The Times, checking more idiot decisions of the Court of Appeal in the law reports, and then, with a peck on the cheek for the long-suffering Lady Sourpuss, a brisk walk to his Club for a pink gin or three and a leisurely lunch of steak and kidney pie, his favourite, and Spotted Dick, which some idiot in the civil service told him was politically incorrect, and must now be referred to as Spotted Richard. The evening would be spent flicking through the court papers for the next day, helpfully delivered by his clerk, another complete idiot but well-meaning, and then a leisurely dinner and idle chit-chat with Lady S, and thence to bed. Instead, here he was back in court, with some idiot called Pertwee prosecuting, with some idiot behind him jerking his strings, and some idiot called Potts who was barely out of short trousers. The index-linked pension couldn't come soon enough.

"Gentlemen," he began, addressing us both, "I have noticed that the defendant in this case is in the service of the Earl of Brockenhurst." We both nodded in unison. "You should know that the Earl and I are very well acquainted. I shoot regularly on his estates, and we have known each other for many years. In fact, we were at school together."

"Slough Grammar I shouldn't doubt," I whispered to Joy sitting behind me, otherwise known as Eton College.

"Quite right, Mr. Potts," retorted Sourpuss, "and despite my advancing years, I still have excellent hearing." I bowed, duly chastened. "In the circumstances, do either of you have an application?"

Giles Pertwee, despite his seniority, was part of the CPS machine, so he turned round to their representative for a hurried conversation and his marching orders. Sourpuss waited impatiently as they whispered away. Finally, his patience snapped.

"Mr. Pertwee?" he asked testily.

"Er, forgive me my lord, but those who instruct me are not sure what application your lordship is inviting me to make."

"This is preposterous! I am not *inviting* you to make *any* application, Mr. Pertwee, but if you have an application that I recuse myself, which, for the benefit of those who instruct you, means that I should stand down from presiding over this case for fear of partiality, then I shall hear you."

"Er," replied Pertwee, clearly shell-shocked from the incoming flak, "would your lordship give me a moment?"

"No I will not! Surely an advocate of your experience can decide for yourself?"

"Er, no your lordship. All decisions affecting the conduct of the trial must be referred to the reviewing lawyer."

Sourpuss, with a monumental effort, just managed to restrain himself. "And pray tell me, Mr. Pertwee, is the reviewing lawyer sitting behind you?"

"Er, no your lordship. He's normally to be found in his office on the fourth floor, although," Pertwee added helpfully, "this is not always the case. It depends on how many reviews he is being asked to review at any one time."

Sourpuss held his face in his hands. Eventually he reappeared. "I am not wasting any more time. Do you have an application or not?"

With the prospect of an unremitting verbal bombardment raining down on him for the next three days, Pertwee broke the habit of a lifetime and made a decision. "Yes, my lord," he replied, "I feel that the interests of justice would be best served if your lordship were to recuse yourself."

"I am not remotely interested in your feelings, Mr. Pertwee," snapped Sourpuss, a self-evident observation. "Mr. Potts?"

I was sorely tempted to dump Sourpuss in favour of a more sympathetic judge, but I chose discretion over valour. And besides, better the devil you know and all that. "I have no application, my lord."

"Put with commendable brevity. I shall not recuse myself. Jury bailiff, summon the jury panel."

Time for me to enter the lion's den. "Before the jury panel is summoned, I am going to ask your lordship to take a view."

"Take a view!?! Take a view!?! What is this gibberish? You make me sound like some sort of a peeping Tom."

"No, no, of course not my lord…." I stammered as the verbal bombardment flew my way.

"If by this curious expression, you mean that you wish to make a submission, then you are at liberty to do so, and I shall thereafter rule upon it. However," he added ominously, "we have wasted enough time already, so it had better be good."

I took a deep breath, and then waded in. To coin a phrase, better to have submitted and lost, than not to have submitted at all. "My lord, it is my submission that the prosecution evidence, taken at its highest, is such that a jury properly directed could not properly convict upon it." Sourpuss raised his eyebrows. "For the purposes of my submission, I assume that the jury would be properly directed by your lordship."

"A wise assumption indeed, Mr. Potts, and I am flattered by the confidence you show in my judicial acumen. That said, I am somewhat bemused by your submission, as I have yet to hear a word of evidence." Sourpuss leaned back heavily on his throne, closed his eyes and gazed heavenwards. Pertwee, having finally recovered his composure, allowed himself a self-satisfied smirk at my expense.

Undaunted, I pressed on. "If your lordship so wishes, we can waste a day listening to the prosecution evidence, and I can then make my submission. But it is clear on the papers that the prosecution cannot prove a material fact in their case, namely that the shot aimed at or in the direction of Chisholm was capable of killing him."

Sourpuss opened one eye. "How so?"

"Has your lordship seen the firearm expert's report? It's at page 26 in the bundle."

He hadn't, but he wasn't about to admit it. "What about it?"

"As your lordship will read, the shot used by the defendant was Number Four, commonly known as birdshot, and used to shoot small game birds such as partridge, snipe and grouse. If larger shot were used, such as Number Eight, the bird would be blown to smithereens, thereby rendering it inedible."

"Are you giving evidence, Mr. Potts?"

"No, No, my lord, I am simply asking you to apply your judicial knowledge."

Sourpuss snorted derisively. "There is no such concept known in the law as judicial knowledge, Mr. Potts, as you should know and evidently do not!" Oh dear, the lion roars, and here I was, thinking it was going so well. "If, however, you wish to refer me to an authority to support your proposition, feel free to do so."

I had earmarked the relevant passage in Archbold, the essential criminal practitioner's guide to the law, and quickly turned to it. I gulped, and felt very small indeed. The passage concerned judicial notice, and clearly didn't apply, as Sourpuss was about to tell me.

"I do apologise, my lord, I had confused judicial notice with judicial knowledge."

"An understandable confusion, which experience will remedy in the fullness of time," replied Sourpuss witheringly. "A more careful reading of this particular legal concept," he continued, "will readily persuade you that I cannot direct the jury to accept judicial notice of a fact that has not been established by evidence unless it is within the sphere of their everyday knowledge and experience, and that has been the law since 1816! It is possible, but unlikely," he continued, even more witheringly, "that twelve jurors chosen at random within the bailiwick of the Bailey have everyday knowledge and experience of Number Four and Number Eight shot. It is possible, but again unlikely, that to a man and woman, they have spent every weekend of the shooting season standing shoulder to shoulder with me on Lord Brockenhurst's Scottish estates, blasting away with Number Four shot, in which case, I should have no option but to recuse myself." I was reeling like a punch-drunk boxer. "Empanel the jury!" snapped Sourpuss, his patience exhausted. I sat down, totally deflated. Joy leaned forward and gave me an affectionate squeeze on the arm.

"You're doing very well, Toby," she whispered, "don't let the miserable old bugger get you down." A friend in need is a friend indeed. I smiled weakly, and hoped Sourpuss hadn't heard.

With the jury empanelled, Pertwee opened the case for the prosecution, and as he was about to call his first witness, I rose again with trepidation.

"My lord, whilst it is for my learned friend to call his witnesses in whatever order he chooses, I ask, for obvious reasons I hope, that he calls the firearms expert first."

"Mr. Pertwee?"

"I propose calling Mr. Chisholm first, my lord."

"Do you indeed! I agree with Mr. Potts, I would like to hear from the expert first."

"If your lordship insists…"

"I do. Usher, call on Mr. Burroughs."

After the expert had been taken through his evidence-in-chief, I rose to cross-examine. Keep it short and to the point, I told myself.

"The cartridge recovered by the police and sent to you for forensic examination contained Number Four shot."

"That is correct."

"It is sometimes known colloquially as birdshot."

"That is also correct."

"And by its very definition, used to shoot small game birds."

"That is also correct. I don't know if your lordship and the jury are familiar with different types of shot loaded into cartridges," Sourpuss grimaced, but held his peace, "but the size and number of the lead pellets can vary considerably, depending on what the marksman hopes to achieve."

"Yes, yes," snapped Sourpuss irritably, "we know all that, don't we, members of the jury?"

Time to assert myself. "Whilst your lordship's knowledge may be considerable," I said mischievously, "the jury may need help from the expert on this important part of the evidence."

Sourpuss glowered at me, then allowed himself a wintry smile. "Touché, Mr. Potts, pray continue."

"Thank you, my lord." I turned back to the expert. "Concentrating on birdshot, if shot at a human being, can it ever be lethal?" Best to grasp the bull by the horns.

"At close range, yes." Not the answer I was looking for, but the race had not yet run its course.

"At close range, how close?" interrupted Sourpuss.

"Virtually point-blank, my lord, and the shot would have to strike a vital organ such as the face or heart. The backside is not generally regarded as a vital organ," he added helpfully. Sourpuss smiled, and I nodded gratefully. Time to wrap it up.

"Have you seen the medical statement in this case, Mr. Burroughs?"

"No."

"Perhaps I can summarise it for you. Mr. Chisholm had a total of fifteen pellets removed from his backside under local anesthetic with tweezers." Burroughs nodded. "It's right, is it not, that a Number Four cartridge normally contains no more than fifty pellets?"

"Correct."

"So that leaves thirty-five pellets unaccounted for. Does that help you in determining the distance between the defendant and Mr. Chisholm when the shot was fired?" I gave up a silent prayer.

"I would estimate the distance between forty and sixty yards. I can explain the formula I use in reaching this conclusion if you wish, which takes into account wind speed, air temperature, mass and velocity."

I looked pleadingly at Sourpuss. "Unless your lordship feels this would be helpful…?"

"No, no, Mr. Potts," replied Sourpuss almost too quickly. "But for the avoidance of any remaining doubt, the jury and I would like to know if this shot was capable of causing grievous bodily harm, or even death."

"Absolutely not, my lord."

Halleluiah!!!!!

Sourpuss made a careful note, then looked up. "Any further questions, Mr. Potts?"

"No thank you, my lord."

"Mr. Pertwee, any re-examination?"

"Er, my lord…"

"No, thank you Mr. Pertwee. I have no further questions. Thank you for coming, Mr. Burroughs, and you are free to go." Sourpuss looked over to the jury. "Members of the jury, there are matters of law to discuss." The jury duly trooped out. "Now Mr. Potts, back to your submission, which I have firmly in the forefront of my mind. Let me hear what Mr. Pertwee says."

"If your lordship is referring to my learned friend's earlier submission that there is no case to answer, I submit in reply that all facts are matters for the jury." It was not in Pertwee's remit to throw in the towel, and counsel's evaluation would make for grim reading if he did so.

Sourpuss was not impressed. "If you are right, Mr. Pertwee, then I am surplus to requirements, and that is not a concept I have ever entertained in all my years on the Bench." He paused. "Are you familiar with the reported case of *Galbraith?*

"I am indeed, my lord."

"Then let's look at it together. Mr. Potts?"

Fortunately, I had flagged it up in support of my submission. "Page 467 in the current edition of Archbold, my lord."

"Excellent. Now, the Court of Appeal have clearly stated, and I refer to paragraph (2) (a), that where the judge, that's me Mr. Pertwee, concludes that the prosecution evidence, taken at its highest, is such that a jury could not properly convict upon it, it is his duty, that's me again, Mr. Pertwee, on a submission being made, to stop the case. Are you with me so far?" Sourpuss was dripping sarcasm.

"Er...."

"Good. So the only matter to be determined is whether you have any other evidence to call to rebut the expert's clear and unequivocal statement that the shot fired at or in the direction of Chisholm was incapable of causing grievous bodily harm or death?"

"Er...no, my lord."

"Splendid, real progress at last." Sourpuss addressed me. "I accede to your submission, Mr. Potts, and I shall direct the jury to enter a verdict of not guilty. Now where does that leaves us, Mr. Pertwee?"

"Er..."

"If you were to apply to add a charge of unlawful wounding to the indictment, I doubt if Mr. Potts could resist such an application. You may need time to consult your reviewing lawyer, so I shall rise for fifteen minutes, not a minute longer." Sourpuss turned to me. "The defendant may have bail within the precincts of the court."

"All rise," intoned the usher as Sourpuss left court.

We found an interview room. Taffy was delighted, and shook me warmly by the hand. So far so good. Joy was equally delighted, and congratulated me on my adversarial skills. What a Joy!

I explained that by firing his gun into the bushes and wounding Randy Andy, the law regarded this as reckless behaviour, and I advised him to plead guilty to this lesser charge. At least it reduced the sentence available from life imprisonment to a maximum of five years.

"However, I make it clear, Mr. Williams, I cannot guarantee that you will leave court a free man. The judge can be unpredictable and has a mind of his own."

"You can say that again, Boyo," replied Taffy, "but I'm in good hands."

We returned to court, Taffy pleaded guilty to unlawful wounding, and the bemused jury returned a verdict of not guilty to attempted murder.

"Now, Mr. Potts," said Sourpuss, turning to sentence, and the whiff of a pink gin in his nostrils, "you have a wealth of mitigation at your disposal which there is no need to rehearse. Unless you seek to persuade me to the contrary, I shall conditionally discharge the defendant for a period of six months."

"I am obliged, my lord, and I have no further submissions to make."

"Very well." Sourpuss addressed Taffy. "Stand up. If you keep out of trouble for the next six months, as I am confident you will, you'll hear nothing further about this matter. Give my kind regards to Lord Brockenhurst, and you may leave the dock."

"Thank you my lord," replied Taffy, tugging his forelock.

Sourpuss snapped shut the court file, and was about to rise, when he looked down at me. "Have we met before, Mr. Potts?"

"Just the once, my lord, when I defended Santa Claus."

Sourpuss allowed himself a smile. "Ah yes, I remember it now. And to my surprise and their delight, my grandchildren had a particularly happy Christmas."

"I never doubted it for a minute, my lord."

"To you and your instructing solicitor, this miserable old bugger wishes you good day. I shall rise."

Joy clapped her hand to her mouth, and turned a whiter shade of pale. We both bowed reverentially at his departing back.

It was a moment to savour as I took her hand, kissed' it lightly, and together we left court.

In the fullness of time, fences were mended, and Blodwen was admitted back to the marital home. Randy Andy moved on the pastures new, and with the shooting season in full swing, Sourpuss and Taffy renewed their acquaintance in more agreeable circumstances.

"Bird over, my lord." What a blast.

CHAPTER 9
LIGHTS CAMERA ACTION

Two days later, to my surprise and delight, Joy phoned to congratulate me, once again, on my great triumph. No word from Mr. Simkins, too busy tugging his forelock at the noble Earl and taking all the credit no doubt, but at least my fees were paid promptly. Thanks to the brilliance of my advocacy, the trial originally listed for three days had ended by midday on the first, so I had argued myself out of two days' work, leaving me poorer to the tune of £500 plus VAT. Never mind, and as the clerks were fond of reminding me, better something than nothing.

Equally to my surprise and delight, Joy accepted my invitation to a drink and a nibble, food-wise of course, and we arranged to meet on one of those overpriced hospitality boats moored along the Embankment and close to the Temple. I wasn't entirely sure why I'd invited her, given that I was promised to another, but I found her great fun to be with, and I was in need of some well-earned rest and relaxation.

Whilst contemplating my forthcoming date, a brief arrived for me in chambers from Peter Rolls, he of Rolls-Royce fame, and my instructing solicitor in the case of Larry King and the porn videos. It was good to be remembered, although the brief hardly filled me with breathless anticipation. I had been to the top of the mountain, it looked good, and I wasn't ready to slide back down again.

Peter Rolls, with an office just north of Cambridge Circus in Charing Cross Road, a stone's throw away from Shaftesbury Avenue and Luvvieland, specialised in representing luvvies of all shapes and sizes, some famous and some infamous. He and his partner Gerald Royce, hand-picked for his name if nothing else, specialised in contract work when the luvvies fell out of luv and started bickering, as well as the occasional breach of copyright, and personal injury, when one of the luvvies fell down an open trap door. The firm also specialised in wills, Gerald Royce's department, advising luvvies who wanted to give their wealth to some obscure dogs' home or retired donkeys' sanctuary. It was all too, *too* divine, my dear. Crime was actively discouraged, it didn't pay, and it was all too, *too* ghastly! However, the occasional brush with HM. Constabulary was tolerated for the favoured few.

A quick skim through the papers told me that the client had been charged with dangerous driving, and a conference had been arranged to advise on plea. The case was listed for summary trial at Bow Street Magistrates' Court, a hop, skip and jump from the Temple, so well-placed for the busy practitioner.

I had to confess, in private of course, that I knew absolutely nothing about the law on dangerous driving, so a brief flirtation with Archbold was *de rigueur*. It told me that a person who drives a mechanically propelled vehicle dangerously on a road or other public place is guilty of an offence. At first blush, that seemed self-evident, and remarkably unhelpful. However, upon further judicious enquiry, I found a definition of dangerous driving, hidden in section 2A (1) *et seriatim*. I learned that a person is to be regarded as driving dangerously if (and, subject to subsection (2) below, only if) – (a) the way he drives falls far below what would be expected of a competent and careful driver, and (b) it would be obvious to a competent and careful driver that driving in that way would be dangerous. As I recalled from my law lectures, it was all about the man on the Clapham Omnibus, going back to the nineteenth century when they had omnibuses, and used to describe the hypothetical reasonable man and a royal pain in the arse.

There then followed examples of dangerous driving and snippets from earlier cases. A person allowing his dog to drive was one such example that preoccupied their lordships in the Divisional Court. I wished I'd been there. It was decided, after much navel-gazing, that whilst the dog owed a duty of care to other road users, it was clearly not a person. However, the submission by its owner that he was not substantially controlling the movement and direction of the vehicle fell on deaf ears.

Then there was the case of the person who had recently purchased a brand-new motor home, and finding himself on the motorway with no traffic in sight, set the cruise control and went back to make himself a cup of coffee. The manufacturer's manual was silent about the motor home self-steering, but that was not conclusive. Equally, the defence that the person was not substantially in control of the movement and direction of the vehicle when it left the road on a trip of its own was doomed to failure from the outset.

It was for the prosecution to prove that the vehicle was a mechanically propelled vehicle, but in my considered opinion, this was a non-starter, as the client was driving a top-of-the-range Range Rover, otherwise known as a Chelsea tractor.

On the day in question, the man in the Vauxhall Cavalier, no doubt related to the man on the Clapham Omnibus, was proceeding in an easterly direction along the Strand and well within the prevailing speed limit when the defendant barrelled into the back of him. Alighting from his vehicle (he had obviously been coached by Plod, as this was pure Plodeeze), he ascertained that his Vauxhall Cavalier had crumpled like a pack of cards, rendering it undriveable, and to make matters worse, as he was later to tell his insurers in his claim for compensation, he had suffered significant whiplash injuries. When he challenged the person driving the mechanically-propelled vehicle that had barrelled into him, he was told in no uncertain terms to "naff off"!

As ill-luck would have it, for the defendant at least, a passing Plod attended the scene and took details. The man in the now-crumpled Vauxhall Cavalier alleged that the defendant, a female by persuasion, given her peroxide blond hair and her very fetching simulated-leather hot pants, had been applying lipstick prior to the accident, and her mind and attention were elsewhere. He had witnessed this through his rear-view mirror. The defendant vehemently denied such a monstrous allegation, although the smear of lipstick running across her left cheek didn't help, and was duly noted.

A small crowd had gathered, attracted more than anything by the peroxide-blond female wearing simulated-leather hot pants and legs going right up to her armpits, but when asked by Plod if they would be willing to make statements and attend court, nobody stepped up to be counted. The thought of wasting a whole day sitting in the witness waiting room only to be told that the trial had been adjourned was not high on their list of things to do, so the evidence was confined to the man in the crumpled Vauxhall Cavalier and the passing Plod.

After she had provided her name and address and signed several autographs, the defendant was allowed to drive away in her top-of-the-range Range Rover which was mercifully unmarked. One in the eye for General Motors.

Autographs? This sounded interesting as I plunged into the background statement. I discovered that my client was none other than Kat Saltmarsh, her screen name I presumed, and a name that rang absolutely no bells with me whatsoever. As I was to discover, she was a star of Eastenders, a soap opera running interminably on BBC television. Mark you, not as interminably as Coronation Street, the original soap opera, which was first aired when Kitchener was making a name for himself in the Boer War, ably assisted no doubt by the youthful Winston Churchill and his faithful companion Bootsy Farmer.

The only Kat I'd heard of was Kat Stevens, the singer song-writer, who converted to Islam and presumably took the name Kat Mohammed Khan. For all I knew, he had dedicated himself to a life of reflective meditation in the Hindu Kush. Better beware the journey home with Amjad's dodgy visas at a premium. I even boasted two of his LPs in my collection, and 'Morning has Broken' was a firm favourite of mine, in and out of church.

Time for some research, as Kat Saltmarsh was paying privately for my services, and telling her I knew nothing about Eastenders was hardly likely to inspire confidence. I learned that it was filmed at Elstree Studios, and depicted life in the East End of London, hence its name. Very little got past me.

When I got home that evening, I watched an episode to bring myself up-to-speed. It centred around Albert Square, with its ficti-tious residents coming and going on, and on, and on about this and that and nothing in particular. They all spoke with cockney accents, which added authenticity if nothing else, and plenty of rhyming slang so beloved of the East End, such as 'mince pies', which meant eyes, 'dog and bone', which meant phone, and so on. One memorable line stuck out above all the others: "It nearly knocked me off me plates of meat. He was wearing a syrup of figs. So I ran up the apples and pears, got straight on the dog and bone to me trouble and strife and said I couldn't believe me mince pies." It was like living in a parallel universe.

I had to say that as soaps go, there was a conspicuous lack of it, as they all looked appallingly grubby. I hadn't a clue who Kat Saltmarsh was, as there were several peroxide-blond characters with legs up to their armpits and all points in between, and not one pair of simulated-leather hot pants to be seen anywhere.

There was the ubiquitous public house where one and all gath-ered to slag and shag each other off, but no sign of dear old Ena

Sharples and her hairnet. Perhaps it was unfair to judge the pro-gramme by one episode, but I couldn't find any semblance of a plot for the life of me.

The next morning, I decided to test viewer opinion, and start-ed in the clerks' room. To a man, they were all avid followers, they didn't say why, and put me down as a degenerate for not joining the fan-club. When I mentioned Kat Saltmarsh, there was a cho-rus of raucous approval, and remarks about her being a 'goer' and 'drop-dead gorgeous' were bandied around. I mentioned casually that I was having a conference with her that very afternoon, and in a trice, my star was in the ascendant.

"We'll see you alright, Mr. Potts," enthused Mike. "Tea and bis-cuits, Paul," he snapped at the chambers gopher, "and the best china."

"That's very thoughtful, Mike," I said, "but from what I saw, tea seems to be slurped out of enormous chipped mugs."

"That's role-play, Mr. Potts. It's called artistic licence." Lights, Camera, action!

Peter Rolls arrived first, closely followed by Kat. Mike hovered in the background, autograph book at the ready.

Rolls was dressed exactly how I remembered him, the same felt trilby hat with an enormous brim, a startling lemon yellow suit with pink shirt and matching socks, suede shoes, and a silk scarf knot-ted lightly around his neck, fluttering provocatively in the breeze as he walked, and every movement accompanied by extravagant theatrical gestures. I wondered if this was his only outfit. I hoped not, as it had been several months since we last met.

"Mr. Potts, what a delight! It's been *too, too* long! You're looking a little piqued, not working too hard I hope." I thought for a mo-ment he was going to embrace me, but he didn't.

"Mr. Rolls, a pleasure to meet you again."

"Yes, I know that, dear boy. Now let me introduce you to our client, as if introductions are needed." He turned to Kat. "Kat, this is the absolutely *divine* young barrister I was telling you about."

I turned to Kat. "How do you do, Miss Saltmarsh," I said, extending the professional courtesies and keeping it formal. "Please take a seat."

"Call me Kat," she replied, "and can I call you Toby?"

"I've been called worse," I quipped, entering into the spirit of the occasion. Rolls roared with laughter. It was all *too, too* lovely.

Kat was hardly in the full flush of youth, but in a valiant attempt to hold back the years, she had obviously made an effort, and I suspected, not just for me. She was provocatively dressed as befitting a star. The hot-pants had given way to full length black simulated-leather trousers, the sort you need a shoehorn to get into, or out of, not that such a thought entered my head, and when she sat down and crossed her legs, they squeaked. Most distracting. She wore boots with vertigo-inducing heels, a white silk blouse showing an ample cleavage, enough to quicken the heartbeat of any red-bloodied alpha male, and a black simulated-leather jacket. She was wearing dark glasses, even though the weather was cloudy and overcast. It went with the territory.

I was about to start the conference when Paul entered, bearing the chambers best china and a plateful of fancy biscuits. Mike was in close attendance to ensure everything went smoothly.

"You're a right poppet," purred Kat as Paul poured the tea, "what are we doing tonight?"

Paul turned bright-red, mumbled something, and left hurriedly. Mike proffered his autograph book and was duly rewarded, and after Kat had blown him a kiss, it was down to business.

"Now, dear boy," Rolls opened the proceedings, "as you know, Kat has a high media profile," I didn't, "and if the paparazzi get wind of this dreadful business, she'll be all over the tabloids."

I nodded. "I understand. But as Oscar Wilde once quipped, there is only one thing worse than bad publicity, and that's no publicity."

"That poor, *poor* man, so badly treated, and such a waste of an enormous talent."

"And an enormous ego, some would say, and so ill-advised to start libel proceedings against Lord Queensberry of all people. They were doomed to failure from the outset."

"A travesty of justice!" Rolls was clearly one of Oscar's greatest fans, "and as we all know," he continued, glaring at me, "Oscar's relationship with Bosie was entirely platonic."

"Well..."

"'ang on a minute," Kat interrupted, "what the drake and duck 'as this got to do with me and me motor?"

"I'm so sorry, Kat, we got carried away," replied Rolls, "now where were we? Ah yes, the paparazzi. We need to keep this low-key."

"I'll leave all that to you, if I may Mr. Rolls," I said, "and I'll do what I can." What about the short and pithy statement on the steps of the court? Toby Potts triumphs again. Sadly, it was not to be. "I'll turn up as usual, well in advance of the hearing, and I suggest that just before the case is called on, you and Kat make your way discreetly into court. You may be advised to park close by, to avoid keeping the judge waiting. I assume you'll be coming," I added.

"An excellent idea, dear boy, and of course I shall be there to hold Kat's hand. I wouldn't dream of abandoning the poor lamb in her hour of need."

"Good. Now the charge is dangerous driving," I continued, getting back to the matter in hand.

"Yeah, I know that darling," Kat replied, fluttering her eyelashes.

"Quite so. I'm afraid you're not exactly on the front foot if I'm to persuade the court it wasn't your fault. Driving into the back of another car, even a Vauxhall Cavalier, is *prima facie* evidence of carelessness at the very least."

"Gerrim, Pete," Kat chortled, "he's got the lingo, whatever that means."

"It simply means there's a case to answer," I replied pompously, "and you'll have to give your version of events, although you're not obliged to do so. The law cannot compel you to give evidence on your own behalf."

"Fair enuff."

"Now from the excellent proof of evidence you gave to Mr. Rolls," lay it on, I thought, keep the punters onside, "you were driving perfectly normally when, to use your own words, the complete Prat in front of you stood on his brakes for no obvious reason, and you were unable to avoid a collision."

"Got it in one, sunshine. If you ask me, he's the one who should be charged with dangerous driving."

"Where were you going?"

"To me hairdresser, Mr. Teasy-Weasy in Bond Street."

"Were you late?"

"No way. Appointments are like hen's teeth, so I always allow plenty of time." I wondered if 'hen's teeth' was cockney rhyming slang, but the moment passed.

"The driver, Gordon Hunt, says you were applying lipstick just before you hit him."

"Is that Hunt with an aitch?" she giggled. "Anyway, he's wrong."

"And the police officer who attended the scene noted a smear of lipstick across your face."

"You make me sound like Big Chief Running Water, which I ain't." She paused. "He had two sons, you know, Hot and Cold." Rolls burst out laughing, although it wasn't that funny. "Anyway," she continued, "immediately after the crash, and before I got out the motor, I tried applying lipstick, but I was so shaken up, I smeared it. I like to look me best for me adoring fans, if you know what I mean."

"I do indeed. And did Mr. Hunt say anything to you after the collision?"

"Yeah, he was rabbiting on about it being me fault, real mouthy, then he recognised me and 'ad the balls to ask me for me autograph. I told him to naff off, and that's when Bottle turned up."

"Bottle?"

"Yeah, you know, bottle and stopper."

It took a moment or two for the penny to drop. "Copper!" I said triumphantly.

"Good one, Toby. We'll make a cockney out of yer yet. Now let's get down to the meat and potatoes," more rhyming slang perhaps, it was becoming a linguistic minefield, "what's the bottom line?"

I was on this one in a flash. "Ten-past five," I replied, consulting my watch and looking well pleased with myself.

"What yer on about?" Kat was not impressed.

"Bottom line, time."

Kat gave Peter an old-fashioned look. She had a moron for a brief.

"I think Kat wants to know what's the worst that can happen if she's convicted," said Rolls helpfully.

"Oh, I see, I'm so sorry." I felt foolish, through no fault of my own. "If convicted of dangerous driving, you face a maximum sentence of six months' imprisonment, or a fine, or both, and you will be disqualified from driving for at least twelve months." No point dressing it up.

"Jesus wept," she replied, "the kitchen sink?"

I hadn't the faintest idea what she was on about, so I chose to ignore it. She could have meant 'clink', but I wasn't about to hazard another guess.

"Sentences of imprisonment are usually reserved for the most serious cases," I replied, trying to reassure her, "so I think it unlikely in the extreme." I had to be careful what I said, as she might not thank me for my learned opinion on her way to the prison van. And that outfit with all those arrows, it was all *too, too* ghastly. "It's more likely to be a fine and disqualification, unless," I added quickly, "you have a string of previous convictions, or you've flattened some old codger on his way to church." Kat smiled weakly and shook her head.

"Two SP30's," Rolls interjected, "whatever they are, and one of them current." He'd checked Kat's licence, but no more than that.

"Exceeding the speed limit," I replied, feeling pleased with myself, "and hardly in the serious category. But we're putting the cart before the horse," I continued encouragingly as poor Kat was in shock, "as yet, you haven't been convicted of anything."

"That's right," Rolls chimed in, "so, dear boy, what do we do?"

"Well, from what Kat has told us," I replied positively, "she has a complete defence to the charge, so I advise her to plead not guilty."

"Excellent advice, and in your young but capable hands, a glorious acquittal. To the victor the spoils!" Rolls was on a roll. I hoped I was equal to the task.

Kat smiled. "So what's the form? Is it trial by jury?"

"No, it's summary trial before a magistrate. No need for me to robe, so I won't be wearing my syrup of figs." I couldn't resist it. Kat and Rolls burst out laughing, lightening the mood.

"And what about me?" she asked, "how should I dress?"

"Well, most magistrates are male, so if you want my advice, your present outfit will fit the bill perfectly. You look drop-dead gorgeous." You young smoothie Potts, I thought to myself. "However, if the magistrate is female, she'll probably want to scratch your eyes out."

"You're a jam-jar, Toby, and I love you. I'll love you even more if you get a result."

"I'll do my best, you can be sure of that. Now, if there's nothing else, I suggest we draw stumps." Kat looked confused. She hadn't heard that one before. "As Oscar Wilde said to Lord Queensberry, see you in court."

"Poor Oscar, a travesty of justice!" lamented Rolls again, and so saying, he swept out of the conference room, closely followed by Kat, followed by Mike, followed by Paul.

The trial was listed at 2pm, although there were several other cases also listed at the same time. By prior agreement, I was to phone Rolls on my mobile phone when the trial was called on, and as they were parked just round the corner, it was barely a two-minute walk away.

To my relief, the presiding magistrate was Henry Fielding, who had a reputation for being fair and efficient, and well-regarded by those who appeared before him. The prosecutor was George Tweedie, I'd never met him before, another in-house lawyer hoping to impress. He was hiding in the CPS office when I arrived. We exchanged common courtesies, and then it was time for some old-fashioned sandbagging.

"Have you had a chance to look at the file?" I asked.

"I have not only looked at it, but I have mastered its complexities," he replied loftily. I wasn't aware of any particular complexities, but for most in-house lawyers, every case had its complexities and challenges, some more quickly mastered than others.

"Then you'll agree with me it's overcharged. This isn't even careless driving. What idiot came up with dangerous driving?"

"You're speaking to him, and I resent your tone. Now, if you'll excuse me, I have work to do," and so saying, he left his office, slamming the door behind him, and walked off to court in high dudgeon. Not a promising start.

I popped into court to test the water. Fielding was already hard at it, setting a furious pace, listening to submissions only when they were necessary, and giving his considered opinion before the proverbial feet could touch the ground. He had no patience with time-wasters, and made it as plain as a pikestaff. But from the handful of cases I witnessed, his reputation for fairness and efficiency went before him.

Checking the court list on counsel's bench, Kat was twelfth in line for summary justice, and by two-thirty, Fielding had disposed of the first ten. That must have been some sort of a record. Time to marshal the troops.

I sidled out of court and made my way to the main entrance. To my surprise and alarm, there were a number of photographers milling around outside. If Kat was their target, how did they know? Too late to do anything about it now. I phoned Rolls. Message received and understood, and two minutes' later, they came round the corner and into sight. They were both wearing the same outfits from our conference, and Rolls in particular stood out like a sore thumb.

This was the signal for a frantic media scrum, as the paparazzi closed in and jostled for position. From his expression, Rolls was mortified. It was all *too, too* frightful. Unbeknown to either of us, Kat's agent had put the word out on the street, he was obviously a fan of Oscar Wilde, and Kat duly obliged with a winning smile and a provocative pose. So much for low-key!

Time and enough for the post-mortem as I escorted them into court, just as case number eleven was concluding. There was a hubbub of activity as the public gallery rapidly filled up with assorted newshounds ready to give their own version of events as the courtroom drama unfolded. Show Time!

Fielding looked up disapprovingly, spotted Kat, and smiled warmly. Was he a fan of Eastenders, I wondered, and if so, why? She returned the compliment, having by now removed her dark glasses.

Fielding opened the file as Kat answered to her name, the charge was read out, she pleaded not guilty and sat back down again.

"Who prosecutes?" asked Fielding.

Tweedie rose and bowed. "I do, sir."

"And Mr. Potts defends."

I rose and bowed. "I do, sir."

"Sit down, Mr. Potts. Now I've read the papers, Mr. Tweedie," Tweedie rose again and bowed again, "and whilst I shall listen to any evidence you choose to call, taking your case at its highest, it's been overcharged. What idiot came up with dangerous driving?"

Poor Tweedie, down and out before he'd even got up and running, and to be called an idiot twice in one afternoon was positively career-threatening. This was not in the script. But he was not going to be browbeaten.

"The appropriate charge was carefully considered, sir, and given the damage to the Vauxhall Cavalier, which was a write-off, excessive speed was but one of a number of relevant issues." I had to give him his due, the man was not for turning. He pressed on. "There is also compelling evidence of the defendant's dangerously wanton behaviour immediately prior to impact, and in all the circumstances, the Crown Prosecution Service determined that dangerous driving was the appropriate charge."

"Very well," replied Fielding after a long pause. "I am not persuaded, but call your evidence, and let's see where that gets you."

Gordon Hunt was brought into court, took the oath and gave his evidence in accordance with his statement, which he had been memorising, line for line, in the witness waiting room.

"Yes Mr. Potts." Fielding looked at me.

"Mr. Hunt," I began, with all the gravitas becoming of a low-key barrister, "your Vauxhall Cavalier was eight years old." He nodded. "Whilst it may have been roadworthy, when was it last serviced?"

"I can't remember."

"That long ago?" I quipped. Tweedie stirred and thought about interjecting, but changed his mind. "The Cavalier is designed to crumple on impact that's right, isn't it? It's in the manufacturer's specifications."

"If you say so."

"And if struck from behind by a Range Rover, which is not designed to crumple on impact, serious damage can be caused even at relatively low speeds?"

"You're running perilously close to giving evidence, Mr. Potts," Fielding interrupted, "but I have your point. Move on."

"As you please, sir." I turned back to Hunt. "You slammed on your brakes for no apparent reason, that's right?"

"No it isn't. There was an elderly pedestrian about to step off the pavement, and to avoid hitting her, I had to brake sharply."

"And where is this elderly pedestrian?" I asked scathingly.

"Alive and well thanks to my quick reactions." One in the eye for me. Nobody said it was going to be plain-sailing. As Nick Ridley used to tell me, if you get the wrong answer, don't dwell on it, move on, so I did.

"Before you slammed on your brakes, were you distracted by anything?"

"Such as?"

"Well, did you notice the defendant following you?"

"Yes I did, and what's more, she was applying lipstick immediately before she crashed into me."

"That's not right, is it, Mr. Hunt? She was applying lipstick immediately *after* she crashed into you."

"I disagree."

"Very well. But you accept you were not watching the road ahead?"

"How do you mean?"

"It's obvious, Mr. Hunt. If you are telling the court that you saw the defendant applying lipstick, you must have been looking at her through your rear-view mirror, unless you actually turned round in your seat?"

"I didn't turn round in my seat, if that's what you're suggesting," replied Hunt indignantly.

"Did you recognise the defendant whilst you were watching her in your rear-view mirror?"

"No."

"Are you sure?"

"Yes I am."

"So why did you ask her for her autograph?"

"I didn't."

"Let me refresh your memory. According to the police officer who attended the scene, after the defendant had driven off,
you said, and I quote: you'll never guess who that was. It's Kat
Saltmarsh from Eastenders. I asked for her autograph, and she
told me to naff off."

There was an awkward silence, eventually broken by Fielding.

"Let me get this straight. Are you denying what counsel has just
put to you, even though the police officer made a verbatim note?"

Another awkward silence. "I can't remember," replied Hunt
lamely.

"No further questions, sir."

"Mr. Tweedie, any re-examination?"

Tweedie rose on a fruitless damage-limitation exercise. "You've
been asked what you said to the police officer," he began. "Can
you clarify?"

Fielding was having none of it. "The witness has already told
us, Mr. Tweedie, that either he didn't say what is alleged, or he
can't remember. What further clarification do you need?"

"Well, sir...."

"Does the prosecution accept that the defendant is indeed an
actress from Eastenders?"

"Yes we do."

"Thank you. Now you were about to call the police officer."

Tweedie wasn't, but with his re-examination stillborn, he had
no choice. The officer read through his notes and confirmed what
Hunt had told him.

"Any cross-examination, Mr. Potts?"

"No thank you sir."

"Very well. Is that your case Mr. Tweedie?"

"I have some questions to put to the officer by way of clarification."

"Have you indeed? However, where a witness has not been cross-examined, you have no right to re-examine. It's a basic principle of jurisprudence, as you should know." Fielding turned to me. "So where does that leave you, Mr. Potts?"

"I submit, sir, that the evidence does not support the charge of dangerous driving."

"Mr. Tweedie?"

"I disagree."

"Yes, thank you. However, I agree with Mr. Potts. As I said at the outset, this case has been overcharged, so I find the defendant not guilty. However, as you know, or should know, on a charge of dangerous driving, I am entitled to consider the lesser alternative of careless driving. What do you say about that, Mr. Potts?"

"I submit, sir, that the prosecution evidence cannot possibly make you sure that the defendant was at fault in any way."

"Mr. Tweedie?"

Tweedie was going down, but not without a fight. "As a matter of law, at this stage, all that is required of the prosecution is raise a case to answer. We haven't heard from the defendant, and I have yet to cross-examine her."

A pleasure in store for all of us, Mr. Tweedie," Fielding sighed. "You are right, of course, but as you know, or should know, the defendant cannot be compelled to give evidence. If she chooses not to do so, Mr. Potts will renew his submission. Mr. Potts?"

I turned round to Rolls, although I couldn't think why. After all, he knew absolutely *nothing* about crime or criminal procedure, it was all *too, too* ghastly. I spoke to Kat in a stage-whisper, she'd know all about that, I advised her against giving evidence, she nodded, and I turned back to Fielding.

"On behalf of the defendant, sir, I call no evidence."

"Thank you. Now on your renewed submission, I find the defendant not guilty of careless driving. I believe that concludes these proceedings. The usual order for costs." Fielding addressed Kat. "You are free to go. I shall rise."

The court erupted as the newshounds scampered off to file their story. Rolls and Kat embraced.

"Now, my poor lamb," Rolls was all but trembling with excitement, "time to face your many fans, and then it's off to the Savoy for afternoon tea. My treat of course," and so saying, they left court hand-in-hand without so much as a backward glance.

I waited for a good ten minutes, not wishing to interrupt Kat's *moment de gloire* on the court steps, and by the time I made my way out, they and the paparazzi had gone. Such were the loyalties of the rich and famous.

I trudged back to chambers, alone, unloved and low-key, but pleased with a job well done.

The next morning there was excitement in the clerks' room. A selection of tabloids had been purchased, with Kat featuring prominently in her skin-tight leathers under a variety of catchy headlines. Mike was particularly excited.

"Fame at last, Mr. Potts," he announced, "there's a picture of you!"

It was a photo of Kat on her way into court, and there in the background, Rolls and me in earnest conversation and he throwing one of his extravagant gestures. Sadly, nothing whatsoever to report about my brilliant advocacy and incisive cross-examination.

My Andy Warhol moment. Famous for fifteen minutes.

CHAPTER 10

THE INCREDIBLE BULK

Even though client gratitude was in short supply, I was giving serious consideration to elevating my professional profile to include standing junior counsel to the aristocracy and the luvvies. After all, I had come, seen and conquered, so time to milk it for all it was worth.

Sadly, the clerks didn't share my proposed elevation, as Fred made clear.

"Time and enough for all that, Mr. Potts," he said ponderously, "there's still a long way to go. Standing counsel are only appointed after a minimum of ten years of selfless devotion and an exceptional track record."

I was crestfallen. "Ten years?! I was hoping to apply for silk by then."

"Think again, Mr. Potts," Fred was doing nothing for my ego, "on average, and if they're lucky, most criminal practitioners take silk after fifteen or even twenty years, and even then, only after three applications and a hatful of glowing references including at least one from a High Court Judge." I wondered if Sourpuss could be relied on to support me, but in fifteen or twenty years, he'd either be dead or fossilised. So much to do, so little time.

"But on the positive side, Mike tells me you're beginning to make your mark with a steady supply of good-quality work coming your way," I wondered if Mike had mistaken me for somebody else, "so be patient. That's my advice."

I returned to my room to lick my wounds. Fifteen or twenty years! It sounded like a sentence of imprisonment without parole. I flicked listlessly through the three briefs gathering dust and which were destined never to see the light of day, usually because the defendant had done a runner and had vanished without trace.

With the clock edging towards six, I popped my head round the clerks' room and looked hopefully at Mike. "What excitement lies in store for tomorrow, Mike?"

"Nothing I'm afraid, Mr. Potts," he replied without the slightest hint of an apology, "it looks like a quiet week all round." So much for the steady stream of good-quality work. "Still, you never know what's round the corner." Cold comfort indeed.

On the positive side, I was in funds, just, after Peter Rolls had paid my fee, so time for affirmative action. I phoned Joy to firm up our date. She paused, a tad too long for my liking, as she consulted her diary.

"How about this coming Friday?" she suggested. "There's a play on at the Barbican Theatre, it's been well-reviewed, and we can have a bite to eat afterwards. Dutch," she added, almost too quickly, but it was a kind offer gratefully accepted.

I paused, a tad too long perhaps for her liking, whilst I consulted the arid wasteland of my diary.

"That sounds great," I replied, "I'll book tickets."

"No need. I'm a Friend of the Theatre, so I get discounted tickets for all their performances." This was getting better by the minute. "The play begins at seven-thirty, so why don't we meet in the foyer at seven?"

I knew little about the Barbican Centre, and I'd never been inside. I knew where it was, and on the few occasions I'd hurried past it on my way to somewhere else, it looked like an enormous concrete multi-storey car park. It's what the luvvies called brutalist architecture, but brutalist or not, it still looked like an enormous concrete multi-storey car park. Still, it was a night out, so what the hell!

For the rest of the week, Mike was as good as his word. It was quiet all round, or certainly quiet all round me. I dutifully spent the day in chambers, whiling away the time with a desultory flick through the latest supplement of Archbold and various in-house journals. At lunchtime I wandered up Chancery Lane to Gray's Inn Common Room for a pie and a pint with colleagues old and new, grumbling to a man about how quiet it was all round and trying, in vain, to lift our collective spirits, and then wandering back to chambers for more of the same.

Friday dawned, and I was still unemployed, and feeling down. Was it time to start searching through the "Situations Vacant" columns, or even applying to the CPS to become an in-house lawyer, with a regular salary, perks and a generous contribution to my pension, but that was defeatist, and besides, I doubted if I could rely on Newman and No Balls to welcome me into the fold.

Just as I was about to resign myself to another wasted day, the phone rang. It was Del, my Saviour in my hour of need and my most loyal solicitor.

"I've got an interesting case coming your way, Tobes," he chuckled. "Are you fit, as this one needs a lot of heavy lifting?"

"Fit as a butcher's dog, Del, and really good to hear from you. I was beginning to think I was the forgotten man."

"Not you, Tobes, but it's been quiet all round, and nothing to test your adversarial skills, just bits and pieces to keep the wolf from the door."

"I'm relieved to hear it, Del. So how can I help?"

"Brief's on its way, you should have it first thing Monday morning, and I've booked a conference for Tuesday afternoon." He paused. "Do you have a ground floor conference room?"

A curious request. "No, but if it helps, I can ask the clerks to reserve the main conference room on the first floor."

"I don't think that'll work." He paused again. "Do you know how many steps there are?"

"Off the top of my head, I'd say about twenty." I paused. "Is the client disabled?"

Del paused. There were a lot of pauses in this conversation, all very ominous. "Yes and no," he replied. "According to the Guinness Book of Records, our client is the fattest man in England. The last time they got him on the scales, he weighed in at over forty-seven stones."

I gasped. "Good Lord! That's enormous!"

"Got it in one, Tobes, so getting him up to the first floor may be Mission Impossible."

"Point taken. I'll see what I can do."

"Good man. I'm a bit tied up Tuesday, so I'm sending Bootsy to sit in on the conference. He's a big strong bloke, so he might come in handy. Must dash, and we'll speak later in the week."

Joy looked absolutely fabulous. Light brown wavy hair, sparkling hazel eyes, and just enough makeup to adorn rather than smother her features. She had dressed for the occasion, and I had no doubt we would capture the couple of the evening award.

The play was hard work. It was a revival of Beckett's **Waiting for Godot** and seriously boring, all about two foreign Johnnies called Vladimir and Estragon waiting interminably for this bloke Godot, who never showed up, and who could blame him? It was a bit like me waiting interminably for my next brief. The review, plastered across the billboard at the entrance, was by the art's editor of the Guardian newspaper, and a man who could obviously interpret things beyond the intellectual compass of the common man:

"Because the play is so stripped down, so elemental, it invites all kinds of social and political and religious interpretations" he wrote. What a twerp!

For Joy's sake, I tried to look riveted, but for me, there were only two memorable highlights: the interval and the final curtain. Thanks to the Friends of the Theatre, the seats were good, pole position, and that was about it.

On our way to the nearby Brasserie, I felt I should say something about the evening's ordeal, if only to please Joy.

"I've always found Beckett intellectually challenging," I ventured, "and because the play is so stripped down, so elemental, it invites all kinds of social and political and religious interpretations." I had a good memory, if nothing else.

Joy burst out laughing, which was a merciful relief.

"Dear Toby," she replied, squeezing my hand, "did you find it that awful?"

"No evening spent in your company could ever be described as awful," I replied, smooth as silk.

She laughed again. "That's not what I meant, and you know it."

Mercifully, our arrival at the Brasserie cut short any further discussion, and by the time we were seated and had ordered drinks, Beckett and Godot were consigned to the back burner. Joy was well-known to the staff, the food was good and we received excellent service. Perhaps she was a Friend of the Brasserie as well.

With the meal over, it was time for coffee. Joy waved away the waiter.

"How about coffee at my place? I live just across the road."

I paused, a tad too long perhaps for her liking, as I weighed the options.

"It's just a coffee, Toby," she said, "not a marriage proposal."

I awoke next morning with Joy sleeping peacefully in my arms, her warm flesh pressed against mine. I blinked a few times to take in the unfamiliar surroundings, and then it hit me. I had made passionate love to a solicitor, not in itself a mortal sin, but I had been unfaithful to my darling Susie, my betrothed and sooner or later my wife to be and the mother of my children, assuming of course she could drag herself away from the primordial beat of the jungle drums and Prince Harry with his matinee-idol charms. Would she ever forgive me? Was this the end? However, what the eye doesn't see the heart doesn't grieve over. It was like that night of passion I'd enjoyed with Camilla Foster-Ward, the drop-dead gorgeous model, and after I'd pleasured her beyond her wildest dreams, I was tossed aside like a used....tissue. It happens!

As Cole Porter put it:

It was just one of those things
Just one of those crazy flings
One of those bells that now and then rings
Just one of those things

Joy stirred, opened her eyes, saw I was awake, and slid out from under the sheets. What a Joy as she walked sleepily towards the bathroom. She was not the only one stirring. Down Boy!

Three minutes later, she emerged, wearing a flimsy robe, and tossed a clean towel towards me.

"Your turn. I'm popping over to the Brazz for fresh croissants, OJ's in the fridge, see you in five."

I was on the horns of a dilemma. To do a Cole Porter seemed ungracious, and it wasn't my style. But I had Susie to think of, so I decided to come clean and let her down lightly.

I had dressed and poured two glasses of OJ by the time Joy returned. After the croissants and coffee, time for a reality check.

"It's been a wonderful evening, Joy, but I have to be honest with you." She looked up enquiringly. "I'm engaged to be married."

"There's a coincidence. So am I!"

"Good Lord!" I gulped. I was speechless.

"Look, Toby, we're both adults, and we both know what we're doing. We've had a great night, I've had better sex, but it was fun." Damned with faint praise, and me thinking I'd scaled the heights. "So let's keep it that way, no commitments, no recriminations."

"Fair enough," I paused. "So what does he do, your fiancé?"

"Duncan? He's a journalist. Served his time on the tabloids, and now he writes for the Guardian. He's a sub-editor on the Arts' desk. As a matter of fact, he reviewed **Godot.**"

Thank Goodness I hadn't said anything about the twerp who'd written that particular review.

"How exciting, free tickets, a glass of complimentary champagne, a couple of backhanders and the power to close a play on the first night."

Joy laughed. "Not quite, but his reviews are generally well received."

"So why me here with you, and not him?"

"Duncan's reviews feature in the Saturday and Sunday supplements, so there are deadlines to meet, and he works quite late into the night. The only quality time we have together is Sunday, which isn't much, but we're both in the early stages of our careers, so it's the price we have to pay. I suppose it's much the same for you, with your busy practice, having to work long hours at short notice."

"Absolutely," I lied. Why spoil the moment? "And how about you? How's life with the redoubtable Mr. Simkins?"

"Actually, quite challenging. Lord Brockenhurst's affairs take up most of the firm's time, as you might imagine." I nodded. "He owns half of Scotland and most of Hampshire, and several estates in between, so there are *fee tails* and inheritance laws to manage. Then there are farm business tenancies, hundreds of them, land disputes, usually over boundaries, and as you know, the occasional brush with hunt saboteurs."

I chuckled. "I remember it well."

"So that's me. Now, how about you?"

I gave Joy a thumbnail sketch of life with and without Susie, and Lesotho and Prince Harry, and how I was awaiting her return with eager anticipation.

"Poor Toby, cast aside for royalty," she giggled. "Now, I've got things to do." She got up and gave me a peck on the cheek, "so push off."

"I can take a hint," I replied. "So what are we doing next Friday?" I surprised even myself with my temerity.

"You decide. Pick me up at seven."

"A reprise of **Godot** perhaps?" We both laughed.

I made my way back to Earls Court feeling a warm glow of contentment. Fortunately, there were no papers requiring my urgent attention at short notice, so I caught the train home, laden as I was with a pile of dirty washing for my mother, Sunday lunch and a relaxing afternoon beckoned, and then back to town to prepare myself for Del's brief on Monday morning. Couldn't be better. How quickly the memory fades.

My client, Billy Brewer, had been charged under the Customs and Excise Management Act of knowingly acquiring possession of goods which were chargeable with a duty which had not been paid and did so intending to defraud Her Majesty of the duty payable. This was very exciting. First the aristocracy, then the luvvies, and now the Numero Uno. I wondered if Her Majesty would have to attend trial. That would be a real feather in my wig, cross-examining her on bended knee whilst suggesting that her evidence was a tissue of lies. That should go down well. Still, if I played my cards right and was sufficiently unctuous, perhaps an inclusion in her birthday honours list, for services to law and order.

Del's helpful summary put flesh on the bones, and as I was to discover, there was a lot of flesh on Billy's bones. It was all about the illegal importation of contraband cigarettes, originating somewhere east of Suez in a variety of seedy sweatshops where labour and life were cheap. All well-known brands were on offer, lovingly rolled between the thighs of hand-picked virgins, packaged and destined for Europe. That's the cigarettes, not the virgins. To the discerning smoker, they were absolutely revolting, but in France and Spain, where all cigarettes were revolting, they sold like hotcakes. They were a welcome relief from the likes of Gauloises and Gitanes and Rumbos Largos, made from factory-floor sweepings in such far-flung places as Morocco and Algeria.

With a corner shop on almost every corner in Her Majesty's realm, there was a ready market for these cigarettes, and everybody made a handsome profit, not least Billy Brewer. Billy had a warehouse down Tilbury way on an industrial estate, where he stored thousands of cigarettes delivered to him by land, sea and air, and from where he distributed them to favoured clients around the Big Smoke. A very apt description in all the circumstances. He'd had a part of the warehouse converted into a 'des- res', with all modern conveniences, a bathroom, rarely used, a kitchen-diner, frequently used, and a specially reinforced double bed with a hydraulic hoist. It was very much home-from-home.

He'd led a charmed life for the best part of ten years, but nothing lasts forever. It may have been a tip-off from a disgruntled client, or simply puffs in the wind, but whatever the reason, word filtered through to Customs and Excise, and affirmative action was authorised from on high, possibly from Her Majesty herself, seeing as she was on a losing wicket. The decision was made to keep Billy's warehouse under round-the-clock surveillance, and no expense was spared. Unmarked vans were parked unobtrusively, with cameras and video recorders, and to add colour, customs officers dressed as stevedores sauntered about trying to blend into the background.

It was day two when Billy got a tip-off from one of his favoured clients. It wasn't the stevedores sauntering around doing nothing that caused concern, after all, that's what stevedores did most of the time, but it was their flat feet and pocket notebooks at the ready that were a dead giveaway.

Billy decided on affirmative action of his own, and that night, under cover of darkness, two trucks sporting the Asda logo "Saving you Money Everyday" thundered out from the warehouse and shot past the unsuspecting officers sitting in their surveillance vans, smoking, doodling and playing cards. Not exactly on the front foot. As soon as the trucks had breasted the perimeter, they split up, and by the time Customs had scrambled for action, they had disappeared into the middle distance. Questions would be asked, and heads would roll, but now was not the time for recriminations.

Billy had not been idle, and by the time the Customs Swat team arrived, the warehouse was as clean as a whistle, save for a strong pungent aroma of rotting vegetable matter that could strip paint at thirty paces.

When interviewed, Billy denied all knowledge, and as was his right, declined to answer any questions. With the overpowering smell of body odour stinging their nostrils, and a rising tide of nausea, Customs elected to charge Billy, and he was bailed to appear at Grays Magistrates Court on a day to be appointed.

More by luck than good judgment, one of the trucks was flagged down on the motorway heading north, and secreted behind a false panel were thousands of foul-smelling cigarettes. When challenged, the driver denied all knowledge, and claimed they must have been loaded onto his truck when he stopped at a roadside caff for a cuppa tea. Believe that, sunshine, and you'll believe anything! He was bailed pending further inquiries, as it said in the manual.

A case conference was called to review the evidence, which was as thin as summer ice. The whole purpose of the exercise was to put Billy in the frame and take him down, and Customs had fallen well-short, even by their own modest standards. Nobody saw fit to take down the registration numbers of the two trucks as they thundered past, and as Asda had over two-thousand identical trucks, it was like looking for a needle in a haystack. When contacted, Asda HQ were buggered if they were going to spend hours trawling through their records to give Customs the exact whereabouts of all their trucks in Greater London on the night in question, so go fly a kite or get a third-party disclosure order. Customs retreated to lick their wounds.

They had the evidence of their tobacco expert, who certified that the cigarettes were contraband, but the country of origin and the transit route remained a mystery. Some bright spark contacted the Malaysian police, a good starting point given that country's track-record, but they were out to lunch, and urgent phone calls were not returned. In short, Customs didn't have much of a case, but they weren't about to throw in the towel, something alien to Billy with his personal freshness problem, so they went with what they had, and hoped something else might crop up to use as ammunition before the trial. As the reviewing officer concluded, inferences could be drawn, and that might be enough.

Like Billy, the day of the conference loomed large. My clerks had persuaded the chambers on the ground floor to make their conference room available at short notice, so that was a step in the right direction. Bootsy arrived early, clutching Del's file, with paper and pen at the ready, and after the usual pleasantries and jokes about beached whales, we stood at the entrance to await Billy's arrival.

Promptly at four-thirty, a people-carrier hove into view, closely followed by Dudley, the keeper of the gate and in charge of parking. Nobody parked in Brick Court without Dudley's say-so and a suitable well-greased palm, so there was a lot of huffing and puffing before the dust settled and Billy was ready to disgorge himself with the help of his driver. This took several minutes. Bootsy and I exchanged glances as Man-Mountain planted his feet on the ground, looked over, broke into a muck-sweat, and began to lumber towards us like the Incredible Bulk. It reminded me of a scene from one of those Hammer horror films! All that was missing was a screaming virgin, she of the lovely rolling thighs, and Bootsy coming to her rescue in the nick of time. Not in his job description.

I stepped forward to meet and greet. "Mr. Brewer?" He nodded, ignoring my outstretched hand. "My name is Potts, Toby Potts, and Mr. Finnan has asked me to represent you." He nodded again. "This is Mr. Farmer, who will sit in on the conference and take notes." He nodded again. Obviously the strong silent type. "We have a room set aside, if you'll follow me." He nodded again.

Fortunately, the entrance to the building boasted double-doors, so that obstacle was easily surmounted. Unfortunately, the entrance to the ground-floor chambers did not, but Billy was up for it. He first tried approaching the door full-on, but that was never going to work. With Bootsy's steadying hand on his back, Billy retreated and tried sideways. Progress of sorts was made as he got halfway in, and then stopped, stuck fast, not going one way or the other.

Members of the ground-floor chambers were beginning to return from court, but it was a bit like Heathrow Airport in meltdown, so they stacked up behind Billy waiting for the all-clear to come on in. One of the junior clerks opened a window to create an emergency entrance as well as much needed ventilation, which was fine for the younger members to clamber through, but a bridge too far for the older members. Doing the best in difficult circumstances, briefs were passed in and out, and progress reports relayed to the senior clerk to update the chambers diary.

A plan of action was needed. I was marooned inside chambers, with Bootsy outside, wishing he were somewhere else. I didn't want to appear sizeist, as overweight people could be very touchy, and besides, it was politically incorrect. Telling Billy to hold it in wasn't going to help.

"Mr. Farmer," I called out over Billy's sweating frame, "any movement your end?"

"None whatsoever, Mr. Potts. Any suggestions?"

"Question is, do we pull or do we push?"

"'ang on a minute, boy," snapped Billy, "you're rabbiting on as if I weren't 'ere, and I am, in case you 'adn't noticed." I had.

"Of course, Mr. Brewer, very thoughtless of me." I replied. "Do you have any suggestions?"

"Of course I don't 'ave any fucking suggestions, you moron!" Billy was losing it. "It's your fucking fault. Even Twiggy would struggle to get through this door!"

Time for Plan B, and twenty minutes' later, the fire brigade arrived, closely followed by Dudley at full gallop.

A case conference was called. It was no good simply removing the doorframe, as Billy was wedged firmly against it. The decision was made by the senior fire officer to remove a section of the wall, which was not well-received by the senior clerk.

"I can't authorise that, officer. This is a listed building, and I'd need the permission of the Honourable Society of the Middle Temple, and they in turn would have to refer it to their listed buildings' sub-committee."

"And how long would that take?"

"About three months."

"And just what do you suggest we do with Mr. Brewer in the meantime?" he asked through clenched teeth.

"I'm afraid that's not my problem."

With a supreme effort, the fire officer just managed to resist decking him. "OK, lads, bring in the equipment."

It took the best part of an hour to demolish a section of the wall. The senior clerk had made an urgent call to the Under-Treasurer of the Honourable Society of the Middle Temple, who together with Dudley, arrived at a gallop and was given short-shrift when he sought to intervene. Bloody pen-pusher!

At last Billy was released from the vice-like grip of the door-frame, and promptly collapsed. Another case conference was called. Although there were eight fire crew in attendance, together with assorted clerks, barristers and Bootsy, nobody saw fit to manhandle Billy. More equipment was brought in, and eventually Billy was hoisted into an upright position, his enormous fat legs dangling some two feet from the ground until he was gently lowered down.

Acting on the senior fire officer's instructions, and with no ambulance equipped to transport him, Billy was guided back to his people-carrier and taken to the nearest hospital for a thorough check-up. As it transpired, that took several hours.

So that was the end of the conference, or my part in it, and I was none the wiser. The only thing it had achieved was a tongue-lashing from Billy, and a half-demolished wall. It was to be several months before our respective senior clerks would speak to each other again. There was an extra-ordinary chambers meeting convened to discuss the bill from the Honourable Society of the Middle Temple for the reinstatement of the wall. Although the wall was within the curtilage of the ground-floor chambers, and on the face of it, their responsibility to repair and reinstate under their tenancy agreement, their lot sought to argue that the damage was caused as a direct result of our lot trying to pour a pint into a half-pint pot. They had a point. Learned opinions were sought, with our lot arguing that their lot had granted us, and by inference Billy Brewer, a licence to enter, and no attempt had been made to qualify or revoke the licence before Billy got stuck.

It was known as the eggshell skull rule, or some such claptrap. I kept my head down and said nothing.

⟞⊹⊹⟝

As soon as he'd recovered his composure, Billy phoned Del to give him an earful, and it took all of Del's persuasive charms to keep him on board. After ruffled feathers were smoothed, it was agreed that Del would attend on Billy in person at the warehouse, to take a full proof of evidence and if I had any supplementary questions, I would ask for clarification. Billy refused to come within a country-mile of the Temple ever again, so it was the best we could do under the circumstances. I agreed to meet Billy in the court foyer at least one hour before his trial was due to start, in case I needed to fine-tune his defence. I hoped to God Del had squared Billy's size and frame with the court office, as none of us wanted a rerun of the Brick Court fiasco.

I had never been to Basildon before, and after my outing with Billy, I vowed never to return. It was the mirror-image of Croydon all over again, only situated to the north-east of London where decent folk feared to tread. The Crown Court was yet another 'fit-for-purpose' court, completed in the mid- 90's, and absolutely ghastly. But for Billy at least, it had one redeeming feature. It had a disabled ramp, so no steps to negotiate. The car park was reserved for essential court users, which expressly excluded counsel, and which left me wondering how much use the court would be put to if we didn't turn up. Such was the skewed thinking of the court service.

I'd left at dawn's early-light to arrive by nine-thirty and my fine-tuning conference with Billy. I needn't have bothered, as Billy didn't turn up until ten-twenty. At least Bootsy was on time, which gave us a chance to chat and for him to go through his 'cop-a-plea' routine. He started as soon as we'd sat down in the coffee-shop.

"I don't fancy his chances, to be blunt Mr. Potts." Bootsy sucked in his breath sharply, "but you're the governor."

"Are you going to tell our client, Mr. Farmer, or shall I?" Bootsy fell silent. "Besides," I continued, "I don't agree. The evidence against him is entirely circumstantial, more smoke than substance," and I chuckled at my unintended wit. Time to rehearse my submissions. "The prosecution have got an Asda truck leaving the warehouse, but as it wasn't followed, nobody can say what was in it." Bootsy wasn't impressed, and it showed. "Some two hours' later, an Asda truck was pulled over and searched, and Customs found a load of contraband cigarettes. Now who's to say it was the same truck?"

Bootsy snorted derisively. "The jury would be my guess," he replied, "and what about the smell in the warehouse? Rotting vegetable matter was how it was described."

"Fair enough, but you've been close and confidential with our client," Bootsy winced at the memory, "and he's got a serious personal freshness problem. I might ask the judge for leave to pass our client round the jury box."

Bootsy burst out laughing. "I'd like to see you try!"

Just then, I noticed Billy on the other side of the coffee-shop door, peering in. "Quick, Mr. Farmer, go and stop him from coming in! We don't want to call the fire-brigade again!"

Bootsy did as he was asked, and I followed. To put it mildly, Billy wasn't at all pleased to see us.

You two," he scoffed, "a couple of fucking losers!"

"Good to see you again, Mr. Brewer," I said, trying to lower the temperature. "Would you like a coffee?"

Billy nodded sullenly. "Yeah, alright, black, no sugar. I'm on a diet."

I just managed to keep a straight face. "Mr. Farmer, would you oblige?"

Bootsy sloped off, and together, Billy and I walked along the main hall trying to find a conference room that would accommodate us. No such luck, so I tried one of the court ushers.

She looked over at Billy, seeing but not believing, then looked back at me.

"I'm afraid the only room I can think of with a large enough door would be the mothers and babies changing facilities."

Not ideal, but beggars can't be choosers. Bootsy returned with the coffee, and in we went. Billy lowered himself gingerly onto the lavatory lid, which juddered and creaked under the strain, I used the baby-changing table to rest my notebook, and Bootsy stood uncomfortably by the door.

The conference lasted precisely four minutes. It wasn't the overpowering smell of rotting vegetable matter that brought proceedings to a sudden and unexpected end, it was the loud cracking of the lavatory lid, which collapsed under Billy's weight and deposited him unceremoniously into the pan with his fat legs sticking up in the air. Oh My God!

Bootsy flung open the door, gasping for air, to be confronted by a mother with a screaming baby. No time for explanations, as the visibly distressed woman reeled back from the noxious fumes. At least the baby stopped screaming.

"I'll get help," I said lamely, turning to a visibly distressed Bootsy. "Perhaps you'd be good enough to stay here and look after Mr. Brewer." Rank sometimes has its privileges.

As I was making my way to the front desk, the tannoy crackled into life. "The trial of Brewer will now be heard in Court Three." You must be joking.

Security were summoned.

"I'm afraid my client is seriously incommoded," I explained, "and will almost certainly need the assistance of the fire brigade. Can you help?"

"We can't go calling the fire brigade just on your say-so, guv, it's more than our jobs worth. We need to assess the situation for ourselves first."

The two security officers followed me and peered in.

"Fucking hell!" said the first, mouth snapped open. "What's the fat fucker doing in here in the first place? Is he a pervert? And what's that disgusting smell?"

"Kindly moderate your language, officer, we're in a court of law. This gentleman is my client, and he's now firmly wedged in the pan."

"Yeah, I can see that for myself."

"Now with goodwill on both sides, it should be possible for the two of you to ease him gently to his feet, and I'm sure my solicitor's representative will help."

That suggestion was met with a vigorous shaking of three heads.

"That's not in our job description, guv, so you can forget about that now! This is a job for the fire brigade."

"Precisely what I suggested five minutes' ago."

"Yeah, I know that, guv, but there are channels, and forms to be filled in." He turned to his colleague. "You call the fire brigade, Bert, and I'll start filling in the forms."

Just then, the tannoy crackled into life again, this time with a heightened tone of urgency: "William Brewer and his legal representatives to Court Three immediately!"

I turned to Bootsy. "I'll go and tell the judge what's happening. You'd better stay with Mr. Brewer." Bootsy nodded.

I hurried to Court Three and, having given my name to the usher, took my place on counsel's bench. No sooner had I sat down, there was a loud rap on the door behind the judge's chair, and in flew His Honour Judge Bagot, known to the local practitioners as "Bushy" and totally devoid of humour. He was visibly angry.

"I require an immediate explanation for this gross discourtesy in the face of the court," he snapped. "This trial was listed to commence at ten-thirty sharp, and here we are, ten-forty-three, and still no sign of the defendant. I shall issue a warrant for his immediate arrest."

"Your Honour…"

"Silence, I shall brook no argument!"

What a complete prat! "Very well, Your Honour, and to assist the bailiff, the warrant can be executed on the defendant who, even as I speak, is firmly wedged in the lavatory reserved for mothers and babies."

"This is not the time for levity, Mr…" Bushy looked down to find my name, "Potts, and unless you moderate your tone, I shall hold you in contempt!" He glowered at me. "Usher, summon the bailiff!"

This was going from the sublime to the ridiculous as we all sat patiently for the arrival of the bailiff. He duly appeared, some seven minutes' later, which, according to the court clock and Bushy's calculations, made the time precisely ten-fifty.

"Bailiff," Bushy snapped at the unfortunate man, "I have signed a warrant for the immediate arrest of William Brewer. Once the warrant has been executed, he is to be brought before me so that I can consider revoking his bail and remanding him in custody. Is that clear?"

"Er…yes and no, Your Honour," replied the hapless bailiff.

"This is intolerable! What do you mean, yes and no?"

"Yes, I can execute the warrant on a gentleman known to me as William Brewer, who is just across the hall in the mothers and babies changing facilities, and no, I cannot bring him before Your Honour, because he is wedged in the toilet and we are waiting for the arrival of fire brigade to release him."

There was a long pause as Bushy took stock of the situation. "What on earth is a male defendant doing in the mothers and babies changing facilities, when he is clearly neither?"

"I can explain, Your Honour," I rose helpfully.

"I don't require any explanations from you, Mr. Potts," snapped Bushy, "kindly resume your seat." Not just a complete prat, a complete idiot as well. "Mr. Murphy," prosecuting counsel rose, "can you help?"

"Er, no Your Honour." Short and to the point.

Bushy sat, grim-faced, pondering his options. Eventually he turned to me. "Mr. Potts, I am determined that this trial will proceed without any further inexcusable delays. With the obvious exception of the defendant, we are all here, the jury panel has been summoned, and we are ready to proceed. As you should know, I have the power to try the defendant in his absence, which I shall do unless you persuade me to the contrary."

Not just a complete prat and a complete idiot, but a complete moron as well.

Time to stir the pot. "With respect, Your Honour, I doubt if the Court of Appeal would be amused in the unlikely event of a conviction secured in the defendant's absence when he is barely seven paces away from Your Honour's court."

A red rag to a bull. "Don't threaten me with the Court of Appeal, Mr. Potts, that will get you nowhere!"

I pressed on, undeterred. "If Your Honour is determined to proceed to trial, I suppose the court could be reconvened in the mothers and babies facilities. It might be a squash, and there is a strong and noxious smell to contend with, but we could try." Bushy was rumbling like Vesuvius. "Of course, rather like the Boy Jesus being shown to the Elders of the Synagogue, the jurors would have to be shown to the defendant, just in case any recognise him, or if he wishes to exercise his right of challenge."

Murphy could contain himself no longer, and burst out laughing.

"This is no laughing matter, Mr. Murphy," snapped Bushy, losing his composure. It was decision time, either dig deeper or withdraw. "I shall rise." The first sensible thing he'd done all morning. He had taken against me, and the feeling was mutual.

I left court for an update, and found Bootsy looking decidedly queasy.

"The fire brigade have just arrived, and are assessing the situation. They're wearing breathing apparatus," he added for good measure. "I need a coffee, how about you?"

"Yes please. I'll wait here for a progress report."

Bootsy shuffled off, and I found the chief officer clutching a large sledgehammer.

"I've instructed court maintenance to shut off the water supply, as we'll have to break the pan. He's wedged in so tight, there's no other way." I nodded. "I've also instructed the court manager to evacuate the building, just in case something blows."

"Good Lord! Isn't that a bit drastic?"

"Are you telling me how to do my job?"

"No, no, of course not."

"Even with the water shut off, there's bound to be some residue in the pipes, and once we break the pan, there's a chance your client could be shot into the air like a cork from a bottle."

I chuckled. "That I'd like to see."

"No you wouldn't. Mind you, he's a big bloke, never seen anybody that big, so he might take some shifting."

"He's on a diet," I replied helpfully.

"It ain't working whatever it is. Now I suggest you leave the building." I turned to go. "There's one good thing that might come out of this," he added.

"What's that?"

"Your client's got a serious personal freshness problem, so a good soaking won't do him any harm. He's also farting like an old horse."

"One last thing," I said, trying not to laugh. "My client's due to stand trial this morning, and he's keeping the court waiting."

"No chance, and besides, what idiot told you that?"

"A complete idiot," I replied.

"Well you tell the complete idiot that once we've released him, he'll be taken to hospital for a thorough examination, and either kept in overnight or sent home to recuperate. The ambulance is on its way."

Just then the fire alarm sounded and the tannoy crackled into life again. "This is not a test, this is an emergency. Leave the building immediately and make your way to the court car park to await further instructions. Do not stop to gather your personal effects. I repeat, this is not a test, this is an emergency."

"Can I have a quick word with my client?" I asked.

"Make it quick."

I popped my head round the door. "Sorry about this, Mr. Brewer, but you're in capable hands."

"Fuck off, you moron!" Billy bellowed back. "Don't come near me ever again!" Such ingratitude.

I found Bootsy clutching two paper cups of coffee, and we made our way out to the car park. An ambulance had turned up and was parked in front of the court, ready to spring into action. A reporter from the Basildon Bizzy-Bee was buzzing around, and two trucks turned up, one from Sky News, they were everywhere, and the other from BBC London. It was 'Camera, Lights, Action' all over again. Very exciting. I spotted Bushy in the car park, still fuming and consulting his watch as if his life depended on it. I gave him a cheery wave, which he ignored.

Ten minutes' later, there was an audible rumbling from the bowels of the court, and the ground shook. Mothers and babies began to scream, old folks held onto each other for comfort, and even grown men began to sob quietly. It was Armageddon.

Billy had survived the ordeal, and was transported to the waiting ambulance, which drove slowly away, blue lights flashing and the axle almost resting on the wheels. The all-clear sounded, and we made our way back to court. The trial was adjourned to a date to be appointed, I collected my robes, and together with Bootsy, I set off for the station.

I saw Security talking to the newshounds and pointing in my direction. In a trice, I was surrounded, and microphones poked into my face. It was my dream come true, a short pithy statement to the press on the steps of the court, but for all the wrong reasons.

When prompted, I explained for the benefit of the readers and viewers that, yes, Mr. Brewer was indeed my client, I was Toby Potts of Counsel, might as well get my name up in lights, and yes, as far as I knew, he was the fattest man in England, weighing in at forty-seven stones, but he was on a diet, I quickly added, black coffee, no sugar.

When asked why he got stuck in the mothers and babies changing facilities, I replied, somewhat pompously as befitting senior and experienced counsel, that this was privileged information and therefore confidential.

The tabloids had a field-day, and the Sun newspaper had a centrefold splash with Billy's Big Breakfast in glorious technicolour, and no sign of the black coffee. So much for the diet, and sadly, no mention of me.

However, all was not lost. Joy phoned me, very excited and laughing herself silly. She'd seen me on Sky News. My mother also phoned. She thought I looked an absolute poppet, but next time I should wear my wig and gown, if only to show my father that his substantial investment was bearing fruit.

Regrettably, that was the last I saw of Big Billy Brewer. As soon as he'd recuperated, he was on the phone to Del, sacking us both. He'd never been so humiliated in his life, not just once, but twice, and he never wanted to see us again.

As somebody once said, size matters, and who was I to argue?

CHAPTER 11

FOREPLAY

Wedged between my two disastrous outings with Big Billy Brewer was my return match with Joy. As it was my treat, I wanted to surprise her with something original, not the usual romantic *dîner a deux* where the prices made the eyes water and the wine list was off the Richter Scale. I remembered vividly dining at the Aurora, Jock McTavish's Michelin starred restaurant in Notting Hill, and thank God somebody else picked up the tab.

The theatre was old hat, been there, done it, and besides, if Joy's idea of a good night out in luvvieland was **Waiting for Godot,** she could wait for him without me.

I couldn't remember who told me about it, but there was a night club in Soho called *Los Jardines Neptuna* specialising in Spanish food and Flamenco. I liked Spain and most things Spanish, so it was worth a try. Even better, the entrance ticket covered the food, selected dishes only, the wine was cheap, and best of all, there was dancing till dawn, cheek to cheek in a hot sweaty embrace.

Despite my best efforts, the evening was an unmitigated disaster. I picked Joy up from her apartment as arranged, but the taxi fare from the Barbican to Soho was well beyond my budget, so we went by Underground. Two changes later, we emerged at

Leicester Square, leaving us with a brisk walk to the night club. Unfortunately, Joy's carefully coiffured hairdo was all over the place, not helped by a light but persistent drizzle, and by the time we arrived, she looked like a wet hen in a thunderstorm. She was not best-pleased and didn't hesitate to tell me.

To describe the lighting in the club as mood didn't do it justice. It was virtually pitch-dark. After we found our table, Joy marched off to the *Señoras* to try and bring forth order out of chaos, groping her way uncertainly in the gloom with only the illuminated sign to guide her, and a few well-chosen expletives to help her on her way.

The club had no atmosphere whatsoever. From what I could see as my eyes gradually became accustomed to the darkness, seating capacity when full must have been eighty, but nobody could remember the last time it was full, if ever. Possibly VE night, although if memory served me well, the Spanish had chosen to sit that one out. On this particular night, there were four of us.

The skeleton staff was drawn from the local recruitment office, so not even a passing acquaintance with the Iberian peninsula, but they had been instructed by the management to affect a sort of Latino twang which sounded positively ridiculous. Some effort had been made to dress the part, with gaily coloured shirts, knotted scarves and cummerbunds, but it was a token gesture.

The floor show was due to start at nine, with a second show at eleven, always assuming the clientele had not drawn stumps by then and headed off for an early bath.

Eventually Joy returned, the hairdo redone, but looking decidedly green around the gills. Two enormous cockroaches had chosen to share her cubicle and had eyed her malevolently before crawling off to the kitchen.

To try and lighten the mood, I ordered two glasses of Spanish champagne, which tasted like battery acid with bubbles. This was going from bad to worse. Peering at the menu with the aid of a flickering candle, I persuaded Joy to share a paella with me. It was one of the selected dishes, which immediately appealed, and paella and Spain went together like peaches and cream, which by hap-chance were also on the menu. I ordered a bottle of *Torres Altos Blanco,* which turned out to be closely related to the Spanish Champagne, but without the bubbles.

The paella arrived with due ceremony. It was hot and steaming like an Andalusian summer night, and that said, there was nothing more to say. The squiggly bits were decidedly chewy, and it may have been a trick of the light, or what there was of it, but some of the squiggly bits still seemed to be squiggling. Some minutes into the meal, there was an audible rumbling, which I took to be Joy's stomach adjusting to the heavy load, and I sensed she was not enjoying it. She was not alone. For dessert, we both chose peaches, fresh from the tin, and heavily diluted cream, more like pasteurised milk.

We slumped back in our chairs, the culinary ordeal over, and after a few pleasantries, it was time for the floor show. This consisted of an ageing *caballero* clutching a Spanish guitar as if his life depended on it, and a matronly flamenco dancer built for comfort not speed. She looked for all the world as if she'd just stepped out of the chorus line of Bizet's *Carmen* as performed by the Billericay Amateur Dramatic Society, with jet-black hair swept back into a tight bun, a carnation stuck behind her ear and castanets poised above her head and ready to take no prisoners.

The small wooden stage shook to the rhythmic and remorseless stamping of her enormous feet as she whirled around like a demented dervish, whilst the *caballero* thrashed away on his guitar, hoping to be heard above the clatter, and moaning away to some Spanish incantation with its roots in the foothills of the Sierra Nevada.

This incessant pounding was giving Joy a raging headache, so she smiled weakly, excused herself, and throwing caution to the wind, set off once more to the *Señoras.* That was the last I saw of her for at least thirty minutes, and at one stage I thought about mounting a rescue party. Eventually she emerged, looking even greener around the gills, and had barely sat down when she shouted above the racket that she was leaving, and she did. I paid the bill and hurried after her. She was propped up in a nearby doorway, gasping for air. She didn't look well.

We found a bistro and I bought two cups of strong black coffee.

"I'm sorry the evening's been such a disappointment," I apologised, "it sounded such fun when I booked."

"It's not your fault, Toby," she replied, smiling weakly, "and it's certainly an evening I'll never forget. Now if you'll excuse me, I need the loo."

Another thirty minutes slipped effortlessly by before she returned to the table. The green hue had turned to ashen white.

"Sorry to be a party-pooper, but I'm not feeling well."

"I quite understand," I replied, "let me take you home."

"No, no," she said, almost too quickly. The thought of another bone-shaking ride on the Underground would have pushed her over the edge. "I'll take a taxi."

Five minutes' later, I stood by the open taxi door, not knowing what to do or say.

"We'll be in touch, Toby," she said, "but all I need now is a good night's sleep," and with that, she was gone.

That was the last I saw of Joy. I phoned a couple of times, but she never returned my calls. Perhaps it was for the best, to have loved and lost and all that, and casual affairs were never really my scene. I had Susie, and it wouldn't be long before she was back in my arms, or so I hoped.

⊱―⊰

After a period of marking time with a few mentions and applications, and the occasional guilty plea with the usual recitation about the defendant having seen the error of his ways and was now determined to make a fresh start living an honest and productive life, a chambers' brief found its way into my pigeon hole. It was common practice for solicitors who briefed chambers regularly to send in work at the bottom of the feeding chain for allocation to suitable junior counsel at the discretion of the clerks, hence the importance of keeping them onside.

Flicking through the papers, I learned that my client faced a serious charge, assault with a deadly weapon. This was very exciting, until I discovered that the deadly weapon was a golf ball!

According to Mark Twain, he of the ready wit, golf is a good walk spoiled. Somewhat harsh perhaps, but he had a point. To others of a similar persuasion, it was a four-letter word. Golfers were a breed apart, with a single-minded obsession second to none, and as far as I could tell, the worst golfers were the most obsessed. Instead of jacking it in for a spot of gardening or putting the world to rights over a pint at the Farmer's Arms, they were out in all weathers, leaving the fairways relatively unscathed as they hacked their way round the course from one clump of impenetrable grass to the next until, after what seemed like an eternity, they found the sanctuary of the green before holing out in double figures and amazingly, feeling well pleased with their efforts. Then it was into the clubhouse to relive every shot over several large pink gins. This in itself was no mean feat, given the scorecard of cricket proportions.

My instructing solicitors were Messrs. Cassell & Cassell, which consisted of Mr. Cassell Senior and Mr. Cassell Junior, and the long-suffering Shirley, receptionist and general dogsbody, with premises located just off the High Street in Esher. The firm had a steady turnover of general common law, enough to keep the wolf from the door, but not enough to strain the sinews. Mr. Cassell Senior's contribution, such as it was, had to fit around his tee-off times at Woodlands Park, which was very much his second home.

As golf clubs go, Woodlands Park in Surrey was very grand indeed. It boasted a magnificent Georgian Clubhouse where members could wine and dine, two 18 hole golf courses set in rolling parklands, tennis courts and a swimming pool. Heaven on earth!

Until recently, Woodlands Park was a male preserve. It was a gentleman's club for gentlemen, and that's how it had been for over one hundred years. Wives were admitted to the clubhouse, with a separate room set aside and approached from the rear of the building, where they could partake of refreshments, read golf magazines and gossip. This was a devilishly cunning ruse to have them on call to drive their gin-soaked husbands home, as good a reason as any to stay married. No partners were admitted, as this was evidence of moral turpitude and not to be tolerated. Any gentleman unwilling to seal his union in the sight of God was no gentleman at all, and was blackballed. Ladies were definitely not allowed on the golf courses, not even as caddies. All too, *too* distracting!

But the winds of change were blowing through Woodlands Park, all to do with equality of opportunity. Humbug! The committee had put in a planning application for an extension to the clubhouse, which in years gone by would have been a formality, but not this time. As ill-luck would have it, the Chief Planning officer of the local council was a woman, and she was singularly unamused about the Club's male only policy, and told them so. Having examined the plans, her department proposed that the new extension should contain a ladies' locker room, together with ablutions, in anticipation of lady members being admitted to the club.

The Committee called an extraordinary general meeting, otherwise known as a Council of War. The antediluvian corner was represented by Colonel Hugo Marjoribanks, pronounced Marshbanks for the uninitiated, who had been a member for thirty years, as had his father and grandfather before him. There was even a Marjoribanks Cup presented annually for the lowest Stapleford round of golf which, by coincidence, was invariably won by Hugo. He had been club captain more times than anybody could remember, as had his father and grandfather before him, so he was a force to be reckoned with. He was implacably opposed to lady members cluttering up the course, powdering their noses, touching up their lipstick and gossiping away when they should be at home dusting and vacuuming and getting the dinner ready.

The progressive corner was represented by Roger Dalziel, pronounced DL for the uninitiated, very much an *arriviste* in Marjoribanks' book, foppish in his manner and dress, wore perfume and was probably a closet-faggot. He had plenty of money but no breeding, so it was hardly surprising the two couldn't stand each other. Dalziel supported lady members, but then he would, wouldn't he?

It was a heated and acrimonious meeting chaired by the Hon. Secretary Earnest Smythe, pronounced Smythe for the uninitiated, but eventually a compromise was reached. Ladies would be admitted, and could play on the New Course twice a week, Mondays and Wednesdays, mornings only. A ladies locker room would be made available to them, otherwise the existing rules would be enforced, with the ladies confined to barracks and out of sight.

The compromise had the desired effect. The clubhouse extension was given the green light by the planning committee, and the dust settled on Woodlands Park. Marjoribanks accepted the arrival of lady members with ill-grace, and vowed to have nothing to do with them. The feeling was entirely mutual.

On the day in question, a Wednesday as it transpired, Marjoribanks and his three companions had arranged a round of golf on the Old Course. No tee time had been booked, as Wednesdays were usually quiet, and besides, when Marjoribanks appeared, the sea parted. Not on this occasion. To his dismay when he approached the first tee, he found it occupied by Nancy-Boy Dalziel and *his* three companions, limbering up and about to tee off. Marjoribanks was decidedly teed-off, but there was nothing he could do about it, as Dalziel had booked in advance and had priority.

To make matters worse, Dalziel was well-known for taking an eternity to play each and every shot as if he were competing for top honours at the British Open Championship, so anybody following him was advised to set aside at least half a day. Marjoribanks had neither the time nor the inclination, so the decision was made to play the New Course.

Although it was ladies' day, there was not a filly in sight, which was good news indeed, and in no time at all, they had teed off and were marching purposefully down the first fairway.

Trouble loomed at the third hole. Four ladies were spotted up ahead, spreading themselves across the fairway and, according to Marjoribanks, powdering their noses, touching up their lipstick and gossiping away, with precious little golf in evidence. One of the four was Ernestine Hibbard, better known to Marjoribanks and his coterie as Old Mother Hubbard, unmistakeable at any distance, a stout woman broad of beam who, as it turned out, had been a close friend of Emily Pankhurst. She was one of the first to join the newly emancipated club, and was now Ladies' Captain, with her own reserved parking space behind the clubhouse and next to the green keeper's hut. It had been hand-picked for her by Marjoribanks, out of sight, out of mind. If only!

Marjoribanks stood on the third tee, glowering at the ladies until his patience snapped.

"May we play through?" he bellowed.

"No you may not!" Ms.Hibbard bellowed back. "It's ladies' day, and you're not supposed to be on the course until after twelve!"

"Don't adopt that tone with me Madam. I am perfectly aware of the rules!"

"Then I suggest you obey them!" and with that, she returned to the game in hand. This meant checking her card for distance to the green, checking the wind, most of it emanating from her, selecting the right club, and taking several practice swings before eventually addressing the ball and sending it on its way. This performance was repeated by her three companions, each in turn, with one, possibly unnerved by Marjoribanks' lowering presence, slicing her ball into the rough. This meant a further delay as they all trooped off in search of it. It took a good five minutes to find the ball, cowering behind a tuft of grass, and begging to be left alone. No such luck, as its owner thrashed it repeatedly until, beaten into submission, it eventually limped onto the fairway barely ten yards ahead of where it started.

In the fullness of time, it was reluctantly persuaded to join the other three balls on the green, and then it was time for the putting ritual. The ball had to be marked and cleaned, the route from the ball to the hole carefully inspected for spike marks or detritus, the squat behind the ball, which in Ms. Hibbard's case was not a pretty sight, the vertical holding of the putter to gauge hidden undulations, checking the knap of the grass, was it with or against the putt, or across it, taking several practice putts to get the feel of the club before impact, and finally, sending the ball scudding on its way with hardly time for a cheery wave as it shot past the hole. And to add insult to injury, all this repeated four times. It made Dalziel look like Speedy Gonzales, and with his oily Latino looks, the two were probably related.

There then followed a trial of strength, neither party willing to give way to the other. On the fourth hole, and heedless of the advice given by his playing companions, Marjoribanks hit his tee shot barely ten yards from where the ladies were powdering their noses, touching up their lipstick, and discussing club selection. This encroachment was duly noted by Ms. Hibbard, who glared at Marjoribanks. He in turn glared back.

The fifth hole was no better. This time Marjoribanks hit his tee shot a good ten yards past the ladies. Ms. Hibbard selected her number three wood, marched up to the ball and struck it firmly back from whence it came. More by luck than good judgment, she made an excellent connection, and the ball whistled back past the astonished Marjoribanks and came to rest on the fourth green.

This was the final straw. Marjoribanks retrieved his ball, thereby incurring a one-shot penalty, teed off again just as Ms. Hibbard was bending over to replace a divot, and with unerring accuracy, the ball took one bounce before embedding itself into her ample posterior. She went to ground like a pole-axed cow.

All hell broke loose. One of her companions scampered off to summon help whilst the other two did what they could to comfort her. Marjoribanks, too little too late, tried to make amends and strode down the fairway to offer his apologies. They lacked the ring of sincerity.

"Sorry?!" she bellowed, wincing with pain. "You'll be sorry, mark my words!"

Unfortunately for Marjoribanks, he had played into Ms. Hibbard's hands, and he didn't have a leg to stand on. She in turn was determined to milk the incident for all it was worth, and she did. At her insistence, the Hon. Secretary reported the matter to the police, and an appointment was made for Marjoribanks to attend interview at Esher Police Station. He was accompanied by Mr. Cassell Senior, who knew absolutely nothing about crime, so he advised his client to remain silent.

Witness statements were taken from Ms. Hibbard's three playing companions, all of which corroborated her account. Marjoribanks' playing companions, like Marjoribanks, had nothing to say. They had no intention of going down with the sinking ship, come hell or high water.

The CPS reviewing lawyer reviewed the evidence. Ms. Hibbard insisted on her day in court, so Marjoribanks was duly charged, assault with a deadly weapon, and summoned to appear at Kingston Magistrates' Court on a day to be notified. It was a public humiliation, the local press had a field day, and Marjjoribanks was hung out to dry. But if that were not bad enough, he received a letter from Smythe notifying him that his membership had been suspended to await the outcome of the criminal proceedings. This was a bitter pill to swallow. Golf was his passion, and Woodlands Park his life. The thought of moping around the house all day, getting under the feet of his good lady wife, pottering in the garden and putting the world to rights at the Farmer's Arms was a fate worse than death.

⟩⊷⊶⟨

Marjoribanks arrived promptly at four-thirty for our conference in Chambers, accompanied by Shirley.

He was tall and fit-looking for his sixty-six years, dressed immaculately in a three-piece tweed suit, greying hair, a matching moustache and a ruddy complexion from endless days on the golf course and too many pink gins. He had an air of authority which would brook no nonsense, as I was about to discover.

"So," he boomed, "you're the young whippersnapper who's going to sort out this mess." He looked at Shirley, then back to me. "Are you sure you're up to it, young man? After all, it's my reputation that's at stake."

"I shall do my best," I replied. The cheek of the man!

"I have no doubt, but will it be enough?"

This was going nowhere, so best to grasp the nettle and plunge in.

"Looking at the charge," I began, trying to show wisdom beyond my years, "the prosecution must prove that you either deliberately drove your ball at Ms. Hibbard, or you were reckless. Your only defence must be that it was accidental."

"As indeed it was, so I'm damned if I know why I've been charged," he blustered. "I blame Old Mother Hubbard, nothing but trouble since she joined the club! I warned the committee against admitting lady members, and I was right!"

"With respect, Colonel, the fact that Ms. Hibbard was a lady member has nothing to do with the case." Marjoribanks was not used to being contradicted and it showed. "Correct me if I'm wrong, but driving through other players is one of the cardinal sins of golf etiquette, and frankly, it's downright dangerous."

This didn't go down at all well.

"And I suppose you're an expert on golf etiquette?" he scoffed.

"Well no," Marjoribanks snorted in derision, "but I used to caddy for my father at weekends."

"Just as I thought, a weekend hacker. Worse than women, cluttering up the course."

"I don't suppose my father would agree. He plays off eight," I shot back. That pinned his ears back.

"Impressive, and where does your father play?"

"Royal St. George's."

Marjoribanks gave a soft whistle. "By Jove, one of the best courses in the country," he conceded, "I've obviously underestimated you, and I apologise."

"No need to apologise, just so we understand each other."

There was a long pause. "So where do we go from here?" asked Marjoribanks. His manner was now more conciliatory.

"Well, there's a faint glimmer of light at the end of the tunnel, but nothing definite."

"Being what?"

"It's the way Ms. Hibbard behaved before your ball struck her posterior."

Marjoribanks perked up. "Go on."

"She hit your ball back towards you and it finished up on the fourth green." Marjoribanks nodded vigorously. "We could certainly argue that she behaved recklessly. In fact, the only difference between her behaviour and yours is that your ball made contact and hers did not."

"By Jove you're right, young man," he replied, slapping his leg in delight. "We've got the old battle-axe over a barrel!"

"Not quite," I hastened to add. I didn't want to raise his hopes prematurely.

"What do you mean, not quite?" Marjoribanks' eyes narrowed.

"The law doesn't allow for the defence that two wrongs make a right. To put it bluntly, just because she nearly poleaxed you doesn't allow you to poleaxe her."

"More's the pity, and if that's the law, the law is an ass!"

I'd heard that one before. "I'm afraid that's no defence either," I continued, metaphorically donning my wig and gown. "It's what we lawyers call 'confess and avoid'. Whilst her behaviour doesn't provide you with a defence, it provides you with some compelling mitigation."

Marjoribanks fell silent as he absorbed the enormity of my peroration. "So what do we do?" he asked at last. "I simply cannot have a criminal conviction against my name. It would ruin me, and the chances of my returning to the club would be zero."

"Point taken," I replied. "I suggest we keep our powder dry, and let's see how the land lies when we get to court."

"Very well. I'm in your hands."

"Just before you go, a word to the wise." Marjoribanks looked at me warily. "If you will permit me to say so, you are a forceful man with strongly held opinions, not least on lady golfers." He nodded. "But if we're to make progress at court, no good going in with all guns blazing." I paused. "A portion of humble pie might be in order."

He scowled, then laughed. "How much?"

"As much as it takes."

He laughed again. "Message received and understood."

I duly arrived on the appointed day in the leafy suburb of Kingston-on-Thames, where Marjoribanks and Ms. Hibbard were to lock antlers and go head-to-head, with the reputation of Woodlands hanging in the balance. Shirley was there to represent Cassell & Cassell, with Mr. Cassell Senior due to tee off promptly at nine, and was therefore unavailable. Mr. Smythe had also put in an appearance.

As luck would have it, my opponent was Tim Dutton. We'd graduated from law school together, got drunk together, and before my fall from grace at Snaresbrook, knocked around together doing low-grade crime.

Leaving the Colonel in Shirley's safe hands, we adjourned to the court cafeteria.

"It's great to see you again, Toby," Dutton enthused, "I suppose you know you're a legend at Snaresbrook."

Good Lord, whatever for?"

"You're the man who saw off Newman. Nobody else had stood up to him until you did, we all wanted to but didn't have the balls. You were brilliant!"

I smiled. "Not quite how I saw it, but thanks anyway. And how is Newman?"

"I gather Yorkshire couldn't stomach him, no surprises there. The last I heard he'd taken early retirement, index-linked pension and all that, and is now running a dog rescue sanctuary. From one old dog to another!" and we both laughed.

"Thanks to you, we're getting much more respect from his replacement, and more work. Time to come back and savour your moment of glory."

"Kind thought, Tim, but the CPS have long memories, and I'm still regarded as the enemy within. Besides, I'm getting plenty of work elsewhere," I lied, "so I can live without Snaresbrook. Now, to the matter in hand," I continued, "is this to be a trial, or can we sort something out?"

"I've spoken to the fragrant Ms. Hibbard, who's determined to have her hour in court. She makes Boadicea look like Mother Theresa, a very formidable woman, and she's got her witnesses lined up like skittles, so I'm not hopeful. Other than that, I'm open to suggestions."

I paused. "Do you play golf, Tim?"

"Good God, no, it's an old man's game!"

"I doubt if Tiger Woods would agree, but no matter." Dutton smiled. "I've caddied enough times for my old man to know something about golf etiquette, and hitting your ball at or near another player is regarded as a cardinal sin."

Dutton nodded. "That's why we're here, Toby."

"Point taken, but did you know that immediately before Marjoribanks had driven his ball at Ms. Hibbard, she had done exactly the same at him."

Dutton's mouth snapped open. "Are you sure? There's nothing in her statement, or the statements of her three witnesses."

"Quite so, but if push comes to shove, I will ask for an adjournment and get the Colonel's three playing companions to give evidence, in which case, Ms. Hibbard's membership will be revoked and she'll be out on her ear. She may get her conviction, but is that a price worth paying? A pyrrhic victory to say the very least, and worse still, all you'll have to show for today is a fifty pound adjournment fee."

That struck a raw nerve. "This is getting more interesting by the minute," said Dutton.

"Ms. Hibbard might also wish to know that Mr. Smythe, the club secretary, is here at court, and will be reporting the outcome of these proceedings back to the committee."

Dutton thought long and hard. "I'm on board, Toby," he said at last, "so what do you suggest?"

"I'm sure I can persuade my client to offer Ms. Hibbard two hundred pounds in compensation for pain and suffering, and in return, she withdraws her complaint." Dutton nodded. "Everyone's a winner, and lunch is on you. All you need to do is sell it to Ms. Hibbard and the CPS."

"Stuff the CPS," brave words indeed, "give me a few minutes to work my magic on Ms. Hibbard, and I'll report back."

Dutton hurried off, and to egg the pudding, I sought out Mr. Smythe. In full view of Ms. Hibbard and her three witnesses, I pretended to be in earnest conversation. It was duly noted as Dutton appeared and took Ms. Hibbard into an adjoining interview room.

I went in search of the Colonel and Shirley. I explained I was in negotiations with the prosecution to see if we could settle the matter without a trial, and asked for their patience. No promises, but I was cautiously optimistic.

Ten minutes' later, Dutton reappeared and gestured towards me. I joined him.

"Nearly there, Toby, but there's one catch."

"Which is?"

"She wants her reserved parking space moved to the front of the clubhouse, as befitting her station as Ladies' Captain."

I laughed. "Let's hope that's not a bridge too far. I'll see what I can do."

Knowing that Marjoribanks would bridle at the suggestion, I thought it best to get Smythe onside. He was perfectly amenable, but it was not his decision.

He looked over to Marjoribanks. "Has the Colonel expressed a view?" he asked nervously, almost anticipating the answer.

"Not yet, but if he doesn't object, may I relay to Ms. Hibbard that her request will be treated sympathetically at the next committee meeting?"

"You may indeed."

"And if Ms. Hibbard withdraws her complaint, will the Colonel's suspension be lifted?"

"Absolutely."

Nearly there, now for the hard part.

As it turned out, after the usual huffing and puffing and blustering, Marjoribanks calmed down and agreed to eat some humble pie.

We went into court. Dutton offered no evidence, the charge was dismissed, no order for costs, and it was honours even. Marjoribanks even managed a wintry smile towards Ms. Hibbard, who cautiously returned it. Not exactly bosom buddies, but a step in the right direction.

Outside court, Marjoribanks shook my hand, and was profuse in his praise of my advocacy skills.

"Well done indeed, Mr.Potts," he gushed, "you have excelled yourself, and I am most grateful." Music to my ears. "I believe I agreed your fee at fifty guineas." He looked at Shirley, who nodded. "Please accept my cheque for sixty, you've earned every penny."

"This is most generous of you, Colonel," I replied, decidedly underwhelmed. "I'm pleased it all turned out for the best."

"And so am I, and if you're ever passing Woodlands, I should be delighted to welcome you as a guest member."

With sixty guineas burning a hole in my pocket, less clerks' commission, chambers' rent, travel and tax, there wasn't a snowball's chance in hell I was going to offer Tim Dutton lunch at the nearby hostelry, it was definitely Dutch. Over a pint and a crusty cheese roll, we reminisced about the good and bad times at the Criminal Bar, and what the future held in store for both of us.

In the fullness of time, I learned that a new cup had been commissioned by Woodlands, mixed doubles, where the Colonel and the fragrant Ernestine partnered each other, and were unbeatable.

The sweet smell of success.

CHAPTER 12

UP AND AT IT

I got an unexpected invitation from Del in the post, very smart, RSVP and all that, drinks and canapés in the Sheraton Room of the Novatel Hotel just off Camberwell Green, twelve noon, to the accompaniment of Spotty Muldoon the resident pianist, dress code casually elegant.

It was to celebrate Del's ten years in private practice, ten eventful years as he was fond of telling me. Topsy's sleeping partnership had become "full-on" and Baby Crispin's arrival on Team Finnan had softened the hard edges as she sought to inject a measure of much-needed sophistication, but it was like drawing teeth, slow and painful.

Needless to say, the celebration was Topsy's idea, carefully costed at Del's insistence, but, as is the way of these things, coming in well over budget.

"It's tax deductible, Del," she said reassuringly.

"Yeah, I know love, but I've got to make it before I can deduct it."

"Don't be so negative all the time. We've got to take the practice to a new level, especially with Crispin's school fees to think about." Del spluttered. "And who can say," she continued, "there might be the patter of more tiny feet on the way."

Del spluttered again. "Oh my God, Topsy, you're not up-the-duff again are you?"

"And what if I was?!" she glared at him. "You men are all the same, all too ready to have your oats, but never ready to live with the consequences. And besides, are you going to deny your first-born the pleasure of a little brother or sister, or the best education money can buy?"

"Of course not, love," he lied, pouring oil over troubled waters. He was a graduate of Camberwell Green Comprehensive, and it didn't do him any harm. Mark you, it didn't do him much good either, but at least it was free. Private school fees were thirty thousand pounds a year, and climbing, and if push came to shove, even if he could afford them, which he couldn't, Del couldn't see Crispin fannying around some overpriced school dressed in white tie and tails. And if he dressed like that on the Green, he wouldn't last five minutes.

Del and Topsy were at the door, ready to meet and greet, a bit like a wedding reception line-up where the proud parents of the bride and groom know only half the guests and wished they were somewhere else. The word had got round the Manor, and where Topsy's careful planning had catered for one hundred guests, at least two hundred turned up. Del had one eye on the guests as they arrived and filtered through, and the other eye on the waiters pouring for England. OK, so it wasn't best end champagne, in fact it wasn't champagne at all, and probably related to the bubbles on offer at *Los Jardines Neptuna,* but with the Novotel mark-up, not cheap. Gawd! This was going to cost an arm and a leg! He couldn't limit his guests to one glass each, although he was sorely tempted, so all he could do was perspire freely and smile through clenched teeth.

I arrived with the reception in full swing, or as Del would describe it, full swig. I tried a glass of bubbles, it was disgusting, so I switched to orange juice and mineral water, and shot to the top of Del's fan club.

"Good to see you, Tobes," he enthused, eyeing my glass approvingly.

"Thanks for the invite, Del." I looked round the assembled multitude. "An interesting selection of guests. I don't think I've seen so many pairs of dark glasses in one room at the same time. It looks like an 'extras' shoot from the Godfather."

"Keep your voice down," Del whispered, "they take themselves very seriously, and so should we. They're members of the five families south of the river here to keep an eye on each other as well as drinking me out of house and home."

"I shouldn't be too depressed Del. As they say in business, you have to spend money to make money. Just look at Topsy, how she's working the room and charming the birds from the trees. You're a very lucky man."

"Yeah, I know."

"And how's Crispin, the son and heir to the Finnan fortune?"

Del burst out laughing, and immediately all eyes turned on him. Why's he laughing? Who's the kid chatting to him? Are they talking about me? If so, what are they saying?

"Topsy's got his name down for Eton," replied Del, "and there's talk about another one on the way. It's getting serious Tobes."

"If anyone can handle it, you're the man Del," I said, keeping well out of the firing line as I saw Topsy bearing down on us.

"Hello Toby," she said, "good of you to come. Now," she continued, turning her big guns on Del, "if this party is to be a success, you've got to mingle, look as if you're pleased to see our guests, and even those who were never invited, don't get bogged down, two minutes max per person, leave them wanting more, and above all, keep it light."

"My thoughts exactly, love, I was just about to start circulating."

"Start now!" she snapped, "and if you need Dutch courage, take Toby with you. He's an up-and-coming young barrister, with hunger in the belly and ready to hit the ground running, so passing him round could work wonders."

"Anything to oblige," I replied, although being compared to a humus dip didn't immediately appeal. But with Topsy booted and spurred, now was not the time to rein her in, best to go with the flow.

Each Family had its own *capo dei capi,* around whom all other members of the Family congregated. They all seemed to be joined at the hip. If the *capo* took a step forward, they all took a step forward. Each *capo* had his 'Moll' draped on his arm, totally sanitized with all moving parts gleaming and in full working order. Peroxide blond was the dominant colour, and not a hair out of place. I suspected that the *capo's* good lady wife was at home, cooking up a storm of spaghetti in readiness for her man's return. Definitely go, not show, but perhaps I'd been watching too many gangster movies, and according to my mother, I was an impressionable lad.

Del and I did the rounds, with Topsy flitting here and there and plugging the gaps. Del did his best to sell me as the best thing since Marshall-Hall, which was kind of him, but barristers were at best a necessary evil and at worst to be avoided at all costs, and nobody rushed forward to introduce himself and take my details. The Family took care of their own business.

Still, as the clerks were fond of reminding me as they tossed another poorly paid brief my way, better to be seen doing something, anything, than nothing at all.

It all went horribly wrong when one of the *capo's* acolytes, a huge bloke with hairy hands, thought he'd recognised me, and had we met before?

"I don't think so," I replied cheerfully. After all, one Heavy behind a pair of dark glasses looked very much like another. "I'm a barrister, you know," I continued, puffing out my chest, "so we might have met professionally."

The wheels were spinning as Man Mountain went through the gears. "So wot's this barrister malarkey?" he asked at last.

"It's a lawyer in wig and gown. I defend criminals in court."

"Wot? You mean a brief, like Dave?" and he nodded in Del's direction.

"You mean Del?" I asked. From his expression, he didn't, and no point arguing the toss. "Yes, I suppose so," I continued, "but I tend to do the more serious work in the Crown Court."

"Wot? Like the Old Bailey?"

"Absolutely," I replied, as if it were my second home.

"I woz at the Bailey once," he said. I nodded, feigning interest. "The Boss sent me there to keep an eye on things and report back." A high-risk strategy if ever there was. "A couple of me best mates went down for something they never done. Some bloody Chink fitted them up. Bloody liberty if you ask me!"

"I think I might have been in that case," I blurted out, the orange juice and mineral water going to my head, "that wasn't the Weasel was it?"

"Who's asking?" Man Mountain looked threatening.

You could hear a pin drop as all eyes turned to me. The Weasel was strictly taboo and far too close to home.

"Dave," snapped the Capo, "leave the nice young man alone!"

"But Boss, he knows the Weasel."

"I don't give a rat's crap who he knows," replied the Boss, losing patience, "now shut the fuck up and get over here!"

Dave did as he was told, and got a clip round the ear for stepping out of line.

A sort of silent Mexican nod went round the room, as first one Family then another put down their glasses and nibbles and moved purposefully towards the exit. Before you could say Ray-Bans, more than half the assembled multitude had taken their leave and pushed off.

Topsy was not best pleased, but Del was over the moon at the thought of all the money he was saving on the refreshments.

"So what happened?" he asked.

"I mentioned the Weasel," I replied, "and that started a stampede to the exit."

"It would, it's still a raw nerve on the Manor. They all know something, but they aren't about to admit it. It's too close to home. It reminds me of the three brass monkeys." I think Del meant the three wise monkeys, but did it matter. "Hang on," he glanced over at Topsy who was beckoning furiously, "duty calls, again!" and with that, he hurried off.

I was just thinking of pushing off and calling it a day when a total stranger wandered over and struck up one of those 'pleased to meet you and what brings you here' conversations. He was about my build and height, mid-thirties, soberly dressed, with dark hair swept back from his forehead. Probably one of the capo acolytes, but I could be wrong.

After the initial pleasantries, he looked down at his glass, then up at me. "Fancy a pint?"

"My sentiments exactly."

We eventually found the bar, took a long draught of bitter and found a corner table.

"My name's Shannon, Dave Shannon." Spooky or what, everybody seemed to be called Dave, including Del. "I'm a solicitor."

My ears pricked up. Solicitors meant work, and work meant money, an irresistible combination. But steady as she goes. Give him the impression you're rushed off your feet, but as a favour you might be able to squeeze him into your busy schedule, and above all, don't look too hungry.

"So how do you know Del?" I asked.

"I've known him for a couple of years, I've not been in the area that long. I moved from Egham, too quiet for me, I wanted to be where the action was, and Del helped me find my feet. He speaks very highly of you," he added.

"The price of fame," I chuckled. "Del's a one-off, and above all, loyal to counsel, a rare breed indeed." I paused. "No offence intended."

"And none taken." He took another long draught of his drink, sizing me up, or so I thought. "I've got a case that might interest you," he said at last, "supplying ecstasy, and as it's still a Class A drug, the client's looking at five to six years." I nodded. "He hasn't a very clever defence, to say the least, but I think it's worth a run." I nodded again, adopting the advice offered by Abraham Lincoln, that it's sometimes better to remain silent and be thought a fool than to speak out and remove all doubt. "Perhaps I have a simplistic approach to crime, but if my client has a defence, it's not for me to act as judge and jury. So long as he knows what he's up against, he should plead not guilty and take his chances, or is that being too naïve?"

In a word, yes it was, but that's not what my new-found friend wanted to hear, so I shook my head and tried to look learned.

"Assuming you can fit me into your busy practice at short notice," I wish, "I'll have the papers delivered to your chambers, and arrange a conference as soon as possible. The trial is in the warned list for the next three weeks, so could be listed at short notice."

"Yes of course, I'll give it my immediate attention," I smarmed. "It's not a criticism," I continued, choosing my words with care, "but any reason for such short notice?" After all, it was usual for counsel to be briefed well in advance of the trial.

"Initially I briefed Ian Glover, perhaps you've heard of him," I nodded again, "and he told my client in no uncertain terms to plead guilty and stop wasting his time." Dave paused. "I hope I'm not treading on professional toes?"

"Not at all," I replied. "I know Glover by reputation. He has his admirers, but I'm not one of them." Dave chuckled. "He's what some in the profession call a 'sharp' practitioner. He gets results, but at a price." I paused. "So what's your client's defence, if you don't mind me asking?"

"Not at all, but a short background check might assist. The client's name is Dave Rumwell," not another Dave surely to God, this was reaching epidemic proportions, "and he's a bit of a wheeler-dealer if you follow my drift." I nodded. "If it can turn a profit, Dave will have it, and he's not too choosy how he goes about it."

"Understood."

"Anyway, some time ago Dave decided to get into Viagra, you've heard of it of course?"

"Only anecdotally," I replied, almost too quickly.

Dave smiled. "It goes without saying. Anyway, by all accounts, Viagra is being sold by the shedload, and the mark up can be considerable. It's a prescription drug, which means a visit to the doctor, a general examination which can be embarrassing, and if you want a dose, it can be as much as ten pounds a pop."

"As much as that?" I asked, trying to put distance between me and the very thought of erectile dysfunction. I had my reputation to think of.

Dave nodded. "So Dave discovered that Viagra, good, bad or downright useless, was being produced in the Far East, mainly Malaysia, at knock-up, I'm sorry, knockdown prices, especially when bought in bulk, and he could make a killing." He paused. "Another pint?" he suggested, and I duly obliged. This was thirsty work.

With glasses refilled, back to the plot.

"Anyway, it was all going swimmingly well, with Dave onto a winner, when a complaint was made by a purchaser that his dose of Viagra was firing blanks. He'd arranged a night of hot passion with a woman who was obviously not his wife, and after popping what he believed was super-strength Viagra to last him all night, he remembered floating around on Cloud Nine for a couple of hours, but no sign of movement down below."

"I can imagine."

"So the disappointed stud, wishing to remain anonymous for obvious reasons, sent the remaining three pills to his local trading standards office with his letter of complaint and Dave's contact details and demanded action, which I suspect was what Miss Right was hoping for on the night in question. It must have been a quiet day at the office, because some officious nerd saw fit to send the pills to the laboratory for analysis, and they came back as low-grade ecstasy."

"So what's his explanation?"

"He's never ordered ecstasy and has never dealt in controlled drugs."

"Fair enough, but he admits he supplied ecstasy to the complainant, even if he thought it was Viagra?"

"Yes and no. Dave's little sweat shop handles thousands of pills daily, and he has half a dozen low-grade workers stuffing envelopes to satisfy demand. I gather immigration have been sniffing round," he added, "but that's another story."

Quite so. It was time to bring this informal conference to an end. After all, this was a freebee, and freebees were to be discouraged at all costs. Perhaps Dave sensed my disquiet, as he stood up, drained the last dregs of his beer, and shook hands. "I'll get the conference sorted out early next week." He paused. "Like Del, I'm a one-man band, so I use outdoor clerks to help me from time to time." I nodded. "If you have no objection, I'll send along one of my most reliable clerks to sit in during the conference, a former police officer, so he knows the ropes. His name is Dave Farmer."

I laughed. "As I live and breathe, surely not my old chum Bootsy Farmer."

"You know him?" Dave asked.

"Bootsy and I are like blood brothers, joined at the hip. A man of strong opinions, but his heart's in the right place." If Ian Glover thought Dave should cop a plea, God knows what pearls Bootsy will be scattering around the conference room. A moment to savour.

"Thanks for taking on Rumwell as such short notice, and if you need any further information after you've read the brief, let me know."

⚊⊹⊹⚊

I arrived early on Monday morning to await the delivery of the brief. The clerks had entered me in the chambers diary as "working on papers", so it was fortuitous that I actually had some papers to work on.

Dave's background summary at Del's party was very helpful, but I had the feeling there were more questions than answers. As in many cases, the most damaging evidence came in a witness statement from the arresting Plod, DC. Dave Morton who, acting on information received, barged his way into Dave's sweat shop brandishing his search warrant and made a beeline straight to a stack of cartons behind Dave's desk. In the top carton, helpfully already opened, Dave found thousands of strips of pills all identical in size and shape to the strip sent by Super-Stud to Trading Standards. Upon analysis, surprise, surprise, the randomly selected pills contained low-grade ecstasy, with a street value of £100,000. Game, set and match if Dave were to be believed.

When arrested and interviewed later that day by Dave, Dave was adamant. He didn't deal in controlled drugs, he had no idea how they were found in his sweat shop, and besides, he wasn't there when they were found.

"So they've been planted, that's what you're saying!" Dave at his most confrontational. He rather fancied himself as the Grand Inquisitor, just like that hard man on the telly.

"It's not for me to say, officer," replied Dave, who was not easily intimidated. "After all, you're the detective, so detect."

"Don't get smart with me, Sunshine. I didn't ride into town on the head of a cabbage!"

"That's not what I heard, officer." Dave was enjoying himself. "I also heard you spell your name without a 'T'."

Dave's brow furrowed. Was this a trick question? He pondered for as long as decency would allow before deciding to move on. "So you claim you're only selling Viagra, is that right?"

"Got it in one, officer. Why, are you after a dose? Special rates for the boys in blue."

"There's nothing wrong in that department, I can assure you of that!"

"If you say so, but if you ever change your mind…."

"Take my word for it; you won't be peddling nothing for the next few years."

There were other bits and pieces in the interview, mostly a low-grade slanging match, but that was the nub of it. I decided to bone up on the law, after all, I was not just a lawyer but learned counsel, and the client would expect me to know these things.

My client had been charged with supplying a controlled drug to another contrary to section 4 (3) (a) of the Misuse of Drugs Act 1971. My trusty Archbold told me that where in any proceedings for an offence to which this section applies, it is necessary, if the accused (Dave) is to be convicted of the offence charged, for the prosecution to prove that some substance or product involved in the alleged offence was the controlled drug which the prosecution alleges it to have been, and it is proved that the substance or product in question was that controlled drug, the accused (Dave) shall not be acquitted of the offence charged by reason only of proving that he neither knew nor suspected nor had reason to suspect that the substance or product in question was the particular controlled drug alleged; but shall be acquitted thereof if he (Dave) proves that he neither believed nor suspected nor had reason to suspect the substance or product in question was a controlled drug; or if he (Dave) proves that he believed the substance or product in question was a controlled drug, or a controlled drug of a description, such that, if it had in fact been that controlled drug or a controlled drug of that description, he (Dave) would not at the material time have been committing any offence to which this section applies. You couldn't make it up if you tried.

It reminded me of one of St. Paul's interminable letters to the Corinthians, which they must have eagerly awaited with all the excitement of children on Christmas Day, when he wrote: "For now we see through a glass darkly, but then face to face; now I know in part; but then shall I know even as I am known." I could imagine them sitting around the kitchen table, poring over this latest missive, and to a man, all asking: "What does he mean?"

It also reminded me of the defence, seldom used for obvious reasons: "I wasn't there guv', but if I was, it was self-defence."

The good news was that nothing in this section shall prejudice any defence which it is open to a person charged with an offence to which this section applies to raise apart from this section. The bad news was that where a person's (Dave's) state of mind falls within section 28 (3) (b) (i) only by virtue of his self-induced intoxication, he cannot avail himself of the defence provided thereby, so tough! You get lashed at your peril!

⟫⊹⊹⟪

Dave Rumwell and Bootsy arrived promptly at four thirty for our conference. In a perverse sort of way, it was good to see Bootsy again. He was predictable and dependable, and provided a good service, even if his heart still belonged to the Met and the best bunch of lads you'd never want to meet.

Dave was a typical East End barrow boy made good. Like Winnie the Pooh, he was short, fat and proud of that, and everything about him was shiny. His well-scrubbed features were shiny, as was his suit, his hair, his watch, his gold bracelet, his tie pin and his two-tone shoes. He positively sparkled.

With some pride, Dave told me he'd worked his way up from street corner trading to white goods, then televisions and stereos, but there was too much heavy lifting, and he wasn't getting any younger.

Then came the Viagra explosion, with the Far East pumping them out in their thousands, and the mark-up was eye-watering. Buying in bulk, he reckoned he was clearing four quid a pop, and that was pure profit. After a few months of building up his contacts, mainly through online advertising, he was off and running, and couldn't spend it fast enough.

"I gather your base of operations was in Shooters Hill." Dave nodded. "Any reason?"

"I'm a born and bred East Ender, Squire," he replied, "it's where I was brought up, and it's where I feel comfortable."

"Fair enough." I paused. "Have you made any enemies recently?"

"Meaning?"

"Well, on your instructions, you've never dealt in controlled drugs, yet when the police pay you a visit, your premises are awash with low-grade ecstasy. So how do you think they got there?"

I sensed Bootsy was stiffening the sinews, rather like a strong dose of Viagra, and ready to jump to the defence of his mates at the very mention of the word 'planting'.

"Well Squire, it's obvious they've been planted. It's not rocket science."

"Any ideas?" I asked before Bootsy could put the boot in. "How about DC. Morton?"

Dave burst out laughing. "Dave Moron? You must be joking! He hasn't the sense God gave apples, and whatever else you say about him, he ain't bent!"

What a relief, as Bootsy relaxed and sank back in his chair. "I'm not aware of a forced entry," I continued, "so how secure are your premises?"

"Obviously not secure enough," replied Dave, stating the obvious.

I paused. "How about your employees? Do you trust them?"

"To be honest, I don't really know them. They come to me from an agency, they're dropped off every morning and collected every evening, I pay in cash, ask no questions, tell no lies, know what I mean?"

I did. Sounds decidedly dodgy. "So where are they now?"

"I hope they're hard at work, that's what they're paid for."

"What, business as usual?"

"Not quite. As part of the terms of my bail, I'm not allowed to go anywhere near my business premises, so I've moved operations to a temporary address." He paused. "It ain't against the law to turn an honest buck, it's called free enterprise."

There was no answer to that.

"I'm really thinking out loud here, Mr. Rumwell...."

"Call me Dave."

"Fair enough. Now as I see it, the prosecution have got this mystery man who receives a batch of low-grade ecstasy tablets when he was expecting Viagra. We've got no statement from him, and no idea who he is, as his details have not been disclosed to us."

"Yeah."

"You are identified by this anonymous man as the supplier."

"Yeah."

"Now we can't challenge the expert evidence, we have to accept that the pills analysed by the expert were what he says, low-grade ecstasy."

"Yeah."

I paused, thinking on my seat so to speak. "Do you keep a record of your customers?"

"Yeah. It's good business practice, once they've bought, we send out follow up messages, special offers, two for the price of one and all that. Repeat customers are the life-blood of any successful business. And then there's the spin offs."

"Such as?"

"Inflatable dolls, all sizes and colours, whips, handcuffs for the bondage freaks, stimulators, dildos, exotic underwear, everything the randy heart desires, great little earners."

"Well," I continued, my eyes watering, "for what it's worth, it looks like somebody's trying to fit you up. Any ideas?"

Dave thought for a moment. "There's quite a drugs trade on my patch," he said, "but it's mainly dealing in the hard stuff, such as high-grade ecstasy, coke, heroin, it's controlled by tight-knit families as they call themselves, basing themselves on the Mafia, like comic-book cartoon characters. Bloody ridiculous if you ask me."

"But what about Viagra? Any takers if you catch my drift?"

There was a long pause. "Now I come to think of it," Dave spoke slowly and deliberately, "I've had hints over the past few months, asking about my business, and would I like a partner. I told them to get lost."

"Who was 'them'?" I asked.

"They didn't say, never face to face, always over the phone, but they seemed to know a lot about me, where I lived, where I did business, that sort of thing. I didn't pay it no mind at the time."

I nodded. Time to bring Bootsy on board. "Mr. Farmer is a retired detective sergeant from the Metropolitan Police, so he's better equipped than I am to help." Bootsy puffed out his chest. "So," I continued, turning to Bootsy, "if one of these gangs wanted to close Dave down and take over his business, they'd plant a stash of low-grade drugs on Dave's premises, tip off the police, and once Dave had been royally kippered and sent down for a spell, they'd have a clear run. All they'd need is a list of Dave's customers and they'd be off and running. How does that sound?"

Bootsy was impressed. "If you ever consider a career change, Mr. Potts, the Met's the place for you, and the finest bunch of lads you'd ever want to meet." I was flattered. "And with a word from me, you're ahead of the competition by a mile."

"Hang on a minute," said Dave, bringing our love-in down to earth, "how do they get my list? Without it, they're stuffed."

Bootsy took over the reins. "It ain't rocket science Dave," he replied, "from what you've told us, I'll bet my pension your staff are illegals, they have full access to the list, they'd soon be traced, and a little gentle persuasion should do the trick. And besides," he added ominously, "how do you think the drugs got planted in the first place? After all, there was no sign of forced entry."

"Fuck me!"

"My thoughts precisely Dave," I said. "The gang will wait until you've been convicted and sentenced, and then they're in business. Sadly, *your* business."

There was a long silence as Dave absorbed the full enormity of his predicament. "So what do we do?" he asked at last.

"Well, we need to find the anonymous complainant who set this particular hare running, to see if we can track him back to the Family trying to put you away. That's got to be our starting point. First thing tomorrow I'll ask your solicitor to contact the Crown Prosecution Service and ask for their anonymous complainant's details. If they refuse, and I expect they will, we'll have to apply to the court to force their hand."

"Fair enough," replied Dave, "you seem to know what you're doing."

Faint praise, but praise nonetheless.

The conference over, I was walking from Chambers to the Embankment Underground Station when I became dimly aware of a slow moving car behind me. I glanced back at the large black Range Rover, which meant nothing to me. I walked on, and was just about to cross the road when it suddenly accelerated towards me. I jumped back, it stopped and the passenger window wound down.

"Hello Dave," grunted the occupant.

It took me a moment to place the face behind the dark glasses, and then the penny dropped. "It's Dave from Del's party. Do we meet by accident or design?"

Dave stared blankly back. "Yeh, whatever."

"Is this a chance encounter, or were you looking for me?"

"Yeah. I've got a message from the Boss. Defending Dave could seriously harm your health, so if you know what's good for you both, get him to plead guilty," and with that, the car accelerated away.

My first reaction was to shrug it off, but I didn't. Del had told me about these families south of the river, and I remembered the Weasel and his untimely fate. I didn't fancy being stabbed to death in some dark alley, especially as I was on the cusp of a glittering career. I also remembered the sudden and unexplained resignation of three police officers from the Weasel's patch, so if I lodged a complaint, what would it achieve? I decided to sleep on it, but as a precaution, I put my Walther PPK under my pillow, or I would have done if I'd had one.

The next morning I settled down in chambers to review the evidence and my notes. Then it was time to phone Dave Shannon.

"Good to hear from you, Toby. I've spoken to Dave Farmer, and the client's well pleased."

"That's good to know Dave," I replied. "Did Dave mention my suggestion that we ask the CPS for their informant's contact details?"

"He did indeed. I've already left a message for the case worker to phone me back, so I hope to hear from him anytime between now and next Christmas." We both laughed. "I like your thinking," he continued, "but I wouldn't hold your breath. You may have to make an application to the trial judge."

"Understood, please keep me informed." I paused, choosing my words carefully. "You remember at Del's party, there was a big bloke, hairy hands, who answered to the name 'Dave'?"

"Yes, he's Slasher Pike's number one heavy. As thick as two short planks, but loyal to a fault. Why do you ask?"

I explained our encounter the night before.

"That's right out of order! Leave it to me, I'll get it sorted."

"Thanks Dave, much appreciated. By the way, who's Slasher Pike, or should I ask?"

"A vicious little hoodlum who started his criminal life by slashing his victims with a cut throat razor, models himself on Pinkie Brown, you remember the book ***Brighton Rock*** by Graham Greene?"

"I do indeed."

"Even if he could read, which he can't, using the nickname 'Pinkie' in his line of work was a bridge too far, 'Pinkie' Pike doesn't exactly instil fear and respect in friend and foe alike, it sounds more like undercooked fish, so it's been Slasher since he nicked his first cut throat razor, if you'll forgive the pun!" We both laughed, although my laugh was a bit on the nervous side. "Most of these hoodlums are all piss and wind, and Slasher's no exception. They're living on borrowed time anyway, it goes with the territory."

"I can't say I feel reassured, but at least I'm better informed. I'll wait to hear from you."

As predictable as summer rain, and in the fullness of time, the CPS refused point blank to disclose the identity of their complainant, and if we wanted to take it further, we would have to make an application to the trial judge. So be it!

To help me marshal my thoughts, if for no other reason, I set out my submissions in writing, with copies to Dave Shannon, George Wetherspoon of the CPS and the court.

My application was listed at short notice before His Honour Judge David 'Not So' Cleverley, the designated trial judge, first on at ten.

Blackfriars Crown Court was another recent creation of the Lord Chancellor's department. It could be found, with difficulty, in Southwark, close to the east end, and a favourite haunt of Charles Dickens, and where many of his stories were set.

It had started life as the reincarnation of Knightsbridge Crown Court, known as 'back of Harrods' in the west end, so its connection with Southwark, a good day's ride across town, was tenuous in the extreme. Still, anything was possible in the Lord Chancellor's department.

Efforts had been made to disguise the total anonymity of the court by the addition of Greco-Roman pillars straddling the front portico but with limited success. The building achieved its primary purpose of functionality without flair, a reputation that the court staff had elevated into an art form.

Acting on my advice, Dave had told Dave there was no need to attend, so he didn't, preferring to sit in his temporary business premises watching his staff like a hawk. If there was a 'stoolie' on his team, he was determined to winkle him out. Bootsy, ever faithful and keen to offer a 'hands-on' service, came along for moral support and to keep an avuncular eye on his potential new recruit.

What I hadn't expected, and lurking at the back of the main hall, was the unmistakeable figure of Dave, Slasher's main man. His bulk and dark glasses were a dead giveaway. Quite how he knew about today's hearing was a mystery, perhaps a friendly police officer had tipped him off.

"There's a surprise," I said to Dave, nodding in Dave's direction.

Dave nodded back. "Leave it to me." He turned to Bootsy. "Dave, a word in your shell-like please," and they walked away from me and out of earshot. Two minutes' later, Bootsy set off at a determined pace towards Dave, and Dave rejoined me. We watched in silent admiration as Bootsy approached Dave, he seemed to be showing him something, could have been a warrant card, but it was difficult to tell from a distance, and after a brief but intense conversation, Dave sloped off to the main exit and out of sight. Bootsy came back, looking well pleased. Say no more!

We were called on at twenty past ten; the bail application listed in front of us went on longer than expected. 'Not So' had a reputation for being firm but fair, and not tolerating fools gladly. Sadly, Blackfriars seemed to have scooped the pot. He was in his late fifties, thinning ginger hair, or as he preferred to describe it, strawberry-blond, which was more of a difference without a distinction, and he'd been appointed long enough to have that air of resignation every time another hopeless application hit his desk. By all accounts, mine was no different.

George Wetherspoon, the reviewing CPS lawyer, had reviewed himself and had deemed himself more than equal to the task. He had experience, he was the CPS senior case officer, and he knew the judge. An irresistible combination, or so he thought. He had also enlisted DC. Morton, more in hope than expectation, to sit behind him and add gravitas. As this was my first appearance at Blackfriars, I knew neither Wetherspoon nor the judge, so as they say in the profession, I came to the task with an open mind.

"I have read the written submissions drafted by Mr. Potts for my consideration," 'Not So' opened the proceedings, "and which I have found most helpful. However," he looked up at me and smiled fleetingly, "I shall need some persuading. Mr. Wiggleswaite, I don't appear to have your written reply."

Wetherspoon, more accustomed to being addressed as Wetherspoon, was initially nonplussed, but regained his sense of importance before any lasting damage could be done. "Your Honour," he bleated in a whining plangent voice, "I considered my learned friend's submissions, but decided they did not merit the time and expense of a written reply."

"A bold statement on any view, Mr. Wetherall, as you are not only pre-empting my judgment, but you are acting as judge and jury. That is not the role of the CPS. And I should add that your failure to reply to Mr. Potts' submissions is a gross discourtesy to him and to me. *He* doesn't matter, but in this court, *I do!*"

Any other advocate would wilt in the face of judicial disapprobation, but Wetherspoon was made of sterner stuff, and besides, he was right and he knew it. In his considerable experience, judges frequently got it wrong, and this judge was no exception. The good news from my point of view was that I had the judge's sympathy, but there was a long way to go.

"Now Mr. Potts," 'Not So' turned to me, "doing the best we can without Mr. Whimsical's input, your defence is planting, is it not?"

"Your Honour has it in one," I replied, ladling it on, "and I submit that the defendant cannot receive a fair trial, even with Your Honour's firm hand on the judicial tiller, unless the identity of the so-called complainant is disclosed."

"Why not? According to my reading of the papers, police officers acting on a tip-off, no doubt originating from your mystery complainant, found thousands of identical low-grade ecstasy pills in premises operated and controlled by the defendant."

"That's correct, Your Honour."

"So Mr. Walthamstowe, had he bothered to reply to your submissions, might well have submitted on behalf of the Crown that section 28 of the Misuse of Drugs Act 1971 applies. Am I right Mr. Williamson?"

Wetherspoon, reeling from the succession of misnomers raining down on him, was not about to abandon the uneven struggle. "Your Honour is quite right," he replied. Wrong answer as it turned out, as Wetherspoon and section 28 were like ships in the night. Besides, it was Counsel's job to sort the wheat from the chaff, so why buy a dog and bark yourself? Too late for regrets.

"How so, Mr. Wetherspoon?"

Wetherspoon stood there, gaping like a fish out of water, stunned in part by 'Not So' actually getting his name right at the fifth attempt, and in part by the fact that he hadn't the faintest idea what he was talking about. For my part, I felt a certain frisson of apprehension as I had read the relevant section and understood very little.

"I wonder if Your Honour would give me a few minutes, as there are matters I need to address."

"You submit that Mr. Potts and I should hang around, twiddling our thumbs, whilst you bone up on the law, a task you should have undertaken well before this application was listed. Request refused. Now where does that leave you?"

Hung out to dry, I thought uncharitably.

"Er....Your Honour."

"Yes, I thought so. It's all about the chain of continuity, or it was when I was at the Bar. You have chosen to charge the defendant under section 4 (3) (a) with supplying the mystery complainant with low-grade ecstasy, and you seek to prove the defendant's guilt by showing that the self-same ecstasy is identical to the ecstasy found on the defendant's premises. Do you agree with my analysis Mr. Potts?"

"I do Your Honour."

"Splendid. But where the mystery complainant is not being called as a witness for the prosecution, all you have, Mr. Wolverine, is evidence that the pills analysed by the expert were low-grade ecstasy identical to the low-grade ecstasy found in the defendant's possession, and identical to thousands of other low-grade ecstasy pills washing around the metropolis. Without the mystery complainant's evidence, there is nothing to link the supply of these drugs with the defendant, and I suspect this is the real gravamen of Mr. Potts' submissions, written or otherwise. Am I right Mr. Potts?"

"Er....Your Honour." It was my turn to be completely wrong-footed, and to make matters worse, played out in front of my solicitor and new-found chum. What a nightmare!

"If the defendant had been charged with possession with intent to supply contrary to section 5 (3) of the Act, different considerations would apply, but he hasn't, and there's an end to it. Now I have a jury waiting, and we are already fifteen minutes' late. Good day gentlemen," and so speaking, 'Not So' rose and left the Bench.

We retired to the court cafeteria to take stock of the situation. To my surprise, Dave and Bootsy were very supportive, and were well pleased with the outcome. Thank God they knew even less about the Misuse of Drugs Act than I did. We agreed to give it to the end of the week and then make tentative inquiries of the CPS.

The best-laid plans and all that, as 'Not So's' trial went short, and our trial was listed the next day, with 'Not So' presiding.

This time Wetherspoon had seen the error of his ways and had instructed John McVitie, experienced counsel, to represent the prosecution.

McVitie and I met in the robing room. We had never met before, so I had no idea what to expect. Upon initial acquaintance, he seemed like a self-important pain in the arse.

Our opening exchanges didn't bode well for an early lunch, as I was soon to find out.

"I assume the CPS have brought you up to speed on yesterday's application?" I asked tentatively.

"I have my instructions, if that's what you mean," he replied rather grandly.

"And they are?"

"None of your business," he snapped. "You seem very young," he sneered, "is this your first jury trial?"

"No it is not!" The cheek of the man!

McVitie gave me a condescending look. "So be it. I can assist you to this extent. There will be a trial, I shall adduce the evidence, and the defendant will be convicted. Does that help?" and so saying, he swept out. Pompous jackass!

Dave had left Dave and me in Bootsy's capable hands. As we assembled in court, there was no sign of Slasher's Dave, but two unknowns in the public gallery who looked suspiciously like plainclothes police officers. I whispered to Bootsy, who turned round slowly and deliberately and stared at them. They shifted uncomfortably in their seats. Time to flush out the vermin.

We all rose as 'Not So' came into court and flopped down in the seat of judgment. I remained standing.

"Mr. Potts? We meet again."

"Your Honour, with your leave, I mention the presence of two gentlemen in the public gallery. In the normal course of events, their presence would be of no concern either to me or to the court. However, in the very recent past I have been threatened by criminal elements in the event that the defendant is acquitted, and I would seek reassurance that these two gentlemen are not party to those threats."

The two 'gentlemen' immediately got to their feet and moved quickly towards the exit, but not quickly enough.

"Stay where you are!" barked 'Not So'. "Usher, I want these men arrested and questioned here at court with a full report to me. Now!"

We sat and waited for the arrival of three police officers, who cuffed and removed the men from the public gallery.

'Not So' addressed both of us. "Now gentlemen, I see no reason why we cannot proceed. Mr. McTavish, you have an application?"

"I do, Your Honour?" McVitie was taken by surprise.

For the next ten minutes, 'Not So' went through the prosecution case in much the same way as he had done the day before. I loved every minute of it, although I couldn't claim any credit, except perhaps for having started the ball rolling.

McVitie wasn't going down without a fight, and with Wetherspoon's eyes and ears sitting behind him, in the form of our Brenda, this was no time to falter under fire.

"In the light of Your Honour's helpful observations," he countered irritably, "I ask for leave to amend the indictment to possession with intent to supply."

'Not So' was not amused. "Do you indeed? Mr. Potts, any objections?"

"I do indeed, Your Honour...."

"Quite so. Application refused. Where does that leave you Mr. McGregor?"

"Your Honour, it leaves me offering no evidence," he replied with an air of resignation.

"Sense at last. I shall enter a formal verdict of not guilty." 'No So' looked over to the dock. "Mr. Rumwell, you are free to go. I shall rise to await the report I have ordered. Both Counsel are to remain until released," and so saying, he left court.

Dave was duly grateful, although he hadn't followed much of the proceedings. All he knew was that he'd been fitted up by person or persons unknown, and he wanted to know why. Thanks to Dave's crude attempt at intimidation, all fingers pointed to Slasher, but as yet, not enough to go on.

Two hours' later, we were summoned back into court. 'Not So' entered at a pace and sat down. He addressed me.

"Mr. Watts, you were right to bring the presence of the two men in the public gallery to my attention. I have read the preliminary report of the court Inspector, who is here at my request, and will correct me if I am wrong." The Inspector smiled deferentially. "It seems that the two men are serving police officers stationed at Woolwich Police Station which covers Shooters Hill. They have provided the Inspector with their names, rank and number, but have otherwise declined to answer any questions or explain what they are doing here. Inquiries with the Station Inspector cannot assist, save only to tell me there is no operational reason that requires their attendance at this trial. It is troubling indeed, and from what I have learned, this whole business has a nasty smell to it. In the circumstances, I shall remand them in custody until tomorrow morning, and in the meantime, I shall expect further inquiries to be made. I assume you are willing to assist the Inspector?"

"I am indeed, Your Honour."

"Excellent, I expected no less. I shall rise."

Looking back, if I had to pick a moment when Slasher's grubby little empire began to crumble, it was that day at Blackfriars. As DC. Dave Morton would put it, acting on information received, the police raided one of Slasher's lockups off Shooters Hill and found thousands of low-grade ecstasy pills identical to the ones found on Dave's premises. To rub salt into the wound, three of Dave's 'illegals' were also present, as was 'Hairy Hands' Dave. Dave, loyal to a fault, had nothing to say after he was arrested, but the three illegals jabbered away as if their lives depended on it, or certainly their work permits. With their help, a further four lockups were raided revealing a smack head's paradise.

Thereafter, it was the dominoes effect, and it wasn't long before Plod had enough evidence to arrest and charge Slasher with possession of Class 'A' drugs with intent to supply. Beaten but unbowed, Wetherspoon had finally seen the light and, as always, was more than happy to take the credit.

There was no direct evidence linking the two off-duty police officers arrested at Blackfriars with Slasher, but there was a wealth of circumstantial evidence, and that was enough for their station commander to offer them Hobson's choice: leave or be damned.

They left, and with Slasher's star in the descendent, they accepted low-grade employment with a twilight security firm.

As for Bootsy, he was the hero of the hour, at least in my book. I had learned from Del early on in our professional relationship that Bootsy fancied himself as a bit of a wine buff, most unlikely, but who was I to judge? So to show my appreciation, I bought him a mixed case of wines, not cheap but just within my budget, and it was as if I had given him the keys to the kingdom. A friend for life!

CHAPTER 13

THE PRODIGAL SON

I had heard nothing back from Dave Shannon after Dave's formal acquittal, which was worrying but not unusual. It was an adage at the Bar that a case won is a brief lost, no rhyme or reason to it, and nothing tangible to explain the crashing silence. As the expression goes, you're only as good as your next brief, so past triumphs counted for little.

In the meantime, there were bills to pay, so the low-grade daily fare was welcome nonetheless, even if it was not exactly intellectually challenging. Bail applications, mentions and the occasional plea in mitigation kept the wolf from the door, but did little to raise my spirits.

After a week of marking time, I was presented with a chambers 'return', nothing special as Mike my clerk had to admit, but it was a jury trial, and at least I would be back on my feet again. In his skewed way of thinking, being seen was all part of keeping my name in the frame, but I had my doubts about being seen peddling complete crap. It was not the reputation I was hoping to cultivate. The icing on the cake, as Mike described it with genuine enthusiasm, was that the trial was listed at Snaresbrook, my old hunting ground before the Anstruther-Browne bust up with the CPS.

'Returns' were a way of life in the profession, especially at the bottom of the feeding chain. Solicitors would send in a brief to their favoured Counsel, knowing that if he or she were detailed elsewhere, the clerks would 'return' it to a suitable replacement within chambers. In the case of the Crown against Rob Roy, I was that suitable replacement. What a thrill!

It had been several weeks since that last outing at Snaresbrook and my spat with the odious Newman, now banished to Yorkshire under the watchful eye of His Honour Judge 'Branston' Pickles. My prosecution practice, such as it was, ended there and then, but I was surprised how quickly my defence practice dried up.

The feedback in the clerks' room suggested that defence solicitors needed to keep the CPS onside during the trial process and, most important of all, to plea bargain and get a reduction in the charge and sentence. As I was *persona non grata* in the eyes of the CPS, any involvement by me in the plea bargaining process was bound to be counter-productive, so I was all but frozen out. Fortunately for Rob, his solicitor was a new kid on the block who, surprisingly, had not yet heard of my reputation for fearless advocacy and my adversarial skills. My colleague's loss was Rob's gain.

The tippex on the backsheet had not totally obliterated my colleague's name. He was below me in juniority, so it irked me that he was too busy to accept the brief. That should be me, picking and choosing my way to fame and fortune, instead of pecking at the crumbs from the clerks' table.

Time to acquaint myself with Rob as I opened the brief. I assumed Rob Roy was Scottish, hairy knees and no knickers and all that, and a'prancing and a'dancing and a'reeling to the strains of Och Aye the Noo and the bonny bonny banks of Loch Lomond, but then, I could be wrong. Best to reserve judgment until I had met the ghastly scrote.

My well-crumpled instructions told me that Rob had been arrested and charged with burglary. In common parlance, he had been caught red-handed, or in even more common parlance, bang to rights. He had been seen leaving premises just off Leytonstone High Street in the early hours of the morning, carrying a bag laden with silver which, as it transpired, did not belong to him but to the owner of the premises. He was a silversmith by trade. The only thing missing to complete Rob's misery was SWAG written in large letters on the bag.

The brief contained a short witness statement from the owner and an equally short witness statement from the arresting officer. Rob was offered an interview at the police station, but as the evidence was overwhelming, there seemed little point.

My instructions began and ended with the cryptic statement: "Counsel is instructed to take instructions from the client in conference, to represent him at trial and mitigate prior to sentence." Was he trying to tell me something?

I arrived early at court, ready for the conference, as I needed to take a proof of evidence from Rob, together with his comments on the prosecution case. Time was of the essence, as the trial was listed at ten, court to be allocated. Above all, I needed to know his defence, if defence there was. As the case had been listed for trial, I assumed there was something to be tried, other than judicial patience.

I hoped for Rob's sake that he didn't draw His Honour Judge 'Bonkers' Clarke as the trial judge. 'Bonkers' was the resident judge, so very much king of all he surveyed, and a man known for speaking his mind. I remembered him well, it was my first jury trial, prosecuting no less in happier times, when Noel Cantwell and I appeared before him in the case of Dwayne Peddler. 'Bonkers' gave Cantwell a right earful about wasting court time in an open and shut case of shoplifting. Cantwell, a seasoned performer, was having none of it, so he stuck to his instructions, and his client was gloriously acquitted within twelve minutes of the jury retiring. It was explained to me at the time that no Snaresbrook jury would convict on any offence of dishonesty, regardless of the weight of evidence. It was against their better nature, and besides, when they weren't sitting on juries, they were all out thieving with the best of them. As far as Rob Roy was concerned, it was his ace in the hole, as he had little else to go on.

As I left chambers on Friday night, I had a clear recollection of asking Paul, the chambers gopher, to ensure that my client and his solicitor met me at court no later than nine. I therefore presented myself, wigged and gowned, just inside the main doors, promptly at nine, waiting to meet and greet and put flesh on the non-existent bones of Rob's defence. I was still there at nine thirty, and again at ten, when at last I saw two likely-looking candidates strolling up the drive without a care in the world.

First there were the introductions. Rob was a sullen brain-dead moron with his mouth snapped permanently open and displaying uneven yellow teeth. He was just twenty, I knew that from the copy of his custody record helpfully enclosed with the brief, and was coping badly with persistent acne. That was evident for all to see. His appearance was depressing. He had long greasy dark hair, and everything about him looked grubby. He reminded me of the contents of a handkerchief after a really heavy cold.

His companion identified himself as my solicitor's outdoor clerk, although from his pallid complexion, he seldom ventured outdoors. He was much the same age as Rob, I didn't catch his name, and did it matter, and it transpired he was doing work experience in preparation for a legal career. Think again Matey! He was under strict instructions to take a careful note and not to make any decisions without prior authority from HQ. Those instructions included me. I was beginning to wish I was still in chambers, "working on papers".

I found a conference room and had just sat down when the tannoy rang out: "All parties with cases listed for trial to attend Court One immediately". This was the Monday morning routine adopted by Bonkers to ensure that court time, *his* court time, was being used to maximum effect. We did as we were commanded.

Twenty minutes' later, twenty minutes that could have been better employed in conference, my case was called on. Rob was directed to surrender to the dock officer. The court clerk rose: "Are you Robert Roy?"

"Oo wants to know?" he snapped.

Oh my God, going down without a shot being fired. I was tempted to leave him to fend for himself, but in front of Bonkers, that would have been a fate worse than death, so I rose from the end of Counsel's Bench where we were all jostling for space.

"Your Honour," I interposed just as Bonkers was about to pounce, "I represent this defendant. I am sure his somewhat flippant remark arose from the gravity of the occasion and understandable nervousness. He meant no disrespect."

"Ah, Mr. Potts," the afterglow of calling the Queen's solicitor as a character witness had not yet faded from his memory, "we meet again. So what is going on?"

"For reasons which the defendant has yet to explain to me, he arrived at ten for a nine o'clock conference, and other than the briefest of introductions, I know very little about his case. It was a late return to me on Friday night."

"I wholly deplore late returns. I have reminded solicitors time and time again that when a case is called on in *my* court, counsel must be fully briefed and ready to proceed. Through no fault of yours, you are not." He paused as he studied the court list. "I shall list your case before Mr. Recorder Longbottom, not before eleven, by which time I expect you to be fully briefed. If not, the case must be returned to me for a full explanation."

The name Longbottom didn't ring a bell with me, and let's face it, it's not the sort of name easily forgotten. I wondered aloud if he boasted a soubriquet, and if so, what it could be.

Bonkers glared at Rob. "Stand up! You are remanded to the precincts of the court until further notice. This means you cannot leave the building unless and until I say so. Is that clearly understood?"

"Yeah, but what about me roll-ups? Oo's gonna buy 'em for me if I can't leave the building? I'm down to me last three, and it's against me 'uman rights to be deprived of me smokes."

Bonkers was about to erupt as I intervened yet again. "I will explain Your Honour's orders to the defendant as soon as Your Honour releases him from your court."

"Very well, Mr. Potts, and tell your client he'll be remanded in custody if I hear any more of this nonsense."

We sloped out and back to our conference room.

"E's a grumpy old sod is that judge," was Rob's opening remark which I chose to ignore.

"I suggest we concentrate on the evidence, as you're looking at a spell of youth custody if convicted."

"Yeah, whatever, been there, done that, so no big deal."

Totally charmless, but at least I'd be spared the wailing and gnashing of teeth if the jury broke ranks and Rob got his just deserts.

"So Rob," Whatshisname chipped in, "Toby here needs to know what you say about the charge of burglary, don't you Toby," he smiled encouragingly at both of us, "and then he can put your defence in front of the jury."

I winced at the note of familiarity, but talking to the defendant as if he were a brain-dead moron hit the spot. I smiled encouragingly back.

"Absolutely, so let's make a start."

"Yeah, whatever."

"So what were you doing on the flat roof of the burgled premises?"

Rob perked up. This was his moment on centre stage.

"Yeah, I'm glad you asked," I groaned inwardly, "'cos I've got a cast-iron defence. Yer see, I'm a thinker, a bit like that bloke Rodin, only I like to do me thinking when walking the streets late at night, it clears me 'ead, unlike Rodin, who likes to do 'is thinking sitting on a rock stark-bollocks naked. Mark you," he added for good measure, "I've been known to do me thinking stark-bollocks naked sitting on the thunder-box, but I don't suppose it's the same thing."

"No, I don't suppose it is," I replied, doing my best to keep a straight face, "but Rodin was the name of the sculptor, his thinker was unnamed."

"Yeah, whatever," Rob grunted, "Yer learn something every day. It's worth thinking abart."

Talking about unnamed, time for Hoojamaflip to make another valuable contribution. "This is most interesting, Rob, isn't it Toby?" and he beamed indulgently. I was in the conference from Hell, with no obvious means of escape and a rising sense of nausea, and I was being spoken to as if I were in the Second Grade. All I could do was go along with this gibberish as politely as possible. After all, as the clerks kept reminding me, a brief was a brief.

"It is indeed," I beamed back with a rictus grin, "but we interrupted your helpful account. Please continue."

Rob's brow furrowed. He was thinking.

"Yeah, right, so I was walking along, thinking and minding me own business, when I woz disturbed by a noise coming from above."

Good Lord, I thought, divine intervention!

"And what was the noise, Rob?" asked Thingamajig.

I was on the edge of my seat with excitement.

"I saw a coupla blokes up on the flat roof next to the silversmith's, coming out of his first floor window and carrying a bag." He paused for dramatic effect. "It looked right dodgy if yer know what I mean."

"I do."

"Yer do wot?"

"I know what you mean," I replied, "so what happened next?" I asked, trying to keep the narrative flowing.

"Yeah, I'm comin' to that." He paused. "Now where woz I?"

I was about to snap, but Howsyourfather came to my rescue.

"I think what Toby wants to know Rob is what happened after you saw the two blokes on the flat roof with a bag? Am I right Toby, as I don't want to speak out of turn?"

Too late for that, as I gave him another of my rictus smiles.

"Right," said Rob as the penny dropped, "got yer!" Another long pause.

"So what's the answer?" I asked at last.

"The answer to what?"

Patience, Toby, patience. "What happened when you saw the two blokes on the roof?" I addressed the brain-dead moron as if I were addressing Johnnie Foreigner, slowly and loudly.

"Well, I reckon they must've seen me at the same time, know what I mean?" Lift off.

"Yes. And.........?"

"They dropped outa sight over the back, and that's the last I saw of 'em."

"Right. So what happened next?"

Another long pause to allow Rob's brain to catch up with his mouth. A fruitless pursuit as it transpired.

"So I'm on the 'orns of a dilemma." I nodded encouragingly. "Do I walk away, or do I do summat abart it, like any law-abiding citizen? Know what I mean?"

"So what did you do?"

"I shinned up the drainpipe to the flat roof, opened the bag wot the two blokes 'ad left, and knock me down with a feather, it was full of silver!"

"Well there's a surprise! So what did you do?" I hurried him on.

"What any law-abiding citizen would do, Guv. I found a length of rope to lower the bag to the ground." I nodded, wondering how a length of rope came immediately to hand on a flat roof in the dead of night. "I was gonna take it round to the Pigsty, but next thing I knew, a squad car came tearing up the road, and before you could say 'filth', I was being cuffed and nicked. So much for being a law-abiding citizen. Instead of a medal and tea and cakes with the Chief Constable, I'm charged with burglary! Fucking liberty if you ask me!"

Well, there you have it members of the jury, I muttered under my breath, believe that and you'll believe anything! The bad news for Rodin was that when he put his law-abiding citizen defence as evidence of good character, his four previous convictions for burglary would be disclosed to the jury, very much the icing on the prosecution cake. Not even the CPS could cock that up, or could they? Come back Newman from Yorkshire, your country needs you.

There was nothing more to be said. I left Hoojamaflip to deal with the formalities as I went in search of my opponent. I found him outside Longbottom's court in earnest conversation with our Tracey, the CPS representative for the day.

It was none other than Giles Pertwee, who prosecuted me at the Bailey in front of Old Sourpuss in the case of Taffy Williams. I recalled he was the darling of Chelmsford Crown Court, who had been seconded to the CPS at the Bailey as a last resort and was somewhat out of his depth. He was obviously a peripatetic prosecutor, have brief will travel.

He greeted me civilly enough, although, like me, I suspected he wished he were somewhere else.

"Bit off your patch," I quipped, "I don't recall seeing you here before."

"You haven't. This is my first time, but as my clerks are fond of saying, go where the work is, and today it's Snaresbrook. What a dump." I nodded sympathetically.

"So, is this to be a trial?" he asked, more in hope than expectation.

"Absolutely," I replied, trying to sound positive, "the defendant has a complete answer to the charge, and is confident of a glorious acquittal."

"As somebody once said, and it wasn't me, hope springs eternal."

"Quite so. Know anything about the judge?"

"Not a thing. He must be from a different circuit, as I've never heard of him."

"Back to the plot," I said, "you can read the loser's statement, as I have no questions to ask him."

"Just as well, as he's not been warned to attend."

"Fair enough. I've got a few obvious questions of the arresting officer," Pertwee nodded, "then the defendant to give evidence, speeches and summing up, job done."

"Agreed. Shall we go in?" He paused. "Where's your client?"

I looked across the hall. "Over there, he's the one with the unfortunate complexion."

"I thought so. I spotted him earlier," replied Pertwee with a straight face.

We entered court, introduced ourselves to the staff, and Rob took his place in the dock, where he immediately struck a Rodin pose. Cue for the Recorder to enter, stage right.

Longbotttom was tall, slim and almost angular. I guessed he was in his early forties, and with his eye on the long game, he looked deadly serious. With journeyman barristers going nowhere fast, a judicial appointment was the only way forward. He took his seat, and looking deadly serious, addressed Counsel's Bench.

"Gentlemen, are we ready to proceed?"

We rose as one. "We are Your Honour."

"Then kindly empanel the jury." He smiled at the court usher, it was in the judicial handbook to do so, and many an aspiring judge had fallen by the wayside for want of a smile. Aspiring judges who don't get on with the court staff are doomed to failure.

The court usher, who in real life was Denise from the back office, left court with a reverential bow and returned some three minutes later, having metamorphosed into the jury bailiff in one seamless transformation.

The court clerk, who in real life was Brenda from the back office, rose with her crib sheet firmly to hand, and addressed Rob, who was deep in thought.

"Robert Roy," Rob, shaken from his reverie, looked up, "the names I am about to call are the jurors who will try you. If you object to any, you should make your objection known before they come to the book to be sworn, and your objection shall be heard. Do you understand?"

"Yeah, whatever."

Eloquently put. I turned to Hoojamaflip, knowing the answer to my question before I asked it. "Have you advised the client on his right of challenge?" I whispered.

"No," he whispered back.

"Why not?"

"I forgot. Sorry."

No point crying over spilt milk as I rose and made my way to the dock. I explained as best I could in a stage whisper as the court clerk waited.

"Yeah, whatever," grunted Rob, and I resumed my seat.

The first two jurors were empanelled without incident, but number three hit the buffers.

"I object," said Rob in a loud clear voice.

This took Longbottom by surprise, as challenges to jurors had to be for a good reason and were therefore a rare event. Challenges on a whim had long since been abolished.

"Why do you object to this prospective juror?"

"Cos ee's deaf, it's plain to see."

Indeed it was, as he was wired for sound and his hearing aid was emitting a low yet audible humming.

"Mr. Potts," I rose, "I would have thought that as the prospective juror has a hearing aid, his hearing is sufficiently enhanced to follow the proceedings. Do you agree?"

"At first blush I agree Your Honour, but perhaps with an abundance of caution…."

"Wait one," he interrupted, as he plunged into his idiot's guide to the criminal law and procedure. Four minutes' later, he looked up.

"Mr. Pertwee, can you help? I am reluctant to draw attention to a prospective juror's disability unless absolutely necessary."

"Quite so, Your Honour, but I agree with my learned friend. Perhaps a discreet enquiry?"

"Very well. I shall ask." Longbottom looked over at the juror. "Mr. Preston?"

There was no response. Mr. Preston had tired of standing whilst his hearing was being picked over, and seeing the other two jurors sitting down, had followed suit, and was now gazing vacantly around the court.

"Jury bailiff," Longbottom decided to try another tack, as progress was painfully slow. He nodded at the vacant Preston. "Please attract his attention."

The jury bailiff did as she was bidden, and Preston looked over to Longbottom.

"Mr. Preston," Preston ignored him. Longbottom addressed us both. "Gentlemen, this is most disturbing. The prospective juror fails to respond to me, so I find as a fact that he is either mute of malice or mute by visitation of God."

Pertwee and I exchanged glances. This was becoming ridiculous. Fortunately, common sense prevailed in the form of the juror sitting next to Preston.

"Oi, Mate," he said, giving Preston a dig in the ribs, "the judge's talking to you."

Preston, cupping his hand to his ear, smiled. "You'll have to speak up, I'm afraid, I'm a bit hard of hearing."

First blood to Rob, although there was a long way to go. Emboldened by his success, he was keen to push his luck. Number Five stepped up to the plate, ready to swing, and gave Rob a nod and a wink. What mischief was afoot, I wondered?

Pertwee had seen this display of familiarity, and was on his feet in a trice.

"Your Honour, before this juror takes the oath, does he know the defendant?"

"Yeah," replied the juror, "Robbie and I go way back."

Longbottom was nonplussed. "What's going on, Mr. Potts? Is this true?"

"If Your Honour will give me a moment." I looked at Thingama-jig. "Go and ask him."

There followed a muttered conversation, duly reported back to me.

"Your Honour, Robbie, I'm sorry, I mean the defendant and this juror do indeed know each other."

"So why didn't the defendant challenge him?" he snapped.

"He is under no obligation to do so. The court clerk's instructions made no mention of challenging a juror who is known to him."

"That's preposterous. Mr. Pertwee?"

"Strictly speaking my learned friend is quite right, Your Honour," replied Pertwee.

"Well, I'm not having a juror sitting on the jury who knows the defendant. It can't be right."

"In the circumstances, perhaps I should apply to stand this ju-ror by?"

"An excellent idea." He looked over to Robbie's friend. "Please leave the jury box and remain at the back of the court in case we need you."

Number Six was a delightful girl, blonde, easy on the eye, with a winning smile.

"Objection."

"And the reason? The defendant must have a good reason."

I turned round to look at Rob. "What's the reason?"

"She looks like a girl I screwed several times, great lay, but we split up when I moved on, and she woz gutted."

I couldn't exactly see the two of them in a hot and passionnate embrace, but there's no accounting for taste.

"Can you help, young lady?" asked Longbottom. "I don't know if you heard the objection?"

"I did," she replied, "and the very thought makes me physically sick. It's disgusting!"

I had to agree, but Longbottom needed guidance and reassurance. "Mr. Potts, I am being asked where the truth lies, and I don't consider this to be my function." Clumsily worded, but I caught the drift. Time to be pompous.

"Your Honour, in a normal situation where a juror is challenged for cause, if Your Honour is satisfied that the challenge is without merit, the juror is duly empanelled and the trial proceeds. However," I paused for maximum effect, "this prospective juror has not only denied carnal knowledge of the defendant, indeed any knowledge of him at all, but her denial was couched in such terms as to suggest that she had already formed a view about him, and this leaves the defendant wondering aloud if he is going to get a fair trial." Brilliantly put, though I say it myself.

"Mr. Pertwee, do you have anything to add?"

Pertwee, the quintessential company man, turned round to Tracey. "Anything to add?" he asked.

Tracey coloured visibly and gawped back. Her remit was to take a careful note, ensure that Counsel takes no decisions without referring the matter to the reviewing lawyer, and to refer everything back to the reviewing lawyer. This included any matter on which she was being invited to 'take a view' which was expressly forbidden.

"I think I should refer the matter to our Mr. Balscott," she replied helpfully.

"Excellent idea." He turned back to Longbottom. "If Your Honour will give me a few minutes to take instructions."

"But I thought that was what you were doing."

"As Your Honour will appreciate, there is a chain of command with the CPS. No disrespect intended, but the CPS representative sitting behind me is like the organ grinder's monkey."

Whilst disrespect may not have been intended, our Tracey was not best pleased. She had been called a lot of things in her time, but never the organ grinder's monkey. She began to scribble furiously on "Counsel's Evaluation Form."

"Yes, yes," replied Longbottom, "I realise there is indeed a chain of command, but for relatively minor matters requiring nothing more than basic common sense, surely you can 'take a view'?"

Pertwee was getting fed up. "If, as Your Honour says, this is a relatively minor matter, I am not sure why you need my input at all," he snapped back.

"Mr. Pertwee, show some respect if you please."

"Of course Your Honour, no disrespect intended," he lied.

"Very well." He turned to the totally bemused jury, sworn or otherwise. "Members of the jury, we will take a short five minute break."

Nothing happens in five minutes at Snaresbrook, or at any court in the land, so fifteen minutes' later, we all shuffled back and Longbottom entered at a brisk pace and with that deadly serious expression of his. He had been trying to phone Bonkers for advice, but Bonkers was in mid tirade. By the time he'd risen to deal with this unacceptable interruption, Longbottom had put the phone down and returned to court. Not a good move, and as far as Bonkers was concerned, these jumped-up recorders were a waste of space.

"Now Mr. Pertwee, as I was saying, do you have anything to add?"

"Sadly no, Your Honour. Rather like Elvis, we know that the reviewing lawyer is in the building, but his exact whereabouts are unknown. Despite our best combined efforts," and he smiled ingratiatingly at Tracey, too little too late, "it is as if he had never been."

I chuckled.

Longbottom may have been down, but not out. "So what do you suggest?"

Pertwee let out a long sigh. "It seems Your Honour has two options. To rise again whilst Tracey and her cohorts of Munchkins dart hither and thither in search of the elusive Mr. Balscott, or to deal with my learned friend's application on the information available and get on with the trial."

Tracey was scribbling again. To be described first as the organ grinder's monkey, and now as one of the Munchkins, was a bridge too far. She'd seen The Wizard of Oz several times, and had a clear picture of the Munchkins as small poisonous dwarfs with high-pitched voices and a malevolent disposition.

"To put it bluntly, Mr. Pertwee, I find myself between a rock and a hard place. If I rise for a further search to be carried out, who knows how long that might take, and I am conscious of the fact that more than an hour has elapsed and we have made very little progress. Notwithstanding, if I rule on Mr. Potts' application without being in possession of the full facts, the Court of Appeal may have something to say on the matter." All Recorders were terrified of the Court of Appeal. It was the kiss of death.

"I understand Your Honour's concerns, but the Court of Appeal will only have something to say on the matter if you rule against my learned friend's application. That, it seems to me, is axiomatic."

I could tell from Longbottom's expression that Pertwee had thrown him a lifeline. Progress at last perhaps?

"Mr. Potts, do you have anything to add?"

I deliberately avoided eye contact with Pertwee in case I lost all self-control. "No thank you, Your Honour," I replied, struggling to retain my composure.

"Thank you gentlemen, I shall now rule on Mr. Potts' application. I have considered his submissions with due diligence, and I find there is a remote possibility, given the prospective juror's comments, that she may be unwittingly prejudiced against the defendant. I therefore propose discharging her from further attendance at this court." He looked at the court clerk.

"Will Ms. Felicity Horton please stand up?" she intoned.

Nobody stood up. Surely not another mute of malice or visitation of God.

"No reply Your Honour."

"Jury bailiff, can you help?"

"When Your Honour rose, the juror was visibly distressed and left court to be sick. That was the last I saw of her."

"Mr. Pertwee?"

Pertwee was getting brassed off. "Perhaps the missing juror can be tannoyed Your Honour."

"Good idea."

We waited patiently for the next five minutes, but no response.

"Gentlemen," said Longbottom, "I need your advice. It appears that Ms. Horton has deliberately absented herself without permission, and that being so, I must hold her in contempt. What are my powers?"

The man was an idiot. Just as one hole got filled, he was digging another. I looked over to Pertwee, who had a glazed expression.

"Contempt of court Your Honour," he began, speaking slowly and deliberately, "is a common law offence which carries imprisonment or a fine or both. However, I urge caution until all the facts are known. After all, the distressed Ms. Horton may be within the precincts of the court and lying down in a darkened room, recovering her composure. I suspect the Court of Appeal may have something to say on the matter if any subject of Her Majesty the Queen is unlawfully deprived of their liberty."

That should put him back in his cage, but Longbottom had a determined streak borne, I suspected, of a lifetime of digging holes, falling into them, struggling to get out of them, and learning absolutely nothing from the experience.

"We need to get on, Mr. Pertwee, if we are to make progress. How long do your propose that we wait?"

"As long as it takes, Your Honour." Not helpful in the circumstances.

Longbottom contemplated his next move. "Can you not stand Ms. Horton by, Mr. Pertwee?" he asked, more in hope than expectation.

"In a word, no. The rules do not permit it. If and when she is found, and if it is still Your Honour's intention to discharge her, she must be present. It's called transparent justice. In addition, if Your Honour is considering contempt proceedings against her, she is entitled to legal representation."

"This is most vexing, Mr. Pertwee."

"It is indeed, Your Honour."

There was a long pause. Finally, Longbottom looked over to me. "You've been very quiet, Mr. Potts. Anything to add?"

"I agree with my learned friend," I replied, "and no, I have nothing to add."

Pertwee was busy thumbing through Archbold in search of inspiration. Not wishing to feel left out, I did the same, and so did Longbottom. That left the jury, or what remained of it, twiddling their thumbs.

After what seemed like an eternity, Pertwee stood up. His Eureka moment perhaps. "I may have a possible solution to the dilemma," he began cautiously. "Is Your Honour familiar with the case of the Mayor and Aldermen of Carmarthen against Evans, decided in 1842?"

"Absolutely Mr. Pertwee, my favourite bedtime reading!"

Good Heavens, I thought, he *does* have a sense of humour.

"Touché Your Honour," replied Pertwee smiling, "but if my learned friend were minded to challenge to the array, and Your Honour were persuaded by his able and incisive submissions, Your Honour could discharge the entire jury panel, whether sworn or not, and start afresh. Those who have already been discharged or stood by can be thrown back into the melting pot, and a fresh panel sworn."

"An excellent idea," Longbottom was almost exultant. "Do you agree, Mr. Potts?"

"A submission worthy of careful consideration," I replied in full flannel, as I had never heard of a challenge to the array and hadn't a clue what it was. Time for some nimble side-stepping. "If Your Honour will rise for a short time, I can take specific instructions on my learned friend's suggestion."

"Yes indeed." He glanced up at the court clock. "I see the hour is upon us. The court stands adjourned until two o'clock. I hope during the adjournment that every effort will be made to find Ms. Horton. I shall rise."

I directed Rob and Hoojamaflip to our conference room. "I suggest we have a short break, so let's meet again at one thirty," and with that, I hurried to the nearest quiet corner out of sight and opened Archbold. The chapter on 'The Jury' was like a short novel, page after page after page. What a nightmare. I went in search of Pertwee. If we could present a united front, we could get away with it.

"I'm up for it," he said, "and the less we argue the toss, the less Longbottom has to worry about."

"What about your reviewing lawyer?"

"Our Tracey is still trying to find him, so if there's no show by two, I'll make the decision and live with the consequences." He chuckled. "It's called living on the edge." I laughed. "All being well, we can discharge this dozy bunch and wheel on a fresh panel. It will work if your boy plays ball. A word in his shell like perhaps?"

"Leave it to me, and thanks for your help."

I scurried off to make our one thirty conference. I explained what was going to happen, with Hoojamaflip repeating in words of one syllable, and in no time at all it was two o'clock.

With the court reconvened, Pertwee put forward his devilishly cunning plan, I supported it, and Longbottom embraced it to his judicial bosom. He discharged the entire jury from further attendance with the thanks of the court ringing in their ears, and they duly trooped out. The still absent Ms. Horton was but a footnote.

"Now gentlemen," said Longbottom, as if a great burden had been lifted from his shoulders, "let us make use of the time remaining to us. Jury Bailiff," Denise rose and bowed, "please summon a fresh jury panel."

"I'm afraid that won't be possible Your Honour. All spare jurors have been sent home. It's part of the Lord Chancellor's new "user friendly" directive. Prospective jurors must not be kept hanging around court unless absolutely necessary."

"But it *is* absolutely necessary," he bleated, "we have a defendant waiting to be tried, and no jury to try him. This is intolerable."

"The decision is not mine Your Honour," Denise bleated back, "I simply follow orders." The Third Reich defence if I'm not mistaken.

Longbottom pulled back, remembering just in time the strictures against judges bullying the court staff. "Please forgive me, I wasn't blaming you."

There was a long pause as Longottom contemplated his next move. Whatever else, he had some explaining to do where a full day of court time had slipped effortlessly by.

"Well Gentlemen," we both rose, "it looks as if we have no choice but to adjourn to tomorrow morning with a clean start at ten."

Brenda, the court clerk, rose with as much gravitas as she could muster. "I'm afraid that won't be possible, Your Honour. Another case has been allocated to this court with a clean start at ten."

Longbottom was dismayed. "That's ridiculous!" he snapped. "What idiot made that decision without consulting me first?"

"It was His Honour Judge Clarke QC, the resident judge, in consultation with the court listing officer."

Poor Longbottom as he reached the nadir of his judicial aspirations. To call the resident judge an idiot was a bridge too far, especially as the resident judge was 'Bonkers' Clarke.

Down but not out, Longbottom pressed on. "It's possible that another trial has befallen the same fate as this one, and this trial can be accommodated at short notice."

"It's possible, Your Honour, but only the listing officer will know."

"Then let him attend upon us forthwith."

It sounded like a Shakespearean tragedy, with the emphasis on tragedy.

In the fullness of time, twenty minutes to be precise, word filtered through that the listing officer, like the reviewing lawyer and Elvis, had entered the building but was nowhere to be found.

The trial was adjourned to a date to be fixed when, hopefully, the listing officer could be found to fix it.

Robbie was readmitted to bail, and was last seen sloping off towards the Underground in the company of Whatshisname. They were made for each other.

Happily, that was the last I saw of either of them, and as soon as professional decency would allow, the brief was returned from whence it came.

CHAPTER 14

LOVE REKINDLED

I t was one of those cases where reputations were made or broken, at the cutting edge of advocacy. Move over Marshall-Hall and F.E. Smith, it was time for Toby Potts to stand up and be counted. I mean, it was hard to imagine anything more testing for the aspiring advocate than the case of Norman Gorman, listed for trial at Acton Magistrates' Court on a day to be fixed. I wondered what possessed the proud parents to christen their bundle of joy 'Norman'. Norman Gorman didn't exactly have a ring to it, or certainly not the ring you'd want to hear, such as Bond, James Bond. The only positive thing I could say about Norman Gorman was that the brief came into chambers in my own name. Fame at last!

Norman was in his late forties, with thinning hair, pasty-faced and pinched features, a bit like a small town bank manager about to refuse an overdraft. He lived alone with his mother Mavis. His Dad had died of boredom some years earlier. Norman had never thrown his cap at anybody, he didn't have the time, he was too busy filing during the day as filing clerk, second grade, for Acton Borough Council, and at night out and about displaying his wares.

He would patrol the streets of Acton, dressed in nothing more than a dirty raincoat, grey ankle socks and trainers, and, come rain come shine, when the opportunity arose, he would open his raincoat and shout: "You don't see many of these to a pound of sausages," before scampering off with a strange high-pitched cackle.

His behaviour was more comical than criminal, given that Norman was not particularly well-endowed in that department, so there was little to shout about. Comments like: "I've seen something like that before, only bigger", were hurtful, but didn't seem to deter him.

It had to happen, and it was only a matter of time. On one of Norman's flashing escapades, he chose a young woman who turned out to have a black belt in Judo, third Dan, and before he could say Chipolata, he was face down and pinned to the ground which, given his state of undress, was decidedly uncomfortable. Plod turned up in their own good time, nicked and cuffed him, and in due course, he was charged with indecent exposure.

For reasons best known to my solicitors, they had arranged a conference "to advise on plea". Other than advising Gorman to plead guilty and take his chances with the Magistrates, I couldn't see what else I could say, and besides, it wasn't Counsel's duty to provide the client with a defence.

If Gorman had legged it, an unfortunate expression in the circumstances, and was later arrested, preferably having dressed, we could always run mistaken identity, in the hope there was nothing remarkable about his pecker save that it was on the small side. Unless the prosecution could show that everybody else living in that area of Acton was hung like an army mule, he might have an argument, but it would need careful handling so to speak.

I tried to sound positive, but it was hard work, and Gorman sensed my mood.

"I get the impression, young man, that you are far from confident about the outcome," he said through pursed lips.

"On the contrary," I replied, batting the ball straight back into his court, "I am entirely confident about the outcome, but it's not the outcome you are hoping for." I was damned if I was going to take the blame for his unrealistic expectations.

There was a long pause as Gorman considered his options, which frankly didn't merit a long pause. As he was wrestling with them, I couldn't get the picture of this ghastly man stark bollocks naked on the rampage in Acton out of my head. I'd shaken his hand when we first met, and I was beginning to feel queasy. The sooner this conference came to an end the better.

"So you're advising me to plead guilty," he said at last.

"That's your decision. I'm simply advising you that you have no defence."

Another long pause.

"So what will happen at court if I plead guilty?"

Progress at last.

"You'll enter your plea of guilty, I will try and persuade the Magistrates that this was a 'one-off', although that might not be easy given the number of sightings of a skinny middle-aged male with a sallow complexion sporting clothes, or lack of them, identical to the clothes, or lack of them, that you were wearing, or not, when you were arrested, and they should sentence you on that basis." I managed to keep a straight face. "Whatever else, they will almost certainly require a psychiatric report."

Gorman was outraged. "A psychiatric report?" he repeated, doing a passable impression of Lady Bracknell. "What on earth for?"

"Picture the scene as presented to the Magistrates by the facts," I replied. "Here we have a perfectly respectable man who, after a hard day's work, goes home, has his supper, and then goes to his room. There he undresses down to his socks, puts on a dirty raincoat, and not long after, he's face down on the ground with the Judo Queen astride him, sitting on his naked bottom. That was your naked bottom." Gorman winced. "In the circumstances, Mr. Gorman, the Magistrates are likely to want some explanation for this behaviour, which a psychiatrist is best qualified to provide. It doesn't mean you're barking mad, but it may mean you have some unresolved mental issues that need resolving."

"Bloody cheek," he snapped back. Actually two to be precise. "I'm not having some trick cyclist prodding me! There's nothing wrong with me!"

I'd touched a raw nerve without knowing why, but it seemed like a good time to bring the conference to an end.

"I think we've had a useful discussion, so if there's nothing else, I suggest we meet at court tomorrow for any additional fine tuning It's listed in the afternoon, no doubt with a dozen or more other cases, at two fifteen. Will one thirty be convenient?"

"As you say, young man, we've had a useful discussion, so what's the point of arriving at least three quarters of an hour before the case is called on, and sitting in a cold and draughty waiting area simply staring at each other and anything else that heaves into view?"

He had a point. "Then I'll see you tomorrow at two fifteen," I replied, and with that, he left, a tad ungraciously. I had no idea what he would do when we got to court, and frankly, I was past caring.

$$\Longleftrightarrow\Longleftrightarrow$$

I trudged my weary way home, a bit like Gray's lowing herd o'er the lea, until I reached the comparative sanctuary of my flat. I had no plans, so it was pizza and a beer or three, and then a dose of telly. I decided to check my emails, heavily laden with junk. One I thought might appeal to Gorman, or Flash Gorman as I was now calling him, was how to increase the size of your penis by at least four inches. The question posed was: "Are you pleased with the size of your love tool, or do the guys laugh at you in the shower?"

There were several offering me riches overnight and beyond my wildest dreams, with pictures of fast and expensive cars, well-stacked blondes, big houses and private jets, and the claim that with this particular fool-proof system, those dreams could become a reality.

And then, like an orchid in a nettle bed, I saw it and trembled with excitement. It was from my beloved Susie. As the days had turned into weeks since she left me, the emails had tapered off from two a day down to two a week as we adjusted to each other's absence and our respective commitments. In my case, it was the cut and thrust of representing the likes of Norman 'Flash' Gorman that held sway on a regular basis. In Susie's case, it was battling against the elements and the last frontiers of civilisation, swatting flies and bringing comfort and joy to thousands of orphaned children. According to her emails, every now and then she'd have R & R in South Africa with 'friends'. Susie was somewhat reticent about describing her 'friends', so I was left to speculate about the king and his forty-nine wives and one hundred and seventy-two children, some of whom may well have reached puberty and beyond.

Anyway, back to the email, and out of the blue, Susie wrote that she was coming back to England and arriving on Thursday. It was the best news ever. I had absolutely nothing against Prince Harry and his dashing ginger good looks and his charitable works in memory of his mother, but time for Susie to move on and give the hundreds of other hopefuls a crack of the whip.

I emailed back. I would be there to pick her up at Heathrow, and after that, we'd play it by ear, so long as she agreed to spend every waking, and sleeping, moment wrapped in my arms. I pressed the send button and waited impatiently for her reply.

It came at nine the next morning, just as I was about to leave for chambers before taking the underground to Acton and my day of destiny with Flash Gorman. She couldn't wait to see me. She loved me, kisses and hugs.

Time and enough to put flesh on the bones of our time together after Flash had been sorted, and I left for court a very happy man.

Everything conjoined to make my outing to Acton Magistrates' Court truly memorable, and for all the wrong reasons. Acton Magistrates' Court was in Acton, and about as fly-blown as you could get without going east of Suez. It was also a stone's throw from Wormwood Scrubs, where I'd first met Bootsy in the case of Tosser Willis and nearly expired from an overdose of passive smoking. Finally, and to add insult to injury, I had a client who was barking mad. Still, I reminded myself, Marshall-Hall and F.E. Smith didn't reach the pinnacles of the profession by throwing in the towel at the first sign of trouble ahead. It was Rudyard Kipling, the darling of the Empire, Gunga Din and Gung Ho and stiff upper lip and all that, who wrote:

If you can force your heart and nerve and sinew
To serve your turn long after they are gone,
And so hold on when there is nothing in you
Except the will which says to them: 'Hold on!'

I should have known, but I wasn't expecting it. In through the main doors walked Flash Gorman, at precisely two fifteen, wearing a grubby raincoat, grey ankle socks and trainers and an inane grin. He spotted me, inclined his head in recognition and walked on into court. Before I had time to react, there was a piercing scream, the court room doors were flung open, and out bounded my client, with a strange high-pitched cackle, his raincoat tails flapping behind him and leaving nothing to the imagination as he left the building, never to be seen again.

As I put my head round the court door, the usher was being revived with smelling salts and a glass of tepid water. The Magistrates had withdrawn to the sanctuary of their retiring room, leaving the court clerk to pick up the pieces. I introduced myself, without which I wouldn't get paid, and after that, there was little else I could do.

After thirty minutes, time and enough to recover their composure, the Magistrates were persuaded to return to court to issue a warrant for Flash's arrest, and that was it. I did wonder if Gorman's somewhat eccentric behaviour might harm his defence, but as Marshall-Hall and F.E. Smith might have said, and probably did, you can only work with the material you're given. Wisdom beyond their years!

$$\blacktriangleright\!\!+\!+\!\!\blacktriangleleft$$

Thank the Lord for small mercies. With Gorman's sudden departure, it left me free to concentrate on more important things, like Susie's impending arrival. I made my excuses with the clerks and caught the train home. Mother was at the station to pick me up, and very excited.

"Such a thrill for all of us, dear. I've spoken to Molly, and we've arranged Sunday lunch together. Just like old times."

I left for Heathrow in plenty of time, and arrived an hour early. Having parked, I checked the arrivals screen. The flight from Johannesburg was on time. Halleluiah! An overpriced coffee and a muffin helped while away twenty minutes as I kept checking my watch and the screen. Finally, and after what seemed like an eternity, the screen showed 'flight landed'. Twenty minutes' later, Susie appeared, looking stunning. We saw each other at the same time, she broke into a smile, we ran towards each other and into a long, lingering embrace. I hadn't fully appreciated just how much I'd missed her until that moment.

Finding the car and escaping the airport perimeter took almost as long as the flight from Jo'burg, but at last we were on our way.

"Our folks are greatly looking forward to seeing you," I said, looking at my watch, "we should be home within the hour."

"Darling," she smiled at me, "do you mind if we don't go home, at least not yet?"

I was a little surprised. "Not at all," I replied. "Where to?"

"Do you still have that flat in Earls Court?" she giggled.

"Of course. Home from home."

"Then that's where I want to go."

I was even more surprised. "It's not up to your usual standards," I said quickly, remembering our first night together at the Savoy, "and my cleaner called in sick, so it's a bit of a mess."

Susie laughed. "Toby darling, I've slept under the stars and in the strangest places over the past few weeks, so your flat sounds perfect. There'll be time and enough for family and friends. Right now I want some quality time with the man I love."

We picked up a slab of strong cheddar, a baguette and a bottle of wine, and then headed on to my flat. I insisted she stay in the living room whilst I changed the bedding and generally tidied up. I heard her talking on the phone to her parents.

"A good flight back, and Toby was there to meet me. We're at his flat, it needs a woman's touch," she added with a giggle. She paused, obviously listening to her mother. "Yes of course, Sunday lunch sounds absolutely perfect, see you then," and she hung up.

Popping her head round my bedroom door, she laughed at my display of domestic bliss. "Toby darling, open the wine and pour us a glass, and I'll finish up here."

I poured the wine, and was just about to set about the cheese and baguette when she came out of the bedroom and took the bread knife from my hand. She kissed me lightly on the lips.

"Let's make love," she said, and we did for the next hour. Then it was a shower together, wine, cheese and baguette, and back to bed. Just feeling her warm body next to mine was exquisite, and at last, we fell into a deep and contented sleep.

The next twenty four hours were bliss, doing all those things Londoners never make the time to do. We took a tour bus full of Chinese, or perhaps Japanese, and did it matter, we went to the Tower of London and saw the crown jewels and the ravens, then over the Millennium Bridge to the Tate Modern, lunch at a pub-bistro overlooking Old Father Thames, then more sightseeing and finally, exhausted but well pleased with our adventures, we returned to my flat. I popped out for another bottle of wine and a bunch of flowers, which Susie loved. She found an old jug and immediately set about arranging them. As she said, my flat needed a woman's touch, and I was happy to oblige.

On that Sunday morning, plans were made in the car on the way down. Susie was staying for the week, returning the following Sunday evening. If I would have her, she would stay with me until Thursday morning, and then return home to spend time with family and friends.

"Is that too much of an imposition, darling?" she asked. "After all, you're a busy practitioner and constantly in demand."

"Absolutely," I lied, "but for you, let them wait. I know I have no commitments tomorrow, so let's see how it pans out."

We'd phoned in advance, and when we arrived, both sets of parents were there to greet us. It was a lovely day, spent in the bosom of our respective families, and the promise of a return match next Sunday with the Sandwells. It was agreed I would take Susie to the airport. More heartache and more tears to be dashed away, but the future was bright.

The week seemed to flash by, and then it was Thursday. I'd managed to keep my professional commitments down to the bare minimum, or as some wag might be tempted to say, business as usual.

The unfortunate Flash Gorman was arrested at his desk, where he was busy filing away as if his brief excursion to Acton Magistrates' Court had never happened. I was obliged to represent him, not that it counted for much, when he was produced from the police cells to face the full majesty of the law. Not surprisingly, he was remanded in custody for the preparation of a psychiatric report. If I had nothing better to do, I'd love to be a fly on the wall during that particular meeting of the minds.

And then it was Sunday. We all tried to stay jolly, but the mood was dampened by Susie's imminent departure. For my part, I'd loved every minute spent with her, our love was rekindled, and as I kept reminding myself, a year, or what remained of it, was a drop in the ocean compared with the rest of our lives together.